# THE WAY IT WAS

# THE WAY IT WAS

## GLIMPSES OF ENGLISH CRICKET'S PAST

**Stephen Chalke**

FAIRFIELD BOOKS

Fairfield Books
17 George's Road, Fairfield Park, Bath BA1 6EY
Tel 01225-335813



Photographs appear by permission, as follows:
Getty Images: front cover and pages 20, 57, 87, 121, 157, 205, 243, 255, 269, 272
PA Photos: pages 42, 72, 162, 167, 187, 263
Patrick Eagar: page 190
Susanna Kendall: pages 79, 81, 196, 199, 211, 218 and 233
Other photographs appear by kind permission of their owners

First published 2008

ISBN: 978 0 9560702 1 0

Jacket design by Niall Allsop

Printed and bound in Great Britain by
Midway Colour Print, Holt, Wiltshire

with thanks to

John Stern, editor of *The Wisden Cricketer*

Marcus Williams of *The Times*

and

Stephen Fay, former editor of *Wisden Cricket Monthly*

whose idea this book was

This book is a collection of articles on English cricket's past,
with one brief foray into the world of football.
They were written originally for the following:
*Wisden Cricket Monthly*, *The Wisden Cricketer* and *The Times*.
105 is made up of extracts from several books by Stephen Chalke.
Where space on the page has allowed, some of these articles
have been expanded slightly for this collection.

## Contents

## Introduction

In November 2000 I wrote to Stephen Fay, the new editor of the *Wisden Cricket Monthly* magazine. I suggested that I could write a monthly column for him, featuring episodes from English county cricket's past.

'Nothing too statistical or authoritative, just some memories and reflections around special moments. County cricket is full of material that hasn't been properly recorded – and it's a good way of reviving interest in the county game. Believe me, there are lots of people out there who would love it.'

'I like your idea,' he replied, 'but I'm not sure how it would fit in the magazine. I'll think hard about it in the next couple of months.'

A few weeks later he asked me to write about the summer of 1946, the story of cricket's post-war reconstruction. We were both feeling our way, and my article went back and forth several times. At one stage it was 1,500 words long, then it was 750. It was 'The Fred Karno summer', then it became 'Old faces, new beginnings'. It appeared eventually in the issue of May 2001, accompanied by a photograph of volunteers laying turf on the Oval outfield.

Stephen asked me to write two more, and I opted for two dramatic stories: Don Wilson's one-handed innings at Worcester in 1961 and Charles Palmer's eight-wicket triumph at Leicester in 1955. On their completion, I asked Stephen anxiously if he wanted any more.

"You can do one every month from now on," he said breezily. "And, when you've done a hundred, you can put them in a book."

The column was called *Only Yesterday*, and it appeared alongside one by Angus Fraser: county cricket past and county cricket present, side by side.

I had already written three books on county cricket. But this was my first venture into journalism, and it took a while to adjust. Most months, after I had conducted my main interview, I would have a panic attack, thinking that I lacked sufficient material. I would undertake a further round of research and, when it came to the writing, the article would always be far too long. I would spend hours squeezing it down to 750 words, reluctantly removing some of the little gems I had collected.

In the autumn of 2003 the magazine amalgamated with *The Cricketer*, Stephen retired and his deputy John Stern became the editor of the new *Wisden Cricketer*. My column survived the merger, but it was decided to give it a new name. *Blast from the Past* was suggested, but I did not like that. They are not blasts. So we settled for a gentler alternative: *The Way It Was.*

Usually John leaves me free to choose my own subjects. In general I like to explore the more obscure byways, and I can finish up a long way from my starting point. I went to interview Stan Cray about the post-war Essex side, and I found myself describing a wartime match in Bombay. I saw Warwickshire's Alan Townsend, and he told me about the Headingley Test of 1934 and about his remarkable cycle journey there. That is the fun of oral history.

Early in 2005, with the excitement of an Ashes summer approaching, I contacted Marcus Williams, the unsung hero of *The Times* cricket desk. Could I write them a series of articles on great Ashes victories, based each time on an interview with a participant? He agreed to five, all games played in England; then, for the tour of Australia in 2006/07, he asked me to do another five, this time on victories down under.

With more than 80 articles for the *Only Yesterday* and *The Way It Was* columns, 10 Ashes articles for *The Times* and a few obituaries and other oddments, I have gone past that magic hundred that Stephen Fay mentioned back in the spring of 2001. It is time to do as he said and to put them in a book.

I have stuck with the title *The Way It Was* because that is what interests me most, that sense of the past as another place that we have left behind. Cricket has always held a quite particular place in English society, so it is good at reflecting our changing way of life.

Born in 1948, I grew up in a world in which the old knew best; we were brought up to respect the experience and wisdom of our elders. Maybe at times we lived too much in the shadow of our history. But, as I grew into adulthood and as austerity gave way to affluence, a new commercial order – thriving on novelty and instant pleasure – gained sway and we swung far to the other extreme. The old suddenly had nothing to tell us.

Yet we all need to know where we have come from, both individually and as a people – and who better is there to tell us than our elders?

So much of the magic and charm of cricket derives from its sense of tradition, its rich historical continuum. There has to be change, but each generation needs to manage that change without destroying the continuum. To shape the future, to plan for the way it will be, we must have a feeling for *The Way It Was*.

Stephen Chalke
Bath, September 2008

# 1. Old faces, new beginnings

*The summer of 1946* WCM, May 2001

The scars of war were at their greatest at The Oval. Bomb craters, a prisoner-of-war cage, an assault course. There was nothing left of the grass on which Hutton stroked 364 in 1938. They brought tens of thousands of turfs from Gravesend Marshes, and Bert Lock the groundsman supervised shilling-an-hour volunteers to lay them. Day after day he pulled the roller up and down.

Meanwhile the Surrey committee looked for a captain. But not a professional, as Leicestershire had been forced to appoint. That would not do at The Oval. They searched for a Major Bennett who had played for the second eleven before the war – but, so the story goes, they appointed the wrong one. Nigel, not Leo. He had popped into The Oval to renew his membership and found himself county captain. He did not impress the professionals but, glad to be playing again, they looked on the bright side.

"I reckon we can cope with him for the summer," one said. "His wife's a real cracker."

By May the Indian tourists were enjoying the rewards of Bert Lock's labours. For the only time in cricket's history, numbers ten and eleven – Sarwate and Banerjee – both scored centuries.

Some counties returned to their pre-war sides. Somerset started with a team with an average age of 38. "We were all strangely nervous," Bill Andrews said. "It was like starting one's career all over again." "Once the initial freshness had worn off," Frank Lee wrote, "we found it all far more strenuous than we anticipated."

Some counties had gaps to fill – and little idea how to fill them. Warwickshire tried 21 new-ball pairings. At the start of one match, the captain sent a debutant fast bowler to the nets to be checked out by leg-spinner Eric Hollies. 'I don't know if he was loosening up,' Eric reported back, 'but he was slower than me.'

Essex had only half a team left. Dickie Dodds, back from service in India, offered himself as a leg-spinner and was told, "You're just the man we need to open the batting."

Runs came slowly for Dickie and, after failing at Hove, he wondered if Essex were going to stick with him. "They didn't have a team sheet. It was all very casual. I didn't know what the drill was. You just tag along automatically. I asked Tom Pearce at Victoria, 'Am I wanted in the next match?' And he said, 'Oh yes, you're very much wanted.'"

Within the fortnight he was at The Oval, anxiously asking his partner Sonny Avery to take first strike. Sonny was using a bat given to him by an Essex member. "It had belonged to this chap's son. He'd been killed in the war, and he wanted Sonny to use it." Together on Bert Lock's turf they put on 270, a new county record.

Yorkshire were reigning champions, but their greatest bowler, slow-left-armer Hedley Verity, had been killed in Italy, and they replaced him with 43-year-old Arthur Booth. His 39-year-old skipper Brian Sellers took to calling him Grandad, but he was a youngster compared with Glamorgan's 48-year-old captain John Clay. Tom Goddard of Gloucester was 45, and he would play for another six years. There were no fast bowlers, just men like these trying to make up for their lost summers.

Some, like Wilf Wooller, were trying to put on the weight they had lost in POW camps. Others, like bomber pilot Bill Edrich, found rationing harsher in civilian life. "I was always hungry," he wrote, "and I had to renew a lot of cricket gear so the coupon situation soon grew difficult."

Rain was never far away all summer, the fielding and bowling had seen better days, but the spectators flocked back. Over 50,000 for the three days of the Glamorgan-India game at Swansea. A ground record for Gloucester-Somerset at Bristol. Vast numbers locked out of the Roses match at Old Trafford.

Wally Hammond dominated as he had done before the war, averaging 84.90 with the bat, while 'Grandad' Arthur Booth and the 48-year-old John Clay took first and second places in the bowling. Yorkshire won the title from Middlesex, as they had done in the last three years before the War.

Normal service had been resumed.

## 2. A fairy tale

*Don Wilson of Yorkshire* WCM, June 2001

Once upon a time. At the County Ground, Worcester. On Tuesday the sixth of June, 1961. Worcestershire thought they had beaten Yorkshire. By 35 runs. Beaten the county champions of the last two years. Beaten them at Worcester for the first time since 1909.

The players were leaving the field, and the crowd were on their feet.

Then Don Wilson came down the pavilion steps, his left arm in plaster from elbow to knuckles. Suddenly there was one more wicket to be taken.

Forty years on, Don recalls the argument in the dressing room.

"You're not batting," his captain Vic Wilson had told him. "You could do yourself incredible damage. If you bat, you'll never play for Yorkshire again."

But that was at 86 for seven, when the game was almost lost. By the time Binks and Illingworth had added 60, Don's pleading had brought a softening: "All right. If there's just five minutes to go, you can bat."

There was half an hour left when Binks was ninth man out, but nobody was going to stop Don Wilson. A broken bone at the base of his thumb. A swelling that throbbed under the plaster. He had been injured on Saturday, and by now he should have back with the specialist in Leeds.

A left-handed batsman, pain shot up his arm when he tried to grip with the fingertips of his bottom hand. "It hurt like hell, but Gifford was bowling, a slow bowler, and I was only defending."

He settled for using his top hand only. "As a coach," he says, "I'm always telling people they should be able to bat with just the top hand."

At the other end Bob Platt resumed his dogged defence. "He wasn't the greatest striker of the ball," Don recalls, "but he was a great blocker."

With ten minutes left, Norman Gifford drifted down leg, and Don swung him away for two fours. Ten in the over, and the target was suddenly 22. "It's funny. When you hit a couple of fours, the pain goes completely, doesn't it?"

Down the wicket came his partner.

"What the hell are you doing? We're playing for a draw."

"We're not, Platty. We're going to win."

"Don't be so bloody silly. The new ball's due. They've got Flavell and Coldwell."

Jack Flavell was at his peak. Day in, day out, he was as fast as anybody in the country, bar Harold Rhodes, and in this summer of 1961 he topped the national averages with 171 wickets. With five minutes left, and 22 runs wanted, he took the new ball and all the Worcester fielders crowded round Don Wilson.

"Waste some time," Bob Platt suggested, no 20-over law in those days. "Adjust your box. Re-do your laces."

But his partner had other ideas. He swung at the first ball, and it flew through the covers for four.

"I thought he'd gone completely out of his mind," Bob tells, "and I don't mind that being quoted."

How do you bowl when a lower-order batsman takes to swinging at you with just one hand on the bat? When you're one of the most feared bowlers in the country? And you thought you'd won the match twenty minutes ago? Maybe Jack Flavell should have stayed calmer.

"Jack's fault, if anything, was he tended to get a bit wild," Worcester's keeper Roy Booth says. "He was going flat out, and Don was swinging the bat. And off the quick bowling, the ball sped away."

Three fours and a two came off the over and, when Flavell did beat the bat, he beat Roy Booth too and the ball ran away for four byes. Now it was only four to win, and there was one last over to be bowled.

Coldwell to Platt.

"Just touch it," Don said, now the senior partner. "Let's get a one."

A push into the covers, and they were scampering to give Don the strike. Three to win.

There was an inevitability about the rest.

"Coldwell ran up, and for some unknown reason it just happened that I hit him straight over his head for four."

Yorkshire had won by one wicket.

It was, in the words of JM Kilburn in the *Yorkshire Post*, 'the only possible finish that would serve the cause of romance.'

"Bob Platt was doing a jig with his bat in the air, I can see him now, but I was stunned. I was speechless."

"If you go out to bat, you'll never play for Yorkshire again."

By autumn the words had acquired a prophetic ring, with Don's replacement Keith Gillhouley proving a great success. "I was feeling very out of it. It wasn't a good winter for me. I was thinking, 'Shall I go and play for somebody else?' But it worked out for me in the end."

It worked out so well that he was back in the side the next summer and played for another 13 years, one of only 13 men to take 1,000 wickets for the county. This year he has become an Honorary Life Member. "What a thrill that was! A real accolade in my cricketing life."

But it was not as incredible as his batting that afternoon.

Worcester, 1961. Wilson, not out, 29. With six fours.

"It was a fairy tale," Don says, and proudly he reads from JM Kilburn's report. 'Figures mark the facts, but this was fancy beyond the fanciful and it began: Once upon a time ….'

## 3. Just one over

*Charles Palmer of Leicestershire* WCM, July 2001

"We're bowling at the wrong ends," the Leicestershire spinners said at tea.

Saturday 21 May, 1955. Grace Road, Leicester. Their captain Charles Palmer remembers the conversation.

"'Fine,' I said. 'I'll alter you round.' And I never gave it another thought until I walked out onto the field."

The game was slipping away fast. Leicestershire, 114 all out on a damp wicket. Surrey, 42 for one and, according to *The Times*, 'May's firm driving looked ominous.' It was a typical day's work for Surrey. They were in the middle of a sequence of 18 outright victories in a row. And now the pitch had dried out.

The first over after tea was to be from the pavilion end and, as he led out his men, Charles Palmer realised that there was a decision to be made. "Oh heck," he thought, "I've got to get someone to bowl one over."

It was easiest to bowl it himself. Except that his back was bad, and he was under orders not to bowl. He had had two experimental overs at the end of the Kent match, but he had not even been bowling in the nets. "Oh, well," he decided, "one over won't hurt me." He turned to Peter May as he went past. "Go easy on me now. I haven't been bowling this year."

A little man with spectacles, he was hardly a fearsome sight with his ten-pace run-up and gentle seamers but, with his second ball, he bowled Peter May. "Back or no back, I had to continue then, didn't I?"

In his next over he had Bernie Constable caught, then he bowled the young Micky Stewart for a first-ball duck. Two overs, three wickets for no runs.

"The pitch was dry," his team mate Terry Spencer recalls, "except for this dinner plate of a patch right on his length." It was a fuller length than Terry bowled, more in line than where the spinners pitched.

"I just bowled straight," he explains. "That's all I could do. I wasn't a bowler really."

Straight enough to hit the stumps of Fletcher in his fifth over, Pratt in his sixth. With balls that pitched on the dinner plate. Five for nought. "He just treated it as a joke," Terry Spencer recalls. "After each wicket, he would say, 'I suppose I'd better have another over now.'"

"I didn't enjoy bowling as much as batting," Charles Palmer recalls. "Only when silly things happened."

Nothing was sillier than the donkey drops he developed the following year. "I was running in to bowl to Jock Livingston of Northants, and I had no idea I was going to do it. Suddenly a yard before the crease I threw the ball up, it must have been thirty feet in the air, and I had the luck of a beginner. Jock's eyes popped out to mid-off and back, he swirled his bat round like somebody tossing the caber, and the ball lobbed off the back of his bat to Maurice Hallam at first slip. We all fell about laughing. In time I took a dozen or more wickets with that ball, including Frank Worrell who trod on his stumps. And the first time I bowled it, it was completely unpremeditated."

Like his decision to bowl one over after tea against Surrey.

In his eighth over he bowled McIntyre. According to *The Times*, 'his medium pace swingers whipped viciously into the batsmen.' Then later in the same over he bowled Surridge. "The Surrey batsmen just played down the wrong line," Charles says. "I bowled down the Metropolitan, they played down the Bakerloo." The scoreboard read 61 for eight, and Charles Palmer had figures of seven wickets for no runs.

"There may have been a wet patch," Bernie Constable remembered, "but it was terrible batting. Charles Palmer was just a dobber."

*Wisden* 1955 lists Remarkable Analyses. Hedley Verity, 10 for 10. Tich Freeman, 9 for 11. Jim Laker, 8 for 2 in the 1950 Test Trial at Bradford.

When Charles Palmer bowled Tony Lock, he had eight wickets for no runs in 12 overs, and seven times he had hit the stumps. "Some of the team suggested I should take myself off and keep the world record."

Who should be on strike for his next over but Jim Laker himself, his eight for two under threat? "He took to smearing me. He hit a two that lobbed into the gap between cover and extra cover, then a two that went off an edge down to fine leg. Then a three. So I finished up with eight for seven. It could so easily have been nine for nil."

Surrey, all out, 77. The crowd ran onto the outfield, the players formed a guard of honour for Charles, and the celebrations began in the bar. "Peter May told my wife that I went into the Surrey dressing room and said, 'Gentlemen, I do beg your pardon.' All I remember was that I learnt how much whisky I could drink. Very quickly, too, I think."

On Tuesday, with no twinges in his back, he bowled another 13 overs, conceding just one run, as May and Constable took Surrey to a seven-wicket victory.

In 27 overs in the match he had taken eight wickets for eight runs. And, if the spinners had been on at the right ends at tea, he would never have bowled that first over.

| | | | | | | | | | | | | | |
|---|---|---|---|---|---|---|---|---|---|---|---|---|---|
| • • | • W | • • | • • | • • | • W | • • | • • | • • | • • | • W | • • | 2 • | • • |
| W • | • W | • • | • • | • • | • • | • • | • • | • • | • • | • • | • • | 2 • | • 3 |
| • • | • • | • • | • • | W • | • • | • • | W W | • • | • • | • • | • • | • • | • • |

## 4. The longest day

*Alan Townsend of Warwickshire* TWC, Aug 2005

"Sometimes I have bad dreams about that journey," Alan Townsend says. "In those days, as a kid, you accepted things as they were, but now I look back and it frightens me to think about it."

From 1948 to 1960 Alan was a popular and successful all-round cricketer with Warwickshire, the outstanding slip fielder of his generation. But he grew up in the North-East where his father Charles, a clerk in a builders' merchants, played his cricket for Thornaby in the North Yorkshire and South Durham League.

"He used to take me with him to matches, ever since I was short. He used to do without his tea and come and throw a ball at me. And I'd be wearing a little straw hat, like all the boys did. So naturally I took to cricket."

Each September there were day trips by train from their Middlesbrough home to the Scarborough Festival, but the journey that stays clearest in his memory took place on Monday 23 July 1934.

To Headingley, to see England playing Australia.

Four years earlier on the same ground the young Bradman had set a new Test record with a score of 334. In the meantime Wally Hammond had eclipsed it with 336 in New Zealand. Now Bradman looked set to regain his record, leaving the field on Saturday evening with 271 not out. He had put on 388 with Bill Ponsford, in front of a crowd of 38,000 spectators, 'packed' – *The Times* reported – 'solidly but cheerfully one against the other, with the more adventurous sitting on the sharp-angled roofs of sheds and swarming up trees.' With the series all-square, excitement was high.

"On the Sunday Dad said to me, 'I'm going to Leeds tomorrow to the Test match. Would you like to come with me?'" Leeds was 65 miles from their home in Middlesbrough, Alan was still a month from his thirteenth birthday – but he was already sufficiently in love with cricket to say yes.

At half past five he was woken by his mother. "She said, 'Your dad's going now. Do you still want to go?' She'd packed beef sandwiches for lunch, tomato sandwiches for tea, and she put them in a haversack which I carried."

They mounted their bicycles. "I didn't have any gears, but Dad had this Remington that had been advertised in the Sunday paper, and it had these three-speed gears."

Soon they were in the countryside. "The sun was coming up, shining brightly. The birds were twittering. And the country lanes were ever so quiet. I don't suppose my dad could afford the bus and train fares, and of course it was door to door on the bike."

His father was a keen cyclist. "He used to take us out biking on Sundays. I'm sure that's where I got my strong legs from. All the years I played county cricket, I never had any trouble from them."

They arrived at Headingley to find that play had already started, and there was quite a queue outside the ground. They parked their bicycles against the wall – "We didn't even lock them up" – and got in just in time to see Bradman complete his 300.

A new world record was drawing close. Then there was a great roar as, according to *The Times*, 'Bowes, with a ball that must have come back inches, knocked Bradman's leg stump almost into the wicket-keeper's throat.'

After six hours of cycling, young Alan longed to sit down – "but we couldn't get a seat anywhere in the ground; we had to stand all day."

The atmosphere was humid, building up towards thunder, and it was only at teatime, as a few people started to leave, that he found a pair of seats. "I put my haversack down, went back for my dad and, when we got back to the seats, I went and sat on the blooming haversack. I had this great wet patch on my backside from the tomato sandwiches, and I couldn't do anything about it."

Whether standing or sitting, he was absorbed by his first sight of Test cricket. The Yorkshire crowd cheered their own bowlers, Bowes and Verity, who shared the wickets as the Australians tumbled from 517 for four to 584 all out. Then, with a first innings deficit of 384 and most of two days still to play, the two of them watched with admiration as Worcestershire's Cyril Walters opened the England innings: "He was very stylish." And they saw Tom Wall race in with the new ball for Australia: "I was like all youngsters. I wanted to be a fast bowler when I grew up. And Wall fascinated me. It must have been dusty. Whenever he bowled and the ball pitched into the crease, all this dust came up."

The great names of English batting came and went: Walters and Keeton, then Hammond run out just as he looked set to play a great innings and the captain Bob Wyatt bowled behind his legs by Grimmett. At this stage England were 152 for four, and for most of the evening session Maurice Leyland and the 45-year-old Patsy Hendren battled doggedly for survival. At close of play the deficit was still 196 runs and, in the words of *The Times*, 'Australia had all but won the match.'

It would be another 23 years before Alan would catch a second glimpse of Test cricket. In June 1957, returning early from Bristol with the Warwickshire team, he saw the final session at Edgbaston of the match in which May and Cowdrey – with a partnership of 411 – smothered the threat of Sonny Ramadhin. "I remember standing in a long queue at the bus stop afterwards, and – to my great embarrassment – Colin Cowdrey pulled up in his car and gave me a lift home."

But there was no such easy journey home from Headingley. "It was very hilly coming out of Leeds, and it had been a hot day. So Dad stopped for a pint. 'I'll go in and have a drink,' he said, 'and I'll bring you out a bottle of lemonade.'"

Then the cycling began in earnest. It was nearly eight o'clock, there were another 60 miles to go, and the sun was fast falling in the sky.

"I never want to go through that journey again. I'm sure it did me mentally. I'd been standing all day in the heat. And somewhere – I can't remember where we'd got to – this thunderstorm came and it absolutely belted down. It was so dark and lonely on the road; we never saw a soul. Just miles and miles of blackness. And Dad kept saying to me, 'Keep going, lad, keep going.' I'm sure I was asleep. I was that wet and miserable, really soaking, fed up and tired with the heat.

"'We're not far off Thirsk,' he said. 'If we get into Thirsk by midnight, we'll catch the fish and chip shop open. And I'll buy you some fish and chips and a bottle of pop.' I suppose it was a spur to keep me going."

In the summer of 2004, seventy years on, he and his wife Hilda had occasion to drive through Thirsk, and he was shocked to find the fish-and-chip shop still there. "And all the memories of that night came flooding back."

"There was a big clock in the square and, sure enough, just before midnight, my dad and I got there and we bought some fish and chips."

There were still another 25 miles to be cycled, and once more they rode on, passing through just a few small villages as, away to their right, invisible in the night, the Cleveland Hills rose above them.

"The hardest part of it was the loneliness. There were no cars in those days, not after night time. We just cycled along, with our capes over the handlebars. It was well after two o'clock when we finally got home."

It was a round trip of more than 130 miles, in the middle of which he had stood for several hours in the heat. He had ridden it on a bike without gears, and he was only twelve years old.

"I met Bill Bowes years later, when I was playing for Warwickshire and he was a reporter. I told him that I'd seen him bowl Bradman that day and how we'd got there. And he couldn't believe what we'd done."

On Tuesday the storms returned to leave the match at Headingley drawn. Play lasted only 90 minutes, but this time neither Alan nor his father was there to see it.

## 5. Lighter bats

*Changes in the bats* TWC, Apr 2004

Two bats for the price of one. That was the closest the professional cricketer of the 1950s came to some free kit. A blazer and a sweater if he was capped, and the rest came out of his wages.

For some, two bats were more than enough. Leicester's Brian Boshier didn't score a run till his 10th innings of 1955, and his bat lasted years, with its distinctive legend on the back: 'Running In – Please Pass'.

For some, a personal bat was not important. Denis Compton picked up whatever was to hand, and Nottingham's Cyril Poole liked to make a bob on the side selling his bats. "This chap came in the dressing room at Trent Bridge," Bomber Wells tells. "He'd got a bat that had been hollowed out and filled with compressed sawdust. It was supposed to revolutionise bat making. We all tried it, and it was dead as a dodo. Then Cyril turned up for a pre-season friendly, and we sent him out with it. We were going to have a laugh, but he hit the ball everywhere. A magnificent innings. Only every time he tapped his block hole, some more of the sawdust fell out."

For others, the state of the bat was everything. "Ron Headley wouldn't put his bat on the luggage rack in the coach," Worcester's Martin Horton says. "He said it might alter the balance. And it had to be absolutely white. We used to clean off the red marks, especially the ones on the edges – you might leave the ones in the middle – but Ron! He was out first ball once, and he came in and spent half an hour sanding down his bat. He was lbw; he hadn't even hit the ball."

Most bats weighed about two pounds three ounces. "Billy Sutcliffe had a two pound six bat," Yorkshire's Bob Appleyard recalls, "and it had to be made specially for him. That was considered exceptionally heavy. One year Len Hutton and Norman Yardley played with harrow bats, which couldn't have weighed more than two pounds. They thought they had more control with a lighter bat."

"Len Hutton picked up one of Ian Botham's bats once," bat-maker Duncan Fearnley recalls. "He said it was the nearest he'd ever come to holding a railway sleeper."

"We were playing on uncovered pitches," Yorkshire's Ken Taylor explains. "The ball deviated much more, and you had to adjust in mid-shot. You can't do that with a heavy bat. Once a three-pound bat starts coming down, you've just got to go through with the shot."

"The bats got so heavy," Tom Graveney says, "that the game lost all the top-hand players. The top hand was always the guiding hand. You took the bat back towards the stumps, and it came down like a pendulum. Now

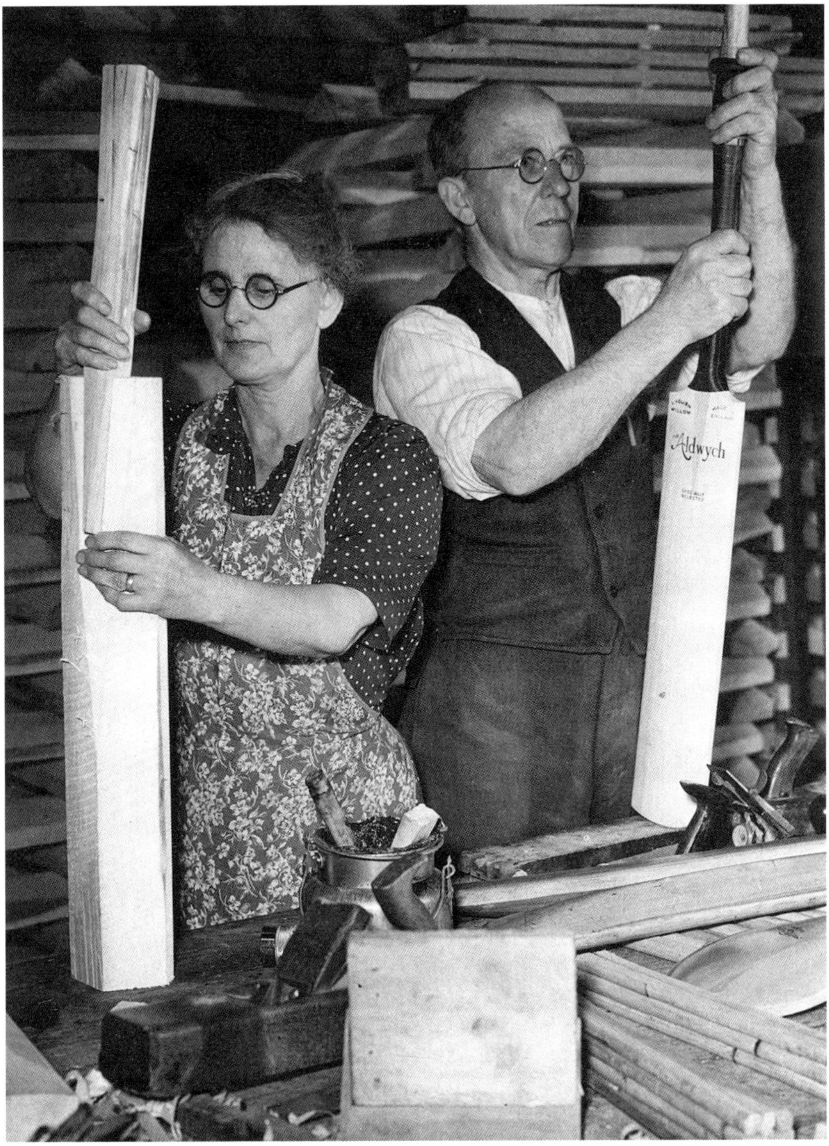
Aldwych

the bat is going out towards third man. I could adjust my shot after the ball hit the seam, and I'm sure I wasn't unique in that."

"It was a different game then," Bob Appleyard thinks. "The bats had a smaller sweet spot, and there was little room for error. You had to time the ball. With these heavier bats, the wood is thicker all the way up. You can mis-hit the ball, and it still goes to the boundary. In a way it's easier to bat with a modern bat, though it probably wouldn't be on turning pitches."

Some say that the change came with one-day cricket, others that in the late '70s the demand for willow became so great that it had to be force-dried, leaving the lighter bats too brittle.

"We plant the trees closer together now," Carleton Wright, Britain's leading willow-grower, says, "so they grow more slowly. It makes a narrower grain. The wood is denser, stronger. It doesn't dry out so much."

"We used to store our bats in damp cellars in the winter," Bob Appleyard recalls. "In fact, there was a theory for a while that they should be left overnight in a bathful of water, to stop them drying out. I don't know how they'd have survived with today's central heating."

"The bats are pressed much heavier now," Carleton Wright says. "They don't need the same knocking in."

"The players have more bats," Duncan Fearnley says. "Really a batsman only needs two bats, and one will always be better than the other. Tom Moody at Worcester was the last one with the old approach. He'd say to me, 'Don't give me two bats. It makes the game complicated.' He'd get a good one, and he'd use it till it disintegrated. It's the tool of your trade, isn't it?"

"I used to be given two bats each summer by Slazengers," Tom Graveney says. "Most years I only used one of them through the whole season, batting four times a week and having a net every day. I only had one pair of gloves, too – and Robin Smith used to change his three times a day."

Tom Graveney. Scorer of 122 first-class centuries. What sort of money did Slazengers pay him?

"My biggest cheque was for autographing some bats. I think it was 27 pounds, 10 shillings."

# 6. A policeman calls

*Old Trafford, 26-31 July 1956, with Alan Oakman* — The Times, 13 July 2005

On Tuesday evening the doorbell rang at Alan Oakman's Hastings home.

"There was a policeman there, leaning on his bike. We weren't on the phone, and Gubby Allen had rung the station. 'Do you know where Alan Oakman lives? … Can you tell him to get to Old Trafford tomorrow?'"

Alan had made his debut in the previous Test at Headingley, when England had levelled the series. But, going in at number three, he had been bowled for 4 and for the Old Trafford Test the selectors, chaired by Gubby Allen, discarded him in favour of David Sheppard, now a young curate in Islington and picked on the back of three first-class innings and some London Clergy cricket.

"That would be a good grounding, wouldn't it?" Alan chuckles. "Lindwall and Miller, you don't meet many of them in clergy matches."

Then Tom Graveney sustained a bruised finger, and the telephone at Hastings Police Station rang.

"We were playing that week at Hastings, and I had to go down to Len Creese, the groundsman. He ran a pub, and I had to get the keys off him to pick up my kit. Then I drove up to London, to stay with some old schoolmates. A road parallel to Baker Street. They put a mattress down, and I slept in the hallway of this basement. The next morning I was off and up to Manchester."

Off, though he did not know it, to one of the most dramatic matches in Ashes history.

According to John Woodcock in *The Times*, the Old Trafford pitch on Thursday was 'a blissful place for batsmen'. Peter Richardson scored a maiden Test century; then David Sheppard, cheered on by a party of boys from his parish, stroked a chanceless 113.

Alan did not bat till Friday morning, making only ten, but by then the pitch was becoming dusty and taking spin. When the Australians went in to bat, Laker and Lock were soon in tandem.

"David Sheppard was fielding in the bat and pad position," Alan recalls. "'I haven't been playing much cricket,' he said. 'My reflexes aren't what they used to be.' He'd just made a hundred against Lindwall and Miller! So Peter May said, 'Oaky, do you mind going in?'"

From then on, the tall man from Hastings alternated between slip and short leg, as the Australians struggled against the turning ball. At four o'clock they were 48 for no wicket; by close, they were two down in their second innings – with eleven of the twelve wickets falling to Laker.

"Jim had a beautiful action, always staying up high. He could spin the ball on anything, and most of the Australians were back-foot players. They tended to push at the ball when they went forward. I was standing very close and, when Keith Miller came in, he said, 'If you don't look out, I'll hit you in the bollocks.' I thought, 'He's kidding me.' I wasn't wearing a box or anything. Then I thought, 'Is he?' But he just stabbed at it, and that helped it on its way to me."

England were over halfway to a victory that would retain the Ashes, then the weather intervened. Saturday was washed out, Sunday saw thunderstorms and on Monday they managed only an hour without further wickets.

The pitch was close to saturation, but the wind was strong and on Tuesday play started only ten minutes late. MacDonald and Craig batted patiently, and they were still there at lunch. Then the sun broke through, and Laker's spin started to bite. Craig was lbw, Miller bowled, and Mackay completed a pair, caught both times by Alan Oakman in the slips.

The Australians were six down at tea, with Colin MacDonald – "He played like an English player would" – looking unmoveable. But, after the break, he edged a fast-spinning off-break into Alan's hands at short leg, his fifth catch in the match, and the end soon followed.

Jim Laker had taken eight wickets for 26 runs in 36 overs in the day. He had captured all ten wickets in the innings, 19 in the match, but such were the times and such was his easy disposition that he 'jogged off the field as though nothing very much had happened.'

Tony Lock, meanwhile, had taken just one wicket in 69 overs.

"I felt a bit sorry for Locky. He was a great trier, but he didn't even look like getting a wicket. He got quicker and quicker, and he finished up bowling at leg stump. At the start he'd been applauding Jim's wickets, but by the end you could see him just folding his arms."

Laker stayed for some interviews, then started the drive home.

'My celebration dinner,' he wrote, 'consisted of a bottle of beer and a sandwich in a pub near Lichfield. I sat in the corner of a crowded bar while everyone talked about the Test. No one spotted me. Beyond asking me how far I had to go, the landlord said nothing.'

David Sheppard would make another comeback, scoring a winning century at Melbourne in 1963, but there were no more calls to Hastings Police Station for Alan Oakman. "I only played in two Tests, both against Australia, and both we won by an innings."

Later that year he and Jim Laker attended a dinner.

"I was introduced as the man who held five catches at Old Trafford, and Jim whispered in my ear, 'You're not still living on that, are you, Oaky?'"

Now working part-time at Edgbaston, where for many years he was Warwickshire coach, he laughs. "Here I am 49 years later, still living on it!"

## 7. Colin at his best

*Colin Milburn of Northamptonshire* WCM, Oct 2001

"You'll have to lose some weight," his county captain Keith Andrew told Colin Milburn. "For a start, why don't you drink halves instead of pints?"

It was August 1965, and that day the big man hit 150 in three hours. In the bar, the captain offered him a drink.

"I'll have two halves, please, guv," he said.

A year later Milburn was at Clacton-on-Sea, opening the batting on the first morning. August the 17th 1966. Sixty miles away at The Oval the England team was assembling with their new captain Brian Close. The idea was to take on the West Indies with a better fielding side – so there was no place for the 17½-stone Milburn.

"If people want to play for England," selector Alec Bedser said, "they've got to think about these things."

Milburn was the leading English run-scorer in the series, with a hard-hitting hundred at Lord's. When he reached three figures, four men ran on to the field and tried to hoist him up, as the West Indian fans had done to their hero David Holford – but, as Colin joked, 'there was a subtle difference – about 7½ stone!'

With the Beatles conquering America and England's footballers winning the World Cup, cricket was crying out for fresh excitement – and Colin Milburn was supplying it. But now, with all eyes on The Oval, he was at Clacton and it was left to the *Northampton Chronicle* to report his efforts: 'He scored only three runs in the first quarter of an hour, patiently pushing and prodding.'

It was a hot morning, the seaside crowd was in shirt-sleeves, and Keith Andrew settled in front of the pavilion with a cup of tea and a sandwich. Before the first hour was up, he was clapping Milburn's fifty and looking out at the Essex fielders scattered all round the boundary. "It was incredible. There was nobody on the off side in any acknowledged position. There was no mid-off, no cover point, no gully. Barry Knight was bowling, and he had four men on the boundary. They were giving Colin the single, and it was still in the first hour. I was spell-bound. I don't think I'd even touched my sandwich."

"The ball came onto the bat at Clacton," Essex's captain Gordon Barker says, "and the outfield was very fast. If I'd left a normal field, he'd probably have holed out. But the way he was going, I thought he'd have 200 by lunch."

They restricted him to 100 – out of 137 for no wicket. At the other end Roger Prideaux was happy to play his own quiet game.

One hundred before lunch, another in the afternoon. He took 18 off one Acfield over, including a six over the sight screen, but with the field back, "I had to run a hell of a lot of singles," he said. It was 297 for 0 at tea.

The temperature was near 80, and in the dressing room he stood red-faced. "It was like he'd got a sweat suit on," Keith Andrew recalls, "and there was a great puddle on the floor where he was standing."

Keith reckons he was too exhausted to add more, but Essex's Robin Hobbs tells a different story. "They came out after tea. Mickey Bear was on his haunches out at cow corner, with the crowd all behind him. Milburn launched into Acfield and, as he hit it, Mickey stood up. 'Oh no,' Colin groaned. He hadn't seen him."

In four hours he had hit 203, with four sixes and 22 fours. One of the only two double centuries of his career. The other was at Brisbane where his 243 included 181 runs in the two-hour afternoon session.

"Colin wasn't really a 200 man," Robin Hobbs says. "Especially when it was warm. He'd rather get back in the bar, wouldn't he?"

But at Clacton he had a point to make, and the next morning in the papers he was 'Clobbering Colin'. The *Daily Mail* rubbed it in: 'Against Essex, home county of chief selector Douglas Insole'.

Not only had he scored 203 but, with all the singles he'd run, he'd lost two pounds in weight.

Keith Andrew looked at him. "You'd better have a pint," he said.

"I never, ever tried to change Colin. He was a genius."

In the second innings Milburn and Prideaux made ducks as Northants won by seven wickets. It was the last time that Essex, struggling financially, staged a festival week at Clacton.

Milburn became one of *Wisden*'s five cricketers of the year. 'A pearl of great price in the modern game,' the almanack called him. But his genius was soon gone; he became a celebrity, got caught up in London's night-club world, and within three years a car accident had cost him his left eye.

"He had a lovely personality," Keith Andrew says. "And he was intelligent, too, a good teacher. There was a lot more to him than people knew. But people took advantage of his nature. It was so sad. I know it sounds sentimental, but I just wish he'd met the girl of his dreams. He'd have made a super father."

Clacton, August 1966. Milburn, caught Baer, bowled Acfield, 203.

"All the years I played cricket, they were worth it just to see Colin at his best."

## 8. A winter in the woods

*The cricketers find employment out of season* WCM, MAR 2002

"I've got just the thing for you this winter," Stuart Surridge told the young fast bowlers at Alf Gover's cricket school. "You can build up your muscles with my tree-felling squads."

Surridge was the Surrey captain, and his family firm made bats from English willow trees. Each winter in the 1950s he took young fast bowlers into the plantations: Tyson, Loader, Moss.

"The idea was to fill us out," Hampshire's Malcolm Heath explains. "Give us an extra yard of pace."

Heath had two winters of tree-felling, the second with the young Somerset bowler Ken Biddulph.

"After the first three days," Loader warned Ken, "you'll want to run away and die. Your hands will be sore and bleeding, and your back will ache more than you can imagine. But it does get better."

The plantation was near Coalville in Leicestershire, and Malcolm Heath and Ken Biddulph set out each Monday morning in a Surridge lorry. Two tall, skinny lads with dreams of greatness. All day they felled trees with a cross-cut saw and chopped them into rounds with axes. Hard manual work before the days of motorised tools.

"The second winter they produced a petrol-driven chain-saw," Ken recalls, "but only the pros were allowed to use it. We had to carry it for them, and even that was hard work."

They stayed at a farmhouse where "we were fed on good home-grown food: steak every night, and lashings of egg and bacon for breakfast." It was the early days of *The Archers*, and each evening the farmer's deaf father pressed his ear against a blaring radio. "He could sit in any part of the room and spit with alarming accuracy into the fire."

Most of his Somerset team-mates found casual employment for the long winter months: cider-making or at the cement works. Harold Stephenson was a qualified sheet metal worker and one year he had half the team making paraffin heaters. Peter Wight, who had come from British Guiana to study engineering, was a car mechanic. Brian Lobb, later a schoolmaster, worked on building sites. In the early sixties Peter Robinson arrived, and he found a job off-loading wagons in Taunton's railway goods yard – with a 5.30 a.m. start. "I couldn't wait to escape at the end of March."

"Around July you'd get members promising you winter jobs," Ken Biddulph recalls. "But they rarely materialised. One chap told me to telephone him in September but, when I did, he just sent me a copy of the local paper. 'I suggest you have a look through that.'"

Gloucestershire boasted five professional footballers, in the days when the seasons barely overlapped, but for the Somerset cricketers there was little romance in the rest of their year – though the debonair Chris Greetham found work as a dogsbody at Bray Film Studios. Look out for *Camp on Blood Island*, and you might even spot him among the prisoners-of-war.

"There were some miserable old buggers at the goods yard," Peter Robinson recalls. "I thought, 'If I finish up doing this for forty years, I'll be a miserable old bugger.' It doesn't make your noughts quite so bad, you know."

The two fast bowlers moved down to Surridge's estate in Surrey, where one day they were beaters for a pheasant shoot. Then they felled more trees near Aldermaston, and Ken earned his evening drinks playing the piano in the local pub. Hard work, good food and plenty of beer.

"The perfect diet for a fast bowler," he reckons. "It's just a pity I didn't become much of a fast bowler."

Heath and Biddulph. They never played for England, but 45 years on their backs are still straight as they bowl to yet another generation of youngsters.

Ken in the Costswolds: "That tree-felling job was the best thing that ever happened to me. I never once had a back problem, not even bowling on that rock-hard surface at Taunton."

Malcolm at Lord's: "It was so healthy, out in the fresh air. They've got a wonderful Keep Fit suite here, but I don't know. I doubt if it makes them as fit as that tree felling made me."

*Ken Biddulph (left) and Malcolm Heath.*

## 9. Rather you than me, old boy

*MCC's first tour of independent India* WCM, DEC 2001

Fifty years ago this winter MCC set out for its first cricket tour of the newly independent countries of India and Pakistan.

They left in mid-September and arrived home in early April. There were twenty of them: 17 cricketers, two journalists (later reduced to one) and a manager, Geoffrey Howard. No physio, no press relations officer, no coaches, no scorer. "We didn't even have a scorebook with us," Geoffrey recalls.

The manager was in his third year as secretary at Old Trafford, a relative newcomer to the world of cricket administration, but he received no pre-tour briefing. "I left my desk at Old Trafford in the afternoon, got together for dinner in the hotel at Paddington and was on the train and boat the following day."

"Well, good luck, old boy," the MCC secretary said, leaning his head into the first-class railway carriage. "Rather you than me. I can't stand educated Indians."

The top players did not expect to tour every year – so none of the party who had spent six months in Australia the previous winter were selected. It was a tour with five full Tests, but England were playing a second eleven. County stalwarts like Jack Robertson and Allan Watkins mingled with young hopefuls like Tom Graveney and Brian Statham.

The accommodation was a hit-and-miss affair. Sometimes they stayed with English families, sometimes in local hotels. At Ahmedabad Jack Robertson turned his back on his breakfast, and a monkey made off with it.

The health care varied, too. The captain Nigel Howard had a spell in a sanatorium, terrified that an Italian nurse would try to convert him to Catholicism, while at Bombay the manager took the Notts batsman Cyril Poole to the local bazaar where, surrounded by flies, an Indian doctor re-broke and set his finger.

"I took his watch while he was being operated on, and I held his hand the whole time. He was so drunk with anaesthesia, it took him hours to come round – and, when he did, quite suddenly, he looked at me and said, 'Here, you've got my bloody watch.'"

The travel was arduous. An overnight train journey to Bahawalpur was luxurious for the amateurs in the first-class coach, but the professionals emerged from their carriage coated in the red sand of the Sind desert and gasping for air.

Geoffrey Howard wrote home each day to his family, and he re-read his letters this summer while I worked with him on his memoirs. "There's something in them that I seem to have forgotten," he rang to tell me. "It seems that sometimes, when we flew, I took the controls of the aircraft."

'Yes,' his letter to his wife read, 'the chaps are always jittery when I take over, but it is as safe as it can be at 8000 feet.'

Some years later, after the Munich disaster, MCC would be dividing their tour parties into two planes. Yet in India the whole party was travelling in a twin-engine Dakota with the manager at the controls. A manager whose only flying experience was as a trainee navigator in the war.

The cricket was played on all kinds of surfaces. Turf at Bombay, then a coir mat at Ahmedabad, then a jute mat at Indore, then back to turf at Amritsar – though here a local protest, that the match had not been allocated to Patiala, led to water being poured over one end.

The Indians were happy to play out draws in the early Tests – unlike the Pakistanis, who were determined to win and to gain Test match status. With the 16-year-old Hanif batting with great maturity, Pakistan won by four wickets at Karachi – though *Wisden* records that 'MCC were very surprised at some of the umpiring decisions, not one of over thirty lbw appeals being granted in their favour.'

At Kanpur Hilton and Tattersall, England's spinners, brought victory in a low-scoring fourth Test, but the rubber was shared when India won a Test for the first time ever at Madras. On the first day of the match the news came of the death of King George VI, and in the only telephone communication from Lord's during the tour the manager was asked to arrange for black arm bands to be worn and for the rest day to be moved forward.

The Pakistanis had celebrated their victory with great jubilation, but the Indians were almost apologetic. "They were all very polite to us," Donald Carr recalls. "They said that the reason we had lost was because we were so upset that the King had died."

*The Times* was less charitable. 'Over the whole series England seem rather lucky to have shared the honours. India looked the stronger side on their type of pitch.'

Back in England, not only was there a new Queen on the throne but Winston Churchill had returned to power during their absence.

As the boat sailed back up the Mediterranean, the manager and Jack Robertson listened together to the radio broadcast of the budget. "The last item reported was that petrol was going up. And Jack said, 'I can't wait to get home and sell the car. I'm not paying three and sixpence a gallon for petrol.'"

## 10. Not given to many

*Arthur Milton of Gloucestershire* WCM, Sept 2002

'PLACID MILTON 104 NOT OUT IN FIRST APPEARANCE,' read the headline in *The Times*.

It was July 1958, the paper ran to just 16 pages, and Arthur Milton's debut century made him the first England cricketer to remain on the field throughout a Test. 'The impression one gained was of a player with a first-rate temperament and a placid disposition. He has the look of one of Nature's games players.'

Seven years earlier, in November 1951, when *The Times* was only ten pages, it reported the late call-up to the England football team of Arsenal's young right-wing. 'Milton, a true games player, progressive and intelligent, for all his inexperience, should not be overawed by the occasion.' But, without his team-mate Jimmy Logie to pass him the ball, he did not shine.

"I was fortunate to be chosen," he says now. "Stanley Matthews was out of favour, and I'd only played a handful of times for Arsenal. I remember Jimmy breaking the news. 'Finney's cried off,' he said, 'and they've picked you, as you're the nearest to Wembley.' I thought he was pulling my leg."

The son of a Bristol factory worker, he had left school in the summer of 1946. "I'd done my Higher School Certificate. Maths was my main subject, and I had the forms to fill out for Oxford, to sit the exams for an exhibition. Quantity surveying was an option, too, I remember."

But a scout arrived from Arsenal, then his National Service papers, and all thought of qualifications was forgotten. "I loved sport – and, when you're young, you don't think about getting old, do you?"

His cricket had developed in his father's team during the War. "They were always short, and I had to take my kit along. So I was playing with men from the age of eleven. Bats were in short supply so Dad sawed the bottom three inches off a full-size one. It was wonderful; you could drive the yorkers."

He made his debut for Gloucestershire in 1948, developing a back-foot technique to cope with Bristol's low, sandy wickets. "He would go right back," his team-mate Bomber Wells says. "He'd follow the ball like a snake." And there was no better close fielder.

His Test career lasted only twelve months, with the 1958/59 tour of Australia a collective disaster. "I was very pleased to get back to my own tump, to my own pals whom I knew how to play with."

He played till 1974. Then he coached Oxford University on an honorarium, but the money was not enough to support a wife and three children. "Joan had had a good job at Barings Bank, but in those days the girls had to leave when they got married."

All his adult life had revolved around sport. Not just cricket and football but golf, tennis and billiards. He was outstanding at them all, a natural games player, and now he had to earn his living another way.

"That's when I started to regret that I hadn't been to university. I loved my years of cricket, they were wonderful days in the sun, but I'd have liked to have worked *and* played. I think that's what sport is for. Recreation and exercise. Away from what we do most of the week. I don't really agree with professionalism."

Eventually he found work delivering the mail in North Bristol. "It turned my whole life around. With cricket I was only interested in my own performance, but with the Post Office I was serving the public; they came first. It was an education in life. It turned me into a better human being."

When he reached retirement, he took to doing paper rounds. You can see him each morning on the Bristol Downs. On his old Post Office bicycle. And the newspapers that he pushes through the letter boxes are not ten pages now. "At weekends there are so many sections I have to take them apart."

He collects the money on Mondays, and he is always happy to stop for a chat. "Over at Cote Paddock, they're mostly old ladies, and they've always got the money out ready for you. I do give them a bit of time. Some of them have had very interesting lives, and they don't see many people."

Arthur Milton. The last man to play football and cricket for England. Imagine the newspaper features if he were playing now, the fees his agent would demand.

"What did you earn at Arsenal, Arthur?"

"I don't know. We never thought about money. I just feel privileged to have been born with the talent to fulfil myself in the games I loved. It's not given to many."

This summer a letter arrived from Bristol University, awarding him an honorary MA. Fifty-six years after he threw away that Oxford application, he and Joan walked with all the young graduates to the ceremony. "It was very flattering, and I had a wonderful response from the hall. But I do wish I'd earned my degree in the normal way and made use of it."

For Jimmy Logie there was no such ending. "It was very sad. We were playing Spartak Moscow at Highbury, and the Russian referee refused us a penalty when we were 2-1 down. After the match Jimmy refused to shake his hand, and he never played for Arsenal again. It ruined his life; he was in love with the club. He ended up selling papers on Piccadilly."

There is no sadness about Arthur as he cycles his paper round.

"It's magical up there. There's always early moisture on the grass and, when the sun comes up over the horizon, it draws it up and forms this low mist that runs all across the downs. I love it. I shall do it as long as I can."

## 11. As the game should be played

*Sydney, Fri 7 Jan 1966, with Bob Barber* THE TIMES, 29 NOV 2006

"Sydney is the essence of Australia," Bob Barber says. "You'd got the Hill, and there was a sense of battle. And I enjoyed that. Maybe for Australians coming to England, Lord's is the place. But for me, there were certain things I wanted to do as a cricketer and Sydney, Australia, was the place to do them. The feeling went right back to when I was a boy, lying in bed with a little radio, listening to Johnnie Moyes' commentaries."

His chance came in January 1966. The boy with the radio was now 30 years old, walking out at 10.30 on a bright morning with Geoffrey Boycott. With the first two Tests drawn and the pitch expected to break up later, a large partnership would be a major step towards regaining the Ashes.

Boycott and Barber. The Yorkshire professional setting out on a long career of run-scoring and the free-spirited Cambridge graduate about to turn to a life in business. They shared a steely determination to succeed, but they differed in the approach.

That morning, while Geoff Boycott sat in a cocoon of concentration, Bob Barber splashed about in the hotel pool with his two-year-old daughter before driving to the airport to collect his father. "To me, cricket is played above the neck," he says, "and I liked to be relaxed."

In a light breeze McKenzie and Hawke swung the new ball effectively, and Boycott was badly dropped at square leg. Then the runs started to come and by noon, according to John Woodcock in *The Times*, 'the famous Hill was a blaze of confetti, and England were safely on their way.'

At lunch the scoreboard read 93 for 0, Barber 57.

Under the captaincy of Mike Smith, England had promised a tour of positive cricket. "It was a time when a bit too much selfishness had come into the game," Bob Barber says. "In one sense it was professionalism – but to me it wasn't professional.

"To my mind we were public entertainers, there to bring in the crowds, not to drive them out. I got runs in the early matches at Perth, and I remember going up in the hotel lift with a group of journalists. 'What I really want to do,' I said, 'is to play one innings as I think the game should be played. And I want to play it at Sydney.' I could have got a first-baller, but within myself I knew this was the one occasion in my life above all others. There's a battle of wills between batsman and bowler, and I always set out to impose myself right away. Once I'd done that and the innings was going well, I didn't mind getting out. But not that day. I was determined to go on."

An hour after lunch he was on 95 out of 168. In Johannesburg the previous winter he had been bowled for 97, trying to reach his maiden

Test century with a six. Now he drove a four, pushed a single, quietly raised his cap and set about the bowling with fresh purpose. In the words of Geoff Boycott, it was 'one of the truly great displays of batting in Test cricket'.

John Woodcock wrote of 'judgment tempered by aggression. In every line of Barber's remarkable innings there showed an independence of character.'

At the start of the tour Boycott had been laid low and, when Bob had visited his sick bed, he had received a typically combative greeting: "Don't you worry. I'll be fit, and I'll have your place." – "I don't remember his exact words. They might have been less polite than that." Now they were working together.

"You have to have a balance. The way I played allowed Geoffrey to play his own game, and he played it very well."

On a gloriously sunny afternoon they took the score to 234 before Boycott chipped the penultimate ball before tea into the bowler Philpott's hands.

For another hour Bob Barber piled on the runs, reaching 185 before 'with a weary-looking stroke' he edged a wide ball from Hawke onto his stumps. His innings stood as the highest ever played against Australia on the first day of a Test till overtaken in 2003 by India's Sehwag.

'Often in bleak moments,' EW Swanton wrote years later, 'do I cast back to that innings. It made blissful watching to English eyes.'

He came off to a standing ovation from the 40,000 crowd. A newspaper cartoon called him 'the only fellow in Australia who can empty the bars', and his delighted father reported the words of a man on the Hill: "Why can't we have a batsman like this Barber?"

John Edrich added a hard-working century. Then, as the pitch became worn and the off-spinners Fred Titmus and David Allen set to work, the Australians fell to an innings defeat.

In the next Test at Adelaide Bob Barber was bowled third ball for a duck, and a batting collapse allowed Australia to level the series.

"It was a hell of a bump," he says, still disappointed that they did not bring back the Ashes.

A successful businessman who follows the game from his home in Switzerland, what advice does he have for the England cricketers this winter?

"You've got to believe in yourself. You're privileged to be given the chance to represent your country, and playing in Australia is the one time in your life above all others when you should grasp the pleasure. You should let your spirit come out. It's a game. It should be fun. I felt it then. I still do."

## 12. The last heyday of Oxford cricket

*Mike Eagar of Oxford University* TWC, March 2006

Mike Eagar went up to Oxford in the autumn of 1955. A classical scholar from Rugby, he won hockey and cricket blues as a freshman. "I'd never have got either if I hadn't done National Service," he says. "I'd had three years between school and university – and, when I joined the Navy, I was posted to the Ministry of Defence so that I could play top-class club hockey."

Having learnt Russian, he had to read *Pravda* and make notes on the leading Soviet admirals. "If I saw a picture of one with a drink in his hand, I'd write, 'Probably an alcoholic'. I'm not sure what it achieved. My successor told me he couldn't read my handwriting and had to start again."

He played hockey for Surbiton, cricket in Navy matches at Chatham. "When I went to Oxford, I was playing the same level of hockey, but the cricket was a big step up."

In his second match, while he struggled against accurate Hampshire bowling, their keeper Leo Harrison coached him, and he top-scored with 34 and 80. Then, in the next three matches, facing the leg spin of Freddie Brown, Bruce Dooland and Richie Benaud, he hit a century and two fifties. "I always think of 1956 as the last really good year of leg-spinners, and I loved playing them. I liked to come down the wicket, and I could read them in the air."

With a fifty in the Varsity match, his name crept into the national averages. "I was about twentieth, but August was wet, it was Laker's great year; by the time the season ended, by not playing, I'd risen to seventh!"

He was above May, Cowdrey, even Neil Harvey, and his uncle on the Gloucestershire committee approached him. "They wanted to groom me for the captaincy." So the following July he stepped into the world of county cricket.

"It struck me immediately that I'd walked out of a conservatory and into a working business. I was always talking theory at Oxford. But there was so much that the professionals knew: about things like using the crease when bowling and how spinners don't spin every ball. I realised that there was a hell of a lot for me to learn."

George Emmett, Gloucestershire's ageing skipper, quietly advised him against the captaincy, and he returned to two more summers in a rapidly improving Oxford side. "We didn't have any coaching to speak of, and at the public schools all the coaching was of batting. So the university sides never had any bowling. Then suddenly we had a really good bowling side."

On a memorable day in May 1958 the seasoned Jack Bailey and the very fast freshman David Sayer bowled out the New Zealanders for 45.

From 1952 to 1955, a period that included Colin Cowdrey's three years,

Oxford played 57 first-class matches without a victory. Yet in the next six years they won 22 matches, eleven of them against county sides. The 1959 Oxford team, EW Swanton reckoned, was good enough to finish in the top half of the championship table.

With several of the side hailing from grammar schools, a wind of change was beginning to blow. Soon the university would stop giving places to less academic sportsmen like Cowdrey, and perhaps later Geography undergraduates would have to do more to gain second-class honours than MJK Smith. "He had to go away in the middle of a match for a viva, and he came back with a broad grin. They'd asked him what relative humidity was, and he was really stuck. Then one of the board said, 'Would you be more likely to put on a swing bowler when it was overcast or when the sun was shining?'"

In the 1959 Varsity match Mike Eagar batted behind the brilliant David Green from Manchester Grammar, the captain Alan Smith, Abbas Ali Baig who later in the month would make a century on debut for India, the Pakistani Javed Burki and CB Fry's grandson Charles. Yet, for all this talent, Mike Eagar was in the middle before lunch, with four wickets down for 68. "Poor Charlie Fry. He went out to bat in his first Varsity match, and off his very first ball he ran Abbas out. When I came out, he was white as a sheet." The two of them took the score to 140, setting Oxford on the way to victory.

The next year, to underline the strength of Oxford's cricket in this period, his place was taken by a freshman, the Nawab of Pataudi.

Meanwhile the Gloucestershire captaincy passed to Tom Graveney and, amid controversy, on to the Old Etonian Tom Pugh. Suddenly in August 1961 Mike Eagar, now a master at Eton, was summoned: "I'd had one village match all summer, and I got a telegram. Would I come and play at Pontypridd?"

His return was not a success. His laboured 29 was slow-handclapped by the Welsh crowd. Back in Bristol, when he messed up a piece of boundary fielding, the Bank Holiday spectators jeered 'Go home, jazz-hat!' Then at Canterbury, as twelfth man, he fielded on the last day while the veteran Sam Cook rested a sore finger. "About three o'clock Sam brought out the drinks. 'I reckon I could bowl this lot out,' he said to Tom Pugh, and I had to go off with the tray. There was a hell of a row. Les Ames the Kent manager came onto the field and, when I reappeared later with a sweater, the crowd slow-handclapped me. So in three games I got barracked three times. It's probably the only record I achieved."

Times were changing. With cricket becoming wholly professional, the role of the universities declined. Excluding the Varsity matches, Oxford won more first-class games in Mike Eagar's four years there than it has done in the last 40 years.

"I never became a star player," he says, "but in many ways I played in the last great years of Oxford cricket."

## 13. The shock of my life

*Allan Watkins of Glamorgan* TWC, Sept 2007

The county championship has thrown up few greater surprises than Glamorgan's first title in 1948. Before that, their 21 first-class summers had yielded 16 bottom-five finishes and none in the top five. Yet, under the ebullient leadership of Wilf Wooller, they pipped the grander Surrey and Middlesex to the championship.

"We weren't a great side," Allan Watkins says. "But we had a skipper who never relaxed. We used to say he skippered both sides. If anything won us the championship, it was the fielding. Wilf was a brainy chap, and he developed this leg theory."

With an attack dominated by in-swing and off-spin, Glamorgan's leg trap took catches all summer – and no one took more than Watkins himself. He was, in John Arlott's view, 'without doubt the best close-to-the-wicket field in the world. He has caught the uncatchable so often as to have made the impossible his normal standard.'

Watkins was a useful middle-order batsman, and that summer he was developing as a left-arm in-swing bowler. He did not score the runs of the classy Gilbert Parkhouse or the highly strung Willie Jones nor did he bowl with the success of the off-spinner Len Muncer, the first in the country to 100 wickets. "People don't talk about Len much," Allan says. "He was a Londoner, and the Welsh like Welsh heroes. He wasn't an athletic type, but he was built for bowling and he'd bowl all day. He'd puff and blow, mind, but he never wanted to come off."

That summer Don Bradman's Invincibles were crushing England, but the selectors – among them the former Glamorgan off-spinner Johnnie Clay – did not turn to Parkhouse, Jones or Muncer, nor to the captaincy of Wooller or the keeping of Haydn Davies. "Haydn was a far better keeper than Godfrey Evans," Allan reckons. "I think he had more up top. Godfrey was all flourish."

But when the team for the final Test was announced, the Welsh county was finally recognised – in the form of Watkins himself. "I had the shock of my life," he says. "I must admit, I wondered why I was picked."

He was the first Glamorgan cricketer to play in an Ashes Test and, according to the *South Wales Argus*, his home town of Usk had not known such distinction since the Marcher Lords made it an important meeting place back in the 14th century.

He had never played a first-class match for any side other than Glamorgan, and the atmosphere in the England dressing room at The Oval was nothing like that of Wooller's rowdy team. "I could be arguing with Wilf every five minutes of the day, all about cricket, all good fun. And

Wilf and Haydn were always arguing. It was never quiet. But England had done so badly there was no joy in the side. Nobody spoke to me."

On the first day, coming in at 35 for five, he went to hook Lindwall and took a fearful blow on his left shoulder that effectively ruined his match. England were all out for 52, and he missed much of Australia's 389 in reply. But he was on the field for Bradman's final Test innings.

"He was a majestic figure, and we clapped him all the way to the wicket. Eric Hollies was bowling from the Vauxhall end, and Norman Yardley said to me, 'You're a close-to-the-wicket fielder, Allan. Up you go. ... See the whites of his eyes.' He played the first ball quietly to me, and I picked it up. The second came down, a googly, and he left a gap. I had a beautiful view of the ball hitting the wickets. He looked back and off he went. I was the last man to field a ball off Bradman in a Test."

Glamorgan pressed forward in the championship. While Allan was at The Oval, his place at Cardiff, in a vital innings victory over Surrey, was taken by the 50-year-old Johnnie Clay, who took ten wickets. "He was an old man by then, but he was still a great spinner. He was tall, with long fingers. The ball came out high and, as it came down, I was at short leg and I swear I could hear it buzzing. He really could spin the ball."

Glamorgan went on to Bournemouth, one victory from the title, and Allan – staying with his sister in London while he had treatment on his shoulder ("I thought, that's the finish of my Test career") – spent the afternoon of Tuesday 24 August buying newspapers from the man at Hither Green Station. "Every hour I was checking the latest score in the Stop Press."

The umpire at Bournemouth was the Glamorgan veteran Dai Davies, and it was his finger that went up for the final wicket. Knott, lbw Clay. "That's out," he is supposed to have said, "and we've won the championship."

Davies always denied the remark. But Allan believes the story. "Everybody told me about it when they came back, and it would have been a thing that Dai would do." According to John Arlott, 'Only a few minutes later Davies' voice was a strong influence in the spontaneous *Hen Wlad Fy Nhadau* of the tiny cluster of Welshmen in front of the pavilion.'

"We'd always been at the bottom with teams like Northants, and the championship gave great pride to the people of Wales."

That winter Allan Watkins was in South Africa, playing for England. He took a brilliant catch to turn the course of the first Test, and at Ellis Park, Johannesburg, he scored his first Test century.

He is 85 years old now, and his house in Oundle is called Ellis Park. "There's a lot of luck in cricket," he says simply. "And I was lucky."

## 14. Deep harmony

*Jack Bond of Lancashire* TWC, Apr 2008

It was February 1968 when Jack Bond got the phone call that changed his life.

He had joined the Old Trafford staff in May 1955, just after his 23rd birthday. "Oh," the Secretary Geoffrey Howard said with shock as the fresh-faced youngster filled in the forms. "We thought you were only about 19."

There followed years of apprenticeship, his greatest progress coming when he played under the second-team captaincy of Geoff Edrich, whose love of cricket was all the stronger for the years he had spent as a prisoner of the Japanese. "He was like a father figure to me. He backed his players, and he was always prepared to take a gamble. Cricket was his life; he ate, slept and drank it. A lot of things in my captaincy I learned from Geoff."

The lessons he learned from the first-team captains were less positive. "Cyril Washbrook would let games drift. As a captain you've got to get a grip. Cricket is a situations game, and the scoreboard tells you what the situation is." Washbrook was a distant figure to the youngsters, a stern disciplinarian, and things did not improve when the committee forced his successor Bob Barber, a young amateur, to stay at separate hotels from the team. "A captain can do more good with his team off the field than on it. You need to know your players, know the home life, know if they've been up all night with the baby, and it's very important for them to know you. The committee didn't give Bob a chance."

Jack Bond won his county cap in 1961, scoring 1,701 runs, and his tally rose to 2,125 in 1962. The last batsman to score 2,000 runs in a summer for Lancashire, he was being mentioned as a possible Test cricketer.

Old Trafford had become an unhappy place, riddled with politics. In 1962 they appointed as captain the 34-year-old amateur Joe Blackledge, who had never played a first-class game and who struggled to make the transition from the Manchester Association. Then came the Australian Ken Grieves, who was sacked after two years, along with several team-mates. "It was in the papers before they'd been told," Jack remembers. "People were shouting at him from the crowd, 'Here, Grievesy, I see you've got the sack.'"

Three years of the genial Brian Statham followed. They rose in the table from 14th to 13th to 12th to 11th, but there was no real progress.

Jack Bond, meanwhile, had his own problems. In May 1963, at the age of 31, he had his left arm broken by a short ball from the West Indian Wes Hall, and his batting never recovered. "They used to say that from 29 to 32 were your prime years, but my arm was so weak that for 18 months I couldn't pick up a shovel full of coal and put it on the fire."

He was in and out of the side, and he nearly left in the autumn of 1964. But the departing secretary Geoffrey Howard persuaded him to stay. "You won't regret it," Howard said. Three years later the telephone rang, and Howard's successor Jack Wood offered him the captaincy. The committee's attempts to recruit an outsider – notably, Garry Sobers – had all failed so they turned to the quiet Bolton man who had worked well with the youngsters whenever he had captained the second eleven. "They asked me to do it on a caretaker basis while they looked round for somebody else."

Jack came from strong Methodist stock. His father had worked as a spinner in the local mill and sat as a Labour member on Little Hulton Council, one year serving as mayor. They had turned the front parlour of their house into a fish-and-chip shop, and his mother worked there from Monday to Saturday. With the only telephone in the area, they were the hub of the local community; Jack, an only child, imbibed the values of their close-knit world.

"Methodism is about friendship and fellowship, people helping other people," he says. "If you only had those things in your life, nothing else, you wouldn't go far wrong."

The chapel at Little Hulton was rebuilt in the 1980s, but Jack and Florence, his wife of 53 years, can still be found there most Sundays. They have had their tragedies – a son, Wesley, was killed in a car accident at the age of 26 – but their faith remains firm, as do their voices. "I love singing," he says. "I know my hymn book better than my bible." His favourite is the old Methodist standard *Deep Harmony*.

*Sweet is the work, my God, my King,*
*To praise thy name, give thanks and sing.*

Before joining the staff at Old Trafford, he had been a promising wing-half for the church football team: "Football was really my first love," he admits. But Florence had made him give it up when he became a professional cricketer. They couldn't afford for him to break a leg so he disposed of his kit with dramatic finality. The next week a scout from Wolverhampton Wanderers turned up. "Where's Jack Bond?" he asked. "He's given up," came the reply. "He's burnt his boots."

The summer of 1968 began badly for the caretaker captain: out of the Gillette Cup in April and only one win in their first 17 matches. But the draws started to outnumber the defeats – "We had to learn how to draw" – then came a run of victories that lifted them to sixth place in the table.

His most important victory came at Northampton. On the second evening he was within seven runs of his first century for three years – but, with a lead of 61, he saw the chance of a crucial half hour with the ball and declared. Three wickets fell, and the match was won by lunch-time the next day. "It made the lads think, nobody can set their own stall out for 100. It's the game that matters."

The Indian wicket-keeper Farokh Engineer had injected a fresh spirit, and there were several younger players coming into the team: David Lloyd, Ken Shuttleworth, David Hughes and Barry Wood. With Clive Lloyd available for half the following summer, the mood at the club was changing. The captain was no longer a caretaker.

The payments were altered – more on the basic wage, less for the match fee – and there was no distinction made between players. "You can't have the fellow bowling the ball earning twice what the fellow catching it at slip is paid. Anyway, I don't believe money is the motivator people believe it is. Pride of performance, pride of playing for the county, that was our motivator."

Lancashire became a family club, with wives increasingly present at matches, and Florence as the captain's wife played her part. "We didn't have people doing the laundry so she used to take home Clive's and Harry Pilling's flannels and wash them."

In 1969 the 40-over Sunday League started, and Jack Bond's Lancashire were its first winners. "Some of the counties, like Yorkshire, weren't interested at all. They thought it was a bit of a joke. But our success created so much interest. We won the title at Nuneaton. It was a two o'clock start, and we had so many supporters come down that they'd run out of pies by one. And they ran out of beer."

Lancashire won ten Sunday matches in a row, but Jack Bond kept them calm. "I've always tried to keep on an even keel. I remember saying, 'Somebody's going to give us a pasting. It's bound to happen. But let it not be today.'"

The tactics emerged. The bowlers' run-ups were limited to 15 yards so the spinners David Hughes and Jack Simmons were crucial. Fitness and fielding were emphasised: "People said they came to watch us field." Then, after an early defeat at Chelmsford, when John Sullivan had had a bad day with the ball, they never again took the field with just five bowlers. It was a fast-moving 'situations game'; Geoff Edrich's example had not been forgotten.

Jack was the only regular church-goer in the side – "Barry Wood used to come sometimes when he was short of runs" – and it wasn't always easy for him to fit in a service on Sunday mornings.

*Sweet is the day of sacred rest,*
*No mortal cares shall seize my breast.*

The Lord's Day Observance Society was strong, but Jack's minister told him, "Bus drivers work on Sundays." So, after 16 afternoons of packed crowds and fast-moving cricket, the new Sunday cup was held aloft by a Methodist. It was Lancashire's first outright trophy for 35 years.

"Winning makes teams happy," he reflects. "But what's important is what you do with that happiness, how you put it to use."

Lancashire built on their success, retaining the title in 1970. Shuttleworth, Simmons and Hughes were all in the first four in the Sunday bowling averages, and the league's leading scorer was little Harry Pilling, nudging and scampering where Clive Lloyd at the other end was strking the ball with power. "If anybody from Lancashire should have played for England in those years, it was Harry."

That year they also reached the Gillette Cup final at Lord's, where their run chase seemed to depend on Clive Loyd. "It was his first full year, and he wanted to win us something. But he got out for 29 and, when he came in, he sat for a long time with his pads on. I think he was thinking he'd let us down and we weren't going to win. There might even have been a tear or two. But Harry got 70, and from then on Clive realised it wasn't all down to him."

Lloyd and Engineer had become Lancastrians, full of Red Rose pride and laughing with their team-mates. "Cricket humour is just the same all the world over."

At Lord's one day the club president Neville Cardus came in to congratulate Peter Lever. "That was the most magnificent spell of bowling I've seen in a decade. Aren't you proud to be a Lancastrian?" "I'm sorry," Lever replied. "I may have been born in Todmorden, but it was on the Yorkshire side." Engineer, sitting next to him, shook his head: "These bloody foreigners."

In the three summers from 1970 to 1972 Lancashire played 13 Gillette matches and won them all, with Jack Bond lifting the trophy for the third time on almost his last day as Lancashire captain, a day made splendid by a vintage Clive Lloyd century.

"They weren't all easy games," he reflects. "We had a load of cliff-hangers."

There was the late-night semi-final at Old Trafford in 1971, when Hughes plundered 24 off a John Mortimore over to bring victory at ten to nine. There were 23,500 in the ground that day, and the ever-steady Bond was at the other end: "I said to David, 'If you can see it and you fancy it, give it the full treatment – but look to hit it straight.'"

Then came the final at Lord's when Kent's Asif Iqbal suddenly seemed to be taking the game away from Lancashire. "I had to bring Jack Simmons on from the pavilion end, which was the wrong end for an off-spinner with the slope. But I couldn't wait another over." Asif cracked the ball into the covers, and the 39-year-old skipper dived acrobatically, rolled over and came up with the catch of his lifetime. A catch that brought forth a great Lancastrian roar around the ground. "The number of people who've told me they were there that day, I don't know how they all got in," he says.

Other trophies slipped away. They lost the 1971 Sunday League on the last day of the season. "We'd been at Clive's wedding the day before, and

*Lancashire at Lord's, Gillette final 1971.*
*(from left) C. Lloyd, D. Hughes, J. Simmons, J. Bond, D. Lloyd,*
*K. Shuttleworth, J. Sullivan, H. Pilling, F. Engineer, P. Lever.*

everybody behaved themselves. But some of the committee thought we'd been drinking." And, to his lifelong regret, the championship was never won. Twice they came close, but it was not to be.

Jack Bond's Lancashire, with five trophies from ten one-day tournaments, are still arguably the finest one-day county of them all.

**Successful county captains in one-day cricket**

| County | Captain | Competitions | Trophies won |
|---|---|---|---|
| Gloucestershire | M.W. Alleyne | 24 | 7 |
| Kent | M.H. Denness | 17 | 6 |
| Lancashire | J.D. Bond | 10 | 5 |
| Essex | K.W.R. Fletcher | 39 | 5 |

"Jack's great strength," Clive Lloyd says, "was that he knew about teamwork. He was such a good man personally, you wanted to do well for him."

"It's so important," Jack says, "to have everybody in the team in complete harmony."

Complete harmony. Deep harmony. He never wore his religion on his sleeve, but the inspiration was always there.

## 15. So close to a cap

*Peter Sainsbury*

WCM, Aug 2002

*'CONFIDENTIAL,'* the paragraph begins, the words typed awkwardly onto the blue aerogramme letter. *'I was called to a meeting yesterday a.m. – PBH, FRB, Kipper, Godders and myself. TEB had gone water-skiing.'*

"Isn't it lovely?" Peter Sainsbury chuckles. "All the initials. I can just hear him saying it."

The letter is dated 17 November 1958. From Sydney. PBH was Peter May, England captain, FRB his manager Freddie Brown. Kipper Cowdrey, Godders Evans, TEB Bailey. And 'myself'? The baggage man and scorer George Duckworth, the old Lancashire and England keeper. Writing to Geoffrey Howard, the Lancashire secretary who had managed the Ashes-winning tour four years earlier.

"You'll enjoy these," Geoffrey told me, as he passed over the bundle. "George always wrote a good letter."

In a pair of fold-up chairs, on a bank overlooking the Hampshire Rose Bowl's second ground, we sit. Peter Sainsbury and I. It is our first meeting since he coached me one Easter holiday at Bournemouth, maybe 1962.

*'Having seen our fourth successive doped wicket, we realise we have a terribly unbalanced side so we decided on a spin replacement. Laker and Lock will have to be preserved for Tests only – they are our only chance. Frank and Loader may as well be in England.'*

Frank Tyson had been the spearhead of the England attack on that tour four years earlier. But the Australians were not to be caught twice that way, and after only a month it was clear that the pitches would be slow and that the tour party was a spinner short. Lock had a bad knee, Laker was never keen to overwork his spinning finger, and they had not replaced Wardle, whose invitation had been withdrawn after writing a series of bitter articles for the *Daily Mail.*

John Woodcock in *The Times* thought the choice lay between Illingworth, Mortimore and Tattersall.

*'Illingworth was mentioned (having played at The Oval last year), but his poor 1958 ruled him out. JCL had mentioned that Mortimore of Glos was promising and had good flight. I plumped for Peter Sainsbury who I saw bowl very well v NZ and also at Scarboro'.'*

"Did he really?" Peter says with a purr.

*'I think he got over 30 wickets at Scarboro'.'*

In fact, he took 21 wickets in three matches. For the Players against the Gentlemen, he twice dismissed the trio of Dexter, May and Mike Smith, and he scored 87 runs for once out against the New Zealanders. 'Throughout the Festival,' *Wisden* recorded, 'his cricket reached a high standard.'

As a family we often watched Hampshire, and our favourite was Peter Sainsbury. He was never a glamorous player, but he was a competitor, always busy in the game. Scampering singles at number six, bowling with that reliable flight and drift, crouching at the batsman's hip and holding the most wonderful catches.

His team-mate Jimmy Gray joins us on the bank.

"I didn't see any better fielders," he says. "Arthur Milton was the only one in Peter's class. They just caught the ball and threw it back. And those people don't get publicity, do they?"

One tea interval my younger brother Andrew ran onto the outfield with his Brownie box camera. "Can I take a snap of you, Peter?" he asked, and for what seemed like ten minutes he wobbled the camera about before finally clonking the shutter. Peter stood there patiently, smiling all the while. He was a nice man, a good county cricketer with no great pretensions.

"I'd love to have worn the three lions," he says now. "It's every cricketer's dream. I got 100 wickets in my first summer, but I went to Pakistan on an 'A' tour with Tony Lock. And I could see the difference in class between us."

That was the winter of 1955/56, when he came back trying to bowl like Lock. "I lost what I did naturally. It took me a couple of years to get it back."

His fielding earned him the chance to be twelfth man in several home Tests. "I was always waiting for somebody to pull a muscle, but I never got on the park. The closest I got was the time I thought Ted Dexter was waving for a hat. I ran out with it. 'What are you doing out here?' he said. 'No, I don't want a bloody hat. Get off.'"

He played till 1976, the only member of both Hampshire's title-winning sides. Then he served the county as coach till 1991 – in the years of Malcolm Marshall. "What a great bowler! How could I tell him what to do? I'd ask him, 'Why do you think you're not getting any wickets, Maco?' And I'd let him tell me."

Twenty cricketers have ended their first-class careers with 20,000 runs and 1,000 wickets, and Peter is the only one of them without a Test cap. And, of these twenty, only six have also taken 600 catches: Grace, Hirst, Rhodes, Woolley, Close and Sainsbury.

"He's up there, isn't he?" Jimmy Gray says. "You can't have the figures he's got and not be up there."

But he didn't play for England. Another of those Hampshire stalwarts who never got the chance: Neville Rogers, Trevor Jesty, Jimmy Gray himself. Between 1932 and 1982, more than 260 cricketers represented England, and only three of them came from Hampshire: Derek Shackleton, Butch White and Bob Cottam. Between them they managed just thirteen caps.

"Had we played for another county," Gray reckons, "we'd have had more opportunities, and that's all you ask for as a player."

That winter of 1958/59, Peter Sainsbury was in South Africa, coaching at Kimberley High School, where his most promising youngster was Frew Macmillan: "a super cricketer, but he chose tennis."

George Duckworth's letter completes the story. *'We decided on Peter and talked of getting him from Kimberley. This a.m. on our way to the ground the skipper told me that they had another recap on the position and decided on Mortimore. What happened last night or who caused the swing round, I don't know.'*

"To think I got that close," he says. "Within twelve hours. Between going to bed and getting up."

What caused the change? Was it Trevor Bailey, back from water-skiing, and offering a different view? Or was it Jim Laker, nursing his sore finger and determined to have another off-spinner, not a slow left-armer? Another letter, ten days later, seems to suggest the latter.

*'This afternoon JCL has been unlucky. Having promised to do all he can for Mortimore (after having done so much to get him here) an extra net has been ordered for the new boy and JCL has missed an afternoon in bed.'*

John Mortimore played the final Test at Melbourne, then two in New Zealand – as no doubt Peter Sainsbury would have done.

He smiles as we part. That same cheerful smile he held for my brother all those years ago.

"I'd like a copy of that letter for the family," he says. "You've made my life!"

## 16. Tenser and tenser

*Melbourne, Thurs 30 Dec 1982, with Geoff Miller* THE TIMES, 14 DEC 2006

"It was the most dramatic finish I ever played in," Geoff Miller says. "In the 1981 NatWest final at Lord's I dived in last ball to level the scores. But this was a Test match at Melbourne. Against Australia."

Bob Willis's England were 2-0 down, needing to win both the last Tests to retain the Ashes, and a see-saw contest was going Australia's way on the fourth afternoon when, chasing 292 for victory, Hughes and Hookes completed a century partnership that took the score to 171 for three.

Four years earlier Miller had set a record for an English off-spinner in Australia, with 23 wickets in the series, but now he was struggling.

"I wasn't bowling particularly well, and Kim Hughes went to lap me. It wasn't a good ball, but it bounced a bit and he gloved it."

Behind the stumps his Derbyshire team-mate Bob Taylor, moving down leg, changed direction and, according to Henry Blofeld, 'held a superb one-handed catch in the middle of a somersault.'

"Bob was very special," Geoff says.

An out-of-form Allan Border took Hughes' place.

"We'd been out on a deep-sea fishing trip: John Dyson, Border, myself and Both. Border just sat at the back of the boat. 'I think this is going to be the end of my career,' he said. 'I can't get a run.' And Both said, 'I'm not surprised with those bats you're using. Get a Duncan Fearnley.' I'm not sure he didn't give him one."

The anxious Border took 41 minutes to get off the mark and, by the time he had reached 16, the innings was in ruins at 218 for nine wickets, six of them taken by Norman Cowans.

"Norman was sharp, but the problem he was creating was lack of bounce. One or two almost shot along the ground."

Australia, needing 74 for victory, were down to their number eleven Jeff Thomson. Willis opted to get him on strike whenever possible, setting the field back for Border and letting the last ball of one over go for four. But by close the 74 runs required had shrunk to 37.

"There was a feeling overnight that we should have wrapped it up, but the new ball was due and we decided to keep the same strategy."

That final day might have lasted one delivery but, with entry free, 18,000 spectators arrived. "You could see them all coming in, realising that something special could be about to happen."

At first Thomson was resolute in defence. Then against the new ball he began to step to leg, trying to slash the ball through the offside. In all Test history no last pair had scored more than 48 for victory and, as a run-out chance ended in two fielders colliding, Border and Thomson took their partnership to 50.

"It was all right giving Border one as long as we were having Thomson in problems. But now Tommo was inventing runs."

When drinks were taken after an hour, only 14 runs were needed.

Occasionally a lone bugler on the terraces could be heard in the moments of quiet, but the crowd roared as Thomson carved Botham to third man and ran two. Border drove a three, glanced and square-cut twos and suddenly it was four to win.

"One hit, one mis-hit," Miller reflects, "and it was going to be all over. It was getting tenser and tenser."

Melbourne, 30 December, 12.24 pm.

Botham to Thomson, with Miller at first slip, Tavare at second.

"The bounce and carry were low so Bob Taylor had gone up a couple of yards. Tav had gone up as well. I only went up a yard."

The ball was bowled.

"Both was a lucky bowler. He bowled good balls, but he also got lucky wickets. When he ran in, you'd always think something could happen."

And this time it did. The ball was wide of off stump.

"Earlier Tommo would have flailed at it but, when they got closer, he started to play properly and he only pushed at it."

Five days of drama had come down to this one moment. An edge. Straight at second slip.

"Both wasn't the slowest of bowlers, the ball went quickly and it hit Tav two yards closer up than he should have been. And he could only parry it."

For a moment, a sickening moment, the last chance seemed to have gone. Then, almost in slow motion, Geoff Miller appeared behind Tavare.

"I caught it, and all I can remember is launching it high into the air and running off. And seeing the crowd as they all got up in silence and left."

Two days later, resting in his bedroom, there was a knock on his door.

"I opened it, and there was Geoff Cook. 'I've got something for you,' he said. And he produced the ball. 'I picked it up, but I think it's more yours than mine.'"

It sits in a mount in his Chesterfield home. "When I got back to England, everybody was coming up to me. 'I was listening to that,' they'd say. 'I had the radio in the bed with me.' And I'd say, 'It's a sad state of affairs if that's the best you can do at two o'clock in the morning.'"

And winning in Australia?

"You've got to look them in the eye. We did that last summer. And we hadn't done that for a long time."

## 17. A remarkable first summer

*Bob Appleyard of Yorkshire* TWC, Dec 2003

"Going from the Bradford League to the Yorkshire second eleven was a quantum leap," Bob Appleyard says, recalling his own step up in the summer of 1950. "I realised that it wasn't enough just to come in and bowl as fast as I could. I had to be doing more with the ball."

In his case that meant experimenting with off-breaks that he had never yet tried in a match. In the League he was a medium-fast bowler: "just another seamer," according to Norman Horner, later of Warwickshire, "there were plenty like him." He was already 26 years old, and the county had its eye on a younger generation: Trueman, Close and Illingworth.

Yet at Knypersley in Staffordshire, in only his second game for the Yorkshire seconds, he mixed pace and off-spin, off a 16-yard run, with such effect that he took 15 wickets for 62 runs. Less than three weeks later he was in the first team at The Oval, and again he experimented. "I took my full run, with the field still set for out-swing, and I bowled this off-break. It landed right on the spot. Fletcher was batting and, because it was slow and different and because he'd never seen me bowl one before, he took a swipe at it, missed and was bowled."

Norman Yardley was the county captain, and he asked the coaches to work with Bob that winter on developing his spin. But none of them can have anticipated what would happen when he turned up one February evening with a blister on his spinning finger.

"So as not to stop bowling, I thought I'd bowl it off the middle finger. I ran up, and I found that I could bowl it much quicker than the normal off-break. I didn't even have to change my action. The wickets were on springs, I hit them, and they went all over the place. Arthur Mitchell came over. 'What's going on here?' he said. I said, 'Just watch this, Arthur,' and I did it again. He looked at me. 'If you can bowl like that, you can bowl any bugger out.'"

Yorkshire had two bowling vacancies: their outspoken fast bowler Alec Coxon had been released, and their young off-spinner Brian Close was on National Service. Now they had a bowler who could fill both gaps.

'Sometimes he bowled like Alec Bedser,' his team-mate Johnny Wardle wrote, 'and sometimes like Jim Laker, and you hardly realised the difference till you were out.'

"I had the best of both worlds," Bob says. "I could bowl with the seam, then if necessary I could revert to spin. So it meant that we could play an extra batsman. I mean, what's the point of being a quick bowler or a slow bowler when you can't get on because it's the wrong type of pitch? If I had my way, I'd take half a dozen bowlers, and I'd teach them every discipline. It can't be all that difficult. Lots of folk could have done what I did. But for some reason you've got to be one or the other."

In the League he had bowled 200 overs a summer. Now he was to play every day for four months and to bowl 1,400 overs, all off a 16-pace run. In the final match at Scarborough he would bowl 79 overs, 40 of them on the last day, as he became the only bowler in the history of the game to take 200 wickets in his first full summer. But Bob, ever the perfectionist, was not content: "I felt I wasn't as fit as I needed to be."

He spent most weekends that winter at the punishingly hilly Halifax Golf Club, playing two rounds each day. "On my own sometimes. One of the holes is twelve hundred feet above sea level, and it can be pretty wild and windy. Sometimes, I remember, I was playing in the snow."

One evening he travelled to Sheffield to present the prizes at a cricket dinner, and he met the old Derbyshire and England bowler George Pope whose leg-cutter was legendary. In the cloakroom Bob produced a ball from his coat pocket and watched closely as the older man showed him how to bowl it. "I couldn't wait to test it out in the Winter Shed."

His stamina, however, did not improve – "I was always feeling tired" – and he soon discovered why. His first match of the summer was at Taunton, and he was sent home with a persistent cough and a high temperature. At Leeds Infirmary an x-ray revealed that the whole top half of his left lung had been destroyed by tuberculosis.

How long had he had the wasting disease? His surgeon Geoffrey Wooler is still alive to give the answer. "At least two years. Probably longer."

It is a remarkable story: a debut at 26, a new style of bowling, 200 wickets in his first summer and all with a debilitating and potentially fatal illness. But it is not as remarkable a story as that of his comeback in 1954.

"After such an extensive disease I would have thought that he would have been wise not to have done much for some time," the surgeon says, "but you couldn't tell him. His main object was to get back and bowl again."

The diseased lobe had been cut away, he had lain in bed so long that he had to learn to walk again, and the Yorkshire committee only wanted to try him out in a few two-day games. Yet at the end of May he was top of the national averages, and – to the cheers of men in sanatoria all over England – he was in the England team for the second Test at Trent Bridge, taking five wickets in the first innings and leading the team off the field.

His season of 200 wickets was a unique landmark in the history of the game, but for Bob "my first season back after tuberculosis was the greater achievement. That's my greatest pride. I gave so much hope to fellow sufferers."

## 18. The new ball

*David Sheppard of Sussex* WCM, Sept 2001

"Don't take the ball out of its wrapping," David Sheppard told Jim Wood, his left-arm fast bowler.

It was June the 9th 1953, the final day of Sussex's match at Grace Road, Leicester. The scoreboard had displayed the white disc for 55 overs, the yellow for 60. Now both discs were showing. 65 overs had been bowled. The new ball was due.

"Have a couple of practice run-ups. I'll re-set the field for you."

His wicket-keeper Rupert Webb remembers the long delay. "It must have lasted three or four minutes."

The Leicester lead was 345, with less than four hours left. Surely Charles Palmer could not keep Sussex in the field much longer. Not once in the last five years had a county side chased so many and won.

"It's about time they declared," the Sussex captain muttered.

"He was only 24," Webb says, "but he seemed older. Even when he was 18 and he skippered the second eleven, he had this bearing, this authority. He led from the front, and the whole team admired him. If I could have been anybody in this life, I'd have liked to have been David Sheppard."

Jim Parks experienced May, Dexter, Cowdrey and Close, but he has no doubts: "David was the finest captain I ever played under."

For just that one summer of 1953 Sheppard led Sussex, and a side that rarely rose above mid-table came as close to taking the title from Surrey as any county in their seven-year reign.

Rupert remembers his captain's fielding: 43 catches close to the wicket. "He stood so close in the gully. Next summer Hubert Doggart took over, and he assumed David's position. Ian Thomson took one look at him. 'Come up from third man, will you, Hubert?' Dear old Hubert, he soon found somebody else to do it."

He remembers his kindness: "David always had time for everybody. If you had anything on your mind, he'd walk round the ground and listen to you." Alan Oakman agrees: "He was the first to say, 'Well caught.' Up till then, the attitude was that you were expected to catch it. And after the season he wrote and thanked me for what I'd done."

And Rupert remembers his batting, which brought him 2,270 runs and seven centuries that summer: 174 at Horsham, when he tried to stop Wilf Wooller swearing at him. "Get on with your f---ing batting," Wooller said. "Which he did. He hit them nearly into the town centre." 105 at Guildford against the full Surrey side. "On a green wicket." 22 in an over off the parsimonious Shackleton at Bournemouth, with three sixes into the beer tent. "He wanted to knock him out of the attack. 'We can't afford

Shackleton and Cannings tying us down,' he said. So he jumped down the wicket and hit him over his head." In his 20-year career, bowling more than 26,000 overs, Shack only once bowled a more expensive one – at Bradford to a belligerent Fred Trueman.

The win at Bournemouth took Sussex to the top of the table. Their seventh win in ten games – and the first of them was that afternoon at Grace Road, when Sheppard hit 186 not out. 'A brilliant and chanceless innings,' *The Times* called it. There were runs for John Langridge, Cox and Oakes, but 'always it was Sheppard who was the dominant figure.' "He looked such a big man," Jim Parks says. Sussex made 346 for two and won with time to spare.

But, before that triumph, he had to secure the declaration.

Leicestershire did not even own the ground. It belonged to a local boys' school, and the only two buildings – the bare-floored pavilion and the gymnasium that they used for a dining room – were in a primitive state. Money was short, and the captain Charles Palmer doubled up as the secretary, husbanding the shillings from the turnstiles: "We were in such a mess," he remembers. "We had to keep players' salaries down to dustbinmen level. And balls were a major item of expenditure. In a three-day match, with four innings, you could get through half a dozen."

It was the same at Somerset, too, where Ken Biddulph was starting out. "I was issued a practice ball for the summer. I had to go along to the office and sign for it. And it wasn't a new ball. By the middle of July it was getting ragged so I went back for another. 'Another ball?' the secretary said. 'You've only had that this summer.'"

At Grace Road David Sheppard moved his fielders with slow deliberation while Jim Wood, re-marking his run, clutched the greaseproof packet that contained the ball. "Don't unwrap it, Woody, and, whatever you do, don't drop it."

Rupert Webb looked across to the pavilion.

"Charlie Palmer appeared. A little man. He didn't walk down the stairs. He came tumbling down, in a great hurry. And he waved the batsmen in."

David Sheppard turned to his Sussex team as they walked off together.

"I knew they couldn't afford a new ball," he said, and they all laughed.

It was a happy summer.

## 19. One thousand in May

*Glenn Turner of Worcestershire* WCM, June 2002

One thousand runs in May. The 1973 *Wisden* listed the same seven instances as it had done every year since 1939.

Grace was the first. In 1895, at the age of 46, he needed only 22 days and ten innings. Then came Surrey's Tom Hayward in 1900 – though he started on April 16 – and in the late 1920s Wally Hammond and Charlie Hallows. Bradman did it on his first tour in 1930, then in 1938 he broke all records, bringing up his 1,000 in just seven innings. The seventh on the *Wisden* list was Bill Edrich, also in 1938 and scoring all his runs at Lord's.

Edrich reached 964 runs by May 21, then the press turned the spotlight on him. "Immediately," he wrote, "I have no excuses, I lost my nerve. I was thoroughly on edge, and my bat was the same." Late on the afternoon of the 31st, he still needed ten runs and only a generous Bradman declaration allowed him a final chance and a place on the *Wisden* list. The achievement won him a call-up for England, but in four Tests that summer he managed only a pitiful 67 runs.

For a while in 1960 Ted Dexter threatened to become the eighth, but the large crowd who flocked to Hove on May 31st were stretching optimism. They watched him score 135, but that left him 123 short.

The next opportunity fell to the New Zealander Glenn Turner in 1973. With the Benson and Hedges Cup reducing the counties to only four or five first-class fixtures in May, it seemed it was now only a tourist who could do it.

Football had ended with the Cup Final on May 5th and, with Turner reaching 796 runs by the 21st, the papers found a story to fill the sports pages before the first Test. "It wasn't something I set out to achieve," he recalls. "I was more concerned to get in form for the Tests. But, once the media made it an issue, I couldn't dodge the pressure."

Turner had already played five summers of county cricket at Worcester. Back in the mid-60s he had worked nights in a Dunedin bakery to afford the fare to England, and he had started out with a trial at Edgbaston that impressed nobody.

"All he did was hit the ball back at me," David Brown recalls. "Mentally he was on the back foot. I thought he hadn't a hope of playing county cricket."

It was the same at Worcester, but they saw something different. "He was a slip of a lad," Roy Booth says, "but he'd got a little bit of hardness. People thought he was going to come good."

In his first county summer he went to bed each night at nine, reliving every moment of his day's cricket. "I used to record every innings I played.

It was detailed to a fault. And I would ask myself, 'What was going through my mind when I got out? What was I thinking? How can I improve on that?' You get so self-analytical, you start to go nutty."

Soon he was following the example of his captain Tom Graveney. "Tom impressed me greatly. He enjoyed his beer at night, but he was the first up in the morning, the first to the ground and the first into the nets." And the young Kiwi impressed Graveney. "He'll be the batsman of the seventies," Tom said in his farewell speech.

The Sunday League took him out of his early cautiousness, so much so that "I got accused of playing too loosely at the end of my career. In 1973 I wasn't yet batting in the more aggressive way, but I'd got past my blocking stage. I was scoring my runs at a reasonable clip."

796 runs on May 21 became 867 on May 25, but the next match at Leicester thwarted his progress. On the first morning he scratched around for 30, then in the second innings, when he looked in better touch, the rain fell.

"It's generally circumstances that help create records," he believes.

He had one more opportunity – at Northampton – to score the last 93 runs, and after more rain the New Zealanders were put in on a treacherous wicket. Surviving a sharp slip chance at 16, he reached the evening on 70 not out. "In some ways," he says, "the pressures off the field were more difficult than the ones on it. I had to do two interviews before I went back out on Thursday morning, and I found that hard to cope with. Back in southern New Zealand, one doesn't make a fuss. That tends to be the way it is; one plays things down."

But the New Zealand press officer was now making a fuss, sending a commentary back home down the pavilion telephone. For 70 minutes Glenn Turner batted watchfully, inching towards the magical figure of 93. Then, off the slow left-armer Bishen Bedi, playing with a vertical bat, he forced the ball to the boundary behind square on the off side, and the cheering began.

"They produced a congratulatory cake," is all that he now remembers.

In the 1974 *Wisden* his name would appear under that of Bill Edrich, to be joined in 1988 by Graeme Hick. But, like Edrich, he would fail in the summer's Tests.

Soon afterwards he analysed his failure in a book. 'On a tour people say you should use the games to build up form for the series, but I had built up to a peak at the end of May and I felt flat. I was not in the right state of mind.'

He was still turning over the reasons for success and failure, but in time he would shake off the introspection – so much so that, when he completed his 100th hundred in 1982, it was in an innings of 311 scored in a day.

So does he now think the pressure of that 1,000 in May took too much out of him? "Who knows?" he replies with a laugh.

## 20. A lost ground

*Nottinghamshire's Steetley ground* WCM, Apr 2002

There were 16 out-grounds on the county championship fixture list last summer – where forty years earlier, back in 1961, there had been 64. Bournemouth, Chesterfield, Weston-super-Mare. Romantics do not need to be reminded what they have lost.

But what about Margam outside Port Talbot, where the wind blew across the exposed ground? In 1962 Gloucestershire set Glamorgan 119 to win on a treacherous pitch, and the home team spent 77 overs struggling to 49 all out. "We came off the field," David Allen recalls, "covered in this red tinge from the steel works."

Or the little ground at Ashby-de-la-Zouch, where many a six would clear the railway line. "The changing room was so small," Maurice Hallam said, "that it was like climbing over an obstacle course. Vic Munden was allocated the task of bringing some six-inch nails to make sure we'd got enough pegs."

There were games at the school grounds of Millfield and Wellingborough, at Ind Coope's brewery ground at Burton-on-Trent and on the Isle of Wight at Cowes: "a testing journey in a slow and rather smelly boat," according to Colin Ingleby-Mackenzie.

But no ground was more obscure than the one at Shireoaks where Notts entertained Sussex in July 1961. In fact, it was so obscure that *Wisden* listed it as Worksop.

Shireoaks was a mining village between Worksop and Sheffield, with a population of barely 1,000, but the Steetley Company, making furnace bricks, had a managing director, Wilf Stocks, with a passion for cricket.

In 1935 he had opened the batting for the village in their famous victory over a Worksop side that boasted five county players.

"He scored 52," his cousin Vic recalls, "in an opening partnership of 179 with Percy Taylor. Percy hit Ken Farnes, the England fast bowler, all over the place. One ball went over the canal and into the next field. Farnes said nobody had ever hit him like that before. I watched every ball; it was like a 'Roy of the Rovers' story."

By 1950 Wilf Stocks was managing director of the Steetley Company, and he spared no expense in creating his own works ground. Recruitment policy discriminated in favour of the best local cricketers – including some when they retired from the county side: Freddie Stocks, his cousin, and Eric Martin, who became the transport manager. "We won a lot of trophies," Eric says.

Wilf Stocks was determined to host county cricket on his immaculate ground and, in 1961, his dream came true.

On Wednesday 5 July, on a beautiful batting track, Nottinghamshire's Norman Hill hit 201, and Sussex's Alan Oakman replied with 229 not out. "It was a nice, small ground," Alan recalls. "Years later I played for Warwickshire Over-50s there, and it was perfect. When you're in your fifties, you don't want to chase the ball too far, you know."

With tennis courts and a bowling club, a lake and a canal, it was a picturesque setting, hidden from the A57 by a row of miners' cottages.

"Unfortunately," Eric Martin says, "there was no room to put in any stands so they just had chairs around the boundary."

"The wicket was superb," the Notts off-spinner Bomber Wells recalls, "but it was in the middle of nowhere. I remember Jim Parks saying, 'The best way of getting us here would have been to have parachuted us in.'"

Shireoaks. It must be the smallest place to have staged county cricket in modern times. Then in 1979 it hosted a one-day international between the England and West Indies women's teams.

Alas, the world of works cricket has not survived our profit-driven times. When Steetley was taken over in 1991, the new American owners did not even know they had bought a cricket ground. The team dispersed, the ground staff were laid off, and for years it was unused, with several proposals to build housing on it.

Peter Wynne-Thomas, Trent Bridge's indefatigable librarian, has visited every field where cricket has been played in the county and, when he found it, "I felt like the discoverer of the Marie Celeste."

"I wouldn't go back," Eric Martin says. "I wanted to remember it as it was."

Other out-grounds had gone: the Erinoid at Stroud under a factory extension, Hastings Central for a shopping mall.

But the Steetley ground has been saved by green belt regulations, and now the field belongs to a local couple who have made their home in the two-storey pavilion. They have brought back the old groundsman, even restored the pavilion clock, and last summer cricket returned – with the ground hired out to the nearby village Woodsetts.

So, if you play in Division 5 of the Bassetlaw League, you can bat on the square where Alan Oakman hit his only double century. He added 66 in the second innings, lofting Bomber Wells out of the ground before being caught next ball on the boundary.

But the takings were poor, and the following summer Notts played just one out-ground match – at Worksop. Now they only play at Trent Bridge.

Alan Oakman paid five more visits to Nottinghamshire, but the runs never flowed as freely for him as they did in that match in 1961. "Every year I used to say to them, 'Why don't we go back to Steetley?'"

## 21. A day out in Bristol

*Bryan 'Bomber' Wells of Gloucestershire* WCM, Aug 2001

The courting couple sat on a bench in Gloucester Park. Friday 13 July, 1951. The sun was dropping below the horse chestnuts as they ate their fish and chips, and they watched as a lone car, an Austin Princess, pulled up and the driver walked towards them. He was a large, middle-aged man with a bronzed face that the lad recognised from the sports pages of the *Citizen*. Tom Goddard, the legendary Gloucester off-spinner.

"Are you Bomber Wells? … Well, get down to Bristol tomorrow. You're playing against Sussex."

"He got back in his car and drove away," Bomber recalls. "Without another word."

The following morning the 20-year-old apprentice printer sat upstairs on the Bristol Tramways bus while it travelled its forty miles through the villages of the old A38. He clutched the brown paper bag that carried his kit and listened to his fellow passengers anticipating the day's cricket. "I never let on that I was playing. I thought it would be my little surprise."

Bryan Wells. A big lad who had never been near a cricket coach in his life. He bowled off a jaunty three-pace run, and he mixed his off-breaks with leg-breaks, floaters and seamers. Two weeks back he was a club bowler on Gloucester Spa. Then he had two days off work to play for the county seconds, taking six wickets in each innings. Now he was replacing the great Tom Goddard.

From club to county in a fortnight: hardly any of his team mates that day had ever set eyes on him. Certainly not the captain Sir Derrick Bailey, whose father had owned diamond mines in South Africa. It was another world from that of Bomber's dad, blacklisted for leading the first strike at the Wagon Works.

"Bomber was just a boy from the sticks," Arthur Milton recalls. "He strolled in, changed, came out. Nothing worried him."

"Why should it?" Bomber retorts. "It was just another game, wasn't it? All I ever wanted to do was to bowl."

Lambert and Scott took the new ball, Mortimore bowled off-spin, and there were five overs of Milton's gentle seamers. Sir Derrick even resorted to his own occasional medium pace. But the newcomer's bulky frame stayed in the outfield.

"I was waiting and waiting," Bomber recalls. "I started to wonder if I was going to bowl at all."

Lunch arrived with Sussex 120 for one.

His turn came early in the afternoon and 'as soon as he came on,' according to the county yearbook, 'the batsmen were struggling.' Two

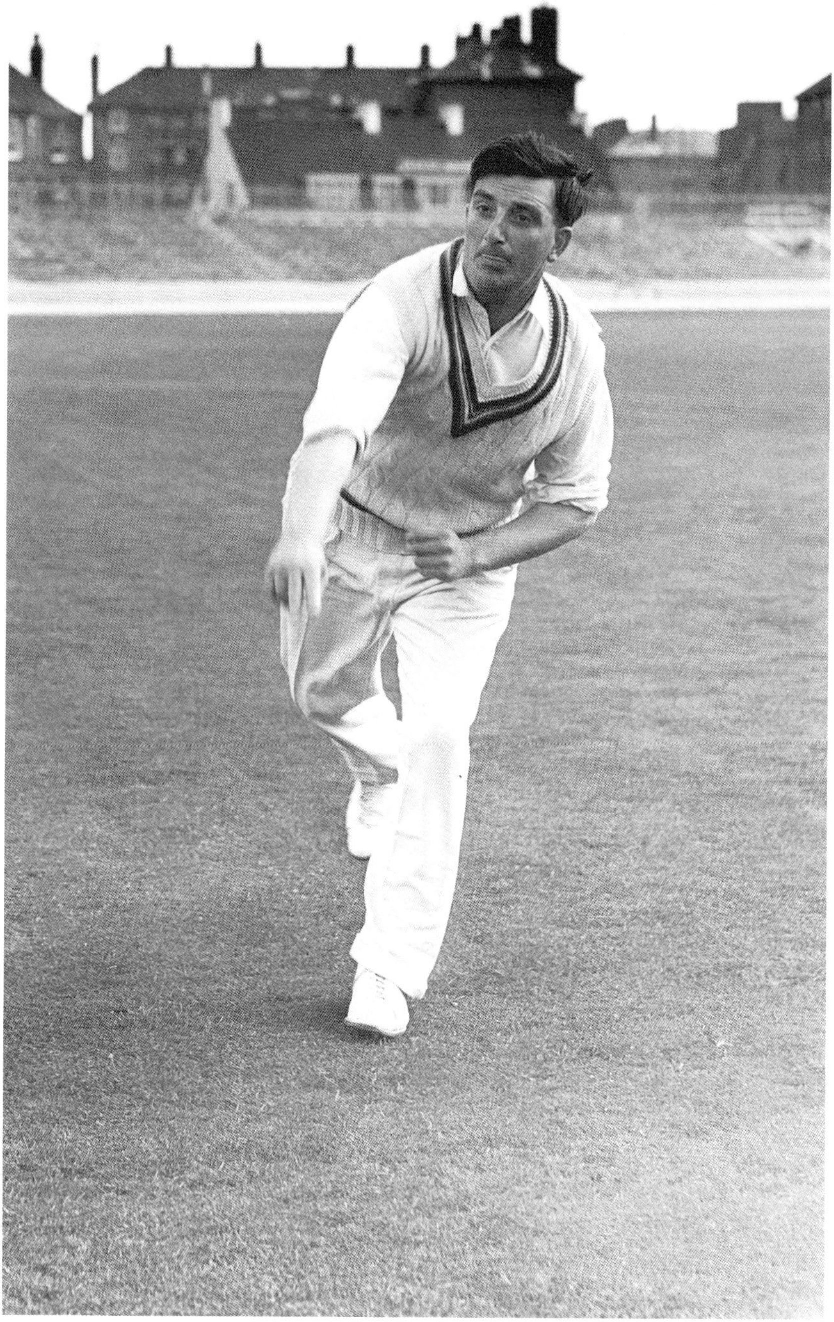

off-breaks beat the left-handed Don Smith's outside edge, and a leg-break was almost chopped onto the stumps. Then David Sheppard, already a Test batsman, played back, and the ball scuttled through and had him lbw. The first of many batsmen to be fooled by Bomber's rolling gait and short run-up.

"I was strong across the shoulders," Bomber explains, "and I had a fast arm. Good spin bowling needs a fast arm."

"The ball used to pitch that much further up than you expected," Arthur Milton says. "People were playing back to half-volleys."

The veteran George Cox was the next to encounter the unknown bowler. 'In his first over to him,' the *Gloucester Citizen* reported, 'Wells bowled a prodigious leg-break which considerably surprised both batsman and fielders.' With Cox and Oakes falling to him, Bomber had figures of three for 33 at the end of his 19-over spell.

"The Sussex batsmen had never seen anything like it," Tom Graveney remembers.

James Langridge and Rupert Webb made runs while Bomber was rested, but he returned to dismiss Langridge, Wood and Cornford in twelve balls, all bowled. His final figures read 25.1 overs, six wickets for 47 runs.

In the second innings he once more dismissed Cox and Sheppard in a marathon 36-over bowl. At the end of the match he stood in the dressing room. "Well," he said. "I can see, if I'm going to play for this side, I'm going to have to do a lot of bowling. I shall have to cut down my run up."

So after that he bowled off one pace. Many a batsman would play the ball back down the wicket, only to look up and find the next delivery already upon him. Many a fielder would be returning to his place when the ball whistled past.

Six for 47. No championship match in the last fifty years has seen a bowler walk off the field on his first day of first-class cricket with better figures.

What glory did Bomber imagine lay ahead of him?

"It was just another day's cricket," he says, still watching his beloved Gloucester City on the Spa ground. "That's all it ever was."

His eyes twinkle behind thick glasses. "All I can remember thinking was, 'Will it finish in time for me to get the bus home?'"

## 22. A summer without equal

*George Hirst of Yorkshire* TWC, SEPT 2006

George Herbert Hirst was 35 years old during the summer of 1906 and was carrying an old injury that required him to bowl with a strapped-up knee. At home his nights were broken by the cries of a baby born in the last week of April. He was a muscular man, a left-arm quick bowler with an awkward run-up and, in the words of one observer, 'a wearing, caring action which takes so much out of him that he ought to be tired out after a dozen overs.' Yet in eight weeks, from May 7 to June 30, playing two three-day matches each week for Yorkshire, he bowled 639 overs and took 104 wickets.

But that was only half his work. In a fragile batting line-up he went in at number five, able to score quick runs or to defend his wicket as the game required, and by the end of June he had scored 1,113 runs. His double remains by a full fortnight the fastest in the history of the first-class game.

Hirst was born in 1871 in the village of Kirkheaton, three miles outside Huddersfield, and he grew up in the Brown Cow inn which his grandparents ran. He left school at ten to work for a local hand-loom weaver, and he spent his evenings playing outside, drawn towards the field where the cricketers practised.

Some say that the loom-owners, for all their religious principles, bet on the inter-village matches and were happy to give their best players time off to practise. Others say that the speed of the shuttle and pick, in those pre-powered days, increased the hand-eye co-ordination of the operators. Whatever the reason, a high standard of cricket was developing in the area, and in 1888 – when Hirst was 16 – Kirkheaton Cricket Club paid the former Yorkshire professional Allen Hill, taker of Test cricket's first wicket, to coach its youngsters. It was the only coaching Hirst ever received.

By 1893 he was a regular in the Yorkshire team. Four years later he was playing for England in Australia. By the turn of the century his bowling was starting to fall away, but in 1901 he developed an extraordinary 'swerve' that saw the new ball swing in several feet from outside the off stump. "Well, really," complained one batsman, "I don't know how I can be expected to play a ball that, when it leaves the bowler's arm, appears to be coming straight but, when it reaches the wicket, is like a very good throw from cover point."

Hirst was a wholehearted cricketer, a man of happy disposition and a great team player. "His smile used almost to meet at the back of his neck," his captain Lord Hawke said. And Pelham Warner, England captain, called him 'the ideal cricketer, so straight, so strong, so honest. It does one good to see him laugh.'

'Cricket is a game, not a competition,' Hirst would say. 'And, when you're both a bowler and a batter, you're twice as happy. You enjoy yourself twice as much.'

Yorkshire had won the championship in four of the first six years of the century, and in 1906 they were locked in a close-fought race with Surrey, Lancashire and Kent. Every game was vital, with the arithmetic of the competition especially hard on a defeat. At Catford against Kent Hirst was the match-winner with a century and 11 wickets, and in the return game at Sheffield he took eight wickets and saved the game with a battling 93. At Bradford his six for 20 demolished Lancashire, and in the return at Old Trafford he turned the match with an 85 that *Wisden* reckoned better than any of his six centuries that summer, though *The Times* thought his 87 on a fiery Oval pitch 'one of the greatest innings he has ever played for Yorkshire.'

In the words of Lord Hawke, 'It was not only what Georgie Hirst did but how he did it, coming off when an effort seemed most necessary and playing his best against the more formidable sides.'

At Bristol on Saturday 25 August, Yorkshire were set 234 to win, and their unexpected one-run defeat cost them the championship. For once Hirst failed, but at that stage of the season he had scored 1,837 runs and taken 184 wickets, and in the next match at Bath he achieved a feat unique in the history of cricket. In oppressive heat he hit a chanceless century on the Monday, then took six wickets in 26 overs on the Tuesday. His captain, conscious that the bowlers needed a rest, opted not to enforce the follow-on, but Hirst was soon back in action, sent in at number three to score quick runs, and he became only the second Yorkshireman ever to score two hundreds in the same match, in the process passing 2,000 runs. On Wednesday he added another five wickets, thus becoming the only man to score two hundreds and take five or more wickets in an innings twice in the same first-class match.

The early finish at Bath allowed them to leave on the 3.13 train, and with two changes they arrived in Scarborough at 11.33. Years later Hirst told the Yorkshire bowler Bill Bowes how in the latter stages of that summer his legs felt like iron and how he massaged them night and morning with Neats-foot oil. When he asked his doctor about it, the reply was blunt: "Don't you realise, Mr Hirst, you've given your legs more use than five ordinary men in a lifetime. You're lucky if you can keep them in order with a drop of oil."

So hot was it that week, the hottest for thirty years, that, when the football season started on the Saturday, in the match between Manchester City and Woolwich Arsenal, two of the City players did not reappear after half-time and three more retired with heat exhaustion before the final whistle.

The first day at Scarborough, Thursday 30 August, saw Yorkshire in the field, and in the heat Hirst bowled 33 overs at 'the strongest team to represent the MCC this season'. In the first over he knocked out the off stump of the Lancashire captain Archie MacLaren; he had Worcestershire's Foster caught at slip in his next, and by lunch he had taken his season's tally to 198, with one more following in the afternoon. At tea he may have resorted to his favourite restorative, a small gin-and-sherry mix, and off the first ball after the interval he had Somerset's Braund caught off a skier at short leg. The cheers rang out, reaching the ears of his mother who had become so anxious that she had taken to walking the streets outside the ground.

In 28 matches, all for Yorkshire, all between May 7 and September 1, he had scored 2,164 runs and taken 201 wickets, and he added a further 221 runs and seven wickets in other matches in September. MacLaren called him 'the most untiring and enthusiastic cricketer who ever wore flannels'.

Bob Appleyard took 200 wickets for Yorkshire in 1951, but he only scored 104 runs. "I was absolutely jiggered after what I'd done," he says. "How he had the energy to bat as well, I can't imagine."

This year Yorkshire are playing at Scarborough on 30 August and at tea-time, one hundred years almost to the minute later, Bob Appleyard, now the Yorkshire President, will go out onto the square with a member of Hirst's family and with the ball with which Hirst took that 200th wicket.

George Hirst was asked if anybody would ever match his achievement. "If they do," he said with a smile, "they'll be very tired." It was a line that Fred Trueman borrowed, adding an adjective or two, when he took his 300th Test wicket. Time has proved Trueman wrong, as the merry-go-round of modern Test cricket has seen bowlers go past 500 and 600 Test wickets.

But time has left George Herbert Hirst and his summer of 1906 on its own. A summer without equal.

## 23. A centenary at Lord's

*Royal Navy v The Army* TWC, Aug 2008

The Royal Navy versus The Army. At Lord's, June 1908. The match was the brainchild of naval commander Hugh Watson and army captain Tom Sheppard, great-uncle of the Reverend David. Both men made ducks, and rain prevented any play on the final day. But such was the standard of the two sides that by 1912 the fixture had joined the first-class list. In 1914 the match was allocated to the second half of the Lord's centenary week.

Most years the Navy lost easily, often by an innings, with one humorist suggesting a new recruiting slogan: 'Join the Navy and bat twice'. The Army were much the larger service, and their team always contained several who had played with success in county cricket, men such as Major 'Bertie' Poore of Hampshire whose 1899 average of 91.23 remained a record till Bradman arrived in 1930.

The Navy won a rare victory on the eve of war in 1914, but they were again defeated by an innings when the teams next met in 1919. *The Times* put it down to lack of practice: 'The bowling was mostly of very moderate quality and occasionally feeble in the extreme.'

'The cricket tended to be run on fairly strict quarter-deck lines,' one naval historian wrote. 'Batting by seniority was not always accidental, and woe betide any cadet who ran out his captain.'

Through the '20s and '30s the fixture remained an essential part of summer at Lord's. The matches were played on the very edge of the square, and the crowds were never large. But a band from the Scots or Irish Guards would accompany the afternoon's play, and around the ground, enjoying a day out, there would be Chelsea Pensioners.

The report was always at the top of the page in *The Times*. And the players had sufficient status that in 1927 the Army wicket-keeper, Ronny Stanyforth, who had never played a game of county cricket, was selected to captain England in the winter Tests in South Africa. The army life could be a good one; within two weeks of his return, Stanyforth was riding a winner at Sandown Park.

In 1928 the game took place on the eve of the Lord's Test. With the Navy's batsmen nearly holding out for a draw, it was six o'clock in the evening before the groundsman could set to work on his pitch for the next morning.

In 1930 the match, reduced from three days to two, lost its first-class status but the teams retained their enthusiasm for the occasion, the Navy's victory owing much to the willingness of the Army to bat the last hour in steady rain. It was the Navy's last success before the Second War, by which time the Army led the series by 17 victories to three.

The fixture was revived unofficially as a one-day match in the latter half of the war. In 1942 the Army took the field with nine men who would play Test cricket, among them Denis Compton, while the Navy – with a team selected through Admiralty Fleet Orders – arrived with an eleven with no wicket-keeper and little in the way of bowling.

The post-war National Service years brought many future Test cricketers to the fixture, none greater than Peter May – though he scored only 13 runs in his three innings for the Navy. The first year he was dismissed by Gunner GAR Lock, the second by Signalman FH Tyson.

May had a clerical posting, and his rank Writer was abbreviated on the scorecard as Wtr. As he walked through the Long Room, he overheard a member working it out. "Waiter," the man said triumphantly. "Chap's the mess waiter."

"In regimental matches," General Richard Peck recalls, "the officers were required to be called sir. But, when we played for the Army, the captain was called skipper, the rest by Christian names."

Peck remembers the thrill of his first selection in 1960, bringing the award of his Army cap. "We stayed in barracks in Regents Park and got paid expenses of about two pounds at the end of the game."

"It was gentlemen's cricket," Captain Derek Oakley of the Royal Navy says. "Fiercely competitive on the field and very social in the evening. I would be playing 60 or 70 days of cricket some summers, and the Army-Navy game was the highlight."

Gradually the fixture was squeezed out of the Lord's schedule. It became a one-day game, and in 1972 it was held there for the last time. The Army won a thrilling match by one wicket, and the day closed with a cocktail party with 450 guests in the Long Room, followed by Beating Retreat by a band from the Parachute Regiment, the first time it had been played at Lord's since 1914.

The Army and Navy have both shrunk in size and have heavy commitments around the world. But the annual cricket match is still a keen one, and this summer for its centenary it returns to Lord's on Tuesday 29 July. There will be an aerial display by the Red Devils, they will toss with a 1908 coin, and the Minden Band of the Queen's Division will play during the day.

But the groundsman has no Test pitch to prepare for the next morning – and it is unlikely that any selector will be there, looking for a captain for England's winter tour.

## 24. An emotional two hours

*Old Trafford, Sat 15 Aug 1981, with Chris Tavare* The Times, 15 July 2005

It was a grey Saturday afternoon in Manchester. That morning England, with a first innings lead of 101, had looked well placed to win the match and retain the Ashes, but they had slumped to 104 for five. The series was back in the balance.

The crowd had seen 34 runs in 34 overs, with Chris Tavare inching from 29 to 41. Then the bare-headed Ian Botham emerged, whirling his bat.

"It was extraordinary how the atmosphere changed," Chris recalls. "From being comatose to being electric. As soon as Ian came down the steps, the level of expectation rose up."

Botham was on a pair, to add to the one he had made at Lord's – when he had returned to the pavilion in an eerie silence and resigned the captaincy. Now, after his match-turning performances at Headingley and Edgbaston, he was brimming with confidence and he played his first ball away for a single. A careful start was called for, and it was over an hour before the 150 came up: Tavare 59, Botham 28. "I realised later that Ian's best knocks were often played when he scratched around at the beginning."

After two Tests the previous summer, Chris Tavare had been recalled to provide steadiness at number three. His first innings 69 had taken nearly five hours; now he had completed the slowest first-class fifty ever made in England.

"I found a little niche for myself," he says. "There were plenty of stroke players. What they needed was somebody to bat for a long time and in that Test, with wickets falling, it worked well."

His obduracy meant that already that day Alderman and Lillee had bowled 30 overs between them so that, when they took the new ball, they were not at their freshest. Botham skied Alderman to long off where Whitney, running back, could not hold the high, swirling catch. Then Lillee tested him with several bouncers.

"He had two men set back. Each time Ian hooked him, I was thinking, 'That's out.' But the ball kept going into the stands. And the crowd got more and more excited."

In eight overs before tea the score raced from 150 to 226. 'One Ian Botham,' the crowd chanted. 'There's only one Ian Botham.'

"You could really see his intensity. The shot I recall best was off Terry Alderman. The ball was just short of a length, and it went like a tracer bullet to mid-wicket for six. The noise off the bat was like a rifle shot. Alderman and Lillee were two of the best bowlers around – but, when someone bats like that, it's very difficult to bowl anywhere."

Nine years earlier, Chris Tavare had been at Lord's, watching his first day of Test cricket. A sixth-former at Sevenoaks School, he had seen Lillee bowl Boycott off his thigh pad. "It looked like he was running in the whole way from the pavilion. He really did roar in. And there I was at Old Trafford, playing for England against him."

After tea Botham swept slow left-armer Ray Bright for six to complete an 85-ball century, adding another six down the ground before being caught behind. He had raced from 28 to 118 while his partner had crept from 59 to 69.

"I can recall all his shots, but not mine. It was really quite an emotional two hours. There I was, trying to be controlled, trying to stop myself being carried away, but I knew that I was witnessing something very special – and from the best seat in the house."

For John Woodcock in *The Times* Botham's century was 'perhaps, of its kind, the greatest innings ever played. I refuse to believe that a cricket ball has ever been hit with greater power or rarer splendour.'

'I couldn't have done it without Tav,' Botham says.

"An uncle of mine sent me a cartoon from the *Telegraph*," Chris recalls. "A little boy breaking a window and his mother saying to him, 'Can't you pretend to be Tavare rather than Botham?'"

His seven-hour vigil came to an end on 78, when he fended an Alderman bouncer to slip. Then the sun finally broke through, the pitch got slower and flatter with each passing session, and for a while the Australians – chasing 506 – looked like snatching an impossible victory.

"Alan Border was so well organised. He was one of the few players whom you felt you were never going to get out. As long as he was there, marshalling the tail, you felt that they had a chance."

The last wicket fell after tea on the final day, and the Ashes were safe.

"It was five days of tension. The game had ebbed and flowed, and I was exhausted at the end."

Now Chris Tavare is back at Sevenoaks School, teaching Biology and looking forward to another Ashes summer.

"I do hope England do themselves justice. To beat the Australians, with Shane Warne and Glenn McGrath in their bowling attack, would be an extraordinary achievement, greater even than what happened in 1981. Cricket really caught the public imagination that summer, more than at any other time in my life."

## 25. Counting the pennies

*Winners and losers of the benefit system* WCM, Feb 2002

"What do you think of it, gentlemen?" the Bath groundsman asked the visiting Lancashire players as they stared at his newly-laid surface.

"We looked down at the wicket," Geoff Edrich says. "You could see the squares where it had been returfed, and they hadn't knitted together properly. If you pushed them, they wobbled like plates of jelly."

It was Saturday the sixth of June, 1953, the weekend after the Coronation, and the players speculated when the match might finish.

"Monday lunchtime at the latest," they hazarded.

"Oh no," the groundsman replied. "The pitches always play better than they look here."

Brian Statham bowled the first delivery of the match to Harold Gimblett.

"It pitched," Geoff Edrich recalls, "and a piece of earth came out of the wicket, half the size of the ball practically. There was the ball and this bloody piece of earth coming at Harold. He looked round to us and he said, 'It's one of those rough days gentlemen.' He didn't stay long."

Gimblett was run out for 0 as Somerset struggled to 55 all out. In reply Lancashire, abandoning caution, hit a quick 158, and by six o'clock it was all over. Somerset had been beaten by an innings, and Bath-based Bertie Buse was left to dwell on the loss of two days' takings in his long-awaited benefit match. A county regular since 1938, he was playing to the age of 43 to top up his modest earnings. By the time the day's costs and his pluvius insurance had been deducted, there was little left.

"He did all right in the end," his team-mate Eric Hill says. "In those days you had to pay the expenses of the away match, and the county let him off. And, of course, lots of people said 'Poor old Bertie' and made extra donations."

With a few Sunday matches and a dinner or two, he finished up with £2,814 – almost £50,000 at today's prices.

His team-mate Johnny Lawrence did better the following year, taking £3,548 – and he was a strict Methodist who would not play the Sunday games. "They were the main source of income," Eric Hill recalls. "But the *Church Times* ran a leader commending him, and he received donations from all over the country."

Committees allocated benefit matches as they saw fit. Lancashire gave Cyril Washbrook the August fixture with the Australians in 1948. He was the first man to have a committee organise his benefit, and he received £14,000 – a record till Northants supporters rallied to the plight of Colin Milburn in 1971.

But few counties were as generous. At Essex Dickie Dodds finished up with a midweek match against Middlesex at Leyton, and he seethed with resentment. Then he heard the voice of his God – "You are on the get; the whole country is on the get" – and he adopted a different approach. He took to prayer rather than pluvius insurance, and he was rewarded with three of the finest days of the summer, a Compton century and a cheque for £2,325, which he donated to Moral Re-Armament for work in India.

Counties did not always pass over the money with such alacrity. In earlier times there had been professionals who had drunk themselves to ruin with their sudden fortunes, and some committees thought it best to invest the money, releasing payments only when they deemed them appropriate.

Surrey's Alf Gover, reflecting the emerging democracy of the post-war world, was frustrated by such paternalism. He was a man who studied the markets – "Money, old boy," he would say, "it speaks all languages, opens all doors" – and he wrote to the county urging them to sell his shares in British Electric. But, as their committee minute makes clear, they thought they knew better and declined his request.

In time Alf prospered – but Yorkshire's Harry Halliday was less fortunate. The county invested his testimonial fund in Australian shares, and he watched helplessly as their value declined to nothing.

At Sussex Rupert Webb was told at one point that he would have to share his benefit year with a team-mate – and there was even a sting in the tail of this. "It won't be 50/50," he was told. "You'll only get 30 or 40%. You're more intelligent. You'll have a higher earning potential when you retire."

Cricket would be over by the age of 35 or 40, and a new life had to be set up. For Sam Cook, the Gloucestershire slow bowler, there was the chance to move out of council accommodation and buy a bungalow. For Alf Gover there was the cricket school to be bought. For Bertie Buse, with £2,814, a public house to take over and run.

It all depended on a good crowd at that one match – and a few Sundays when team-mates and opponents would give up their day off.

"Nutty Hazell was the one at Somerset who did worst," Eric Hill says. "The year he had his benefit, the Lord's Day Observance Society started going to court. He had one very big event at Glastonbury – a lot of big names and a funfair – and they got it cancelled."

Perhaps he would have done better if he had curried favour with the *Church Times* – or said his prayers.

## 26. What might have been

*Two championships decided by the same man* WCM, MAY 2002

Wooller of Glamorgan. Ingleby-Mackenzie of Hampshire. Kenyon of Worcestershire. They will always hold a special place in their county histories. The first to lead their sides to the championship.

Maybe this summer we will add Cox of Somerset or Adams of Sussex.

Sussex have been trying since 1864, the only one of those first counties never to have won and, when John Barclay took over in 1981, he was all too aware of it. "I wanted passionately to put that right," he says, "and I felt we had the side to do it."

From April to September they never let up. They bowled out Derbyshire at Eastbourne when the game seemed dead. They even tried to score 225 in 25 overs at Tunbridge Wells.

"Jeez, mate, are you all on pills?" the umpire Bill Alley asked. "You can't play like this all the time."

The vital match was at Trent Bridge in mid-August. Nottinghamshire were championship leaders, preparing pitches for their bowlers and winning ten home tosses in a row, but on the final evening Sussex had them nine wickets down and playing for the draw. The light was poor, and Imran and le Roux were at full speed.

Mike Bore, the Notts number eleven, stepped out with five overs to survive. "He was wearing a motorcycle crash hat," John says, "and he looked petrified."

Imran bowled, Bore shuffled back, and the ball thudded into his pad. There was a great appeal, and Peter Stevens the umpire thought long and hard.

"Not out," he said and, with both sides winning their four remaining fixtures, Notts pipped Sussex to the championship by two points. It was their first trophy in any competition since 1929, and the Trent Bridge crowd was ecstatic. "It really hit home," Mike Bore recalls, "when I saw Reg Simpson in tears."

So John Barclay joined Ranji, Duleep and David Sheppard, men who have captained Sussex to second place.

"At the end of the summer," he recalls, "our abiding feeling was that we would win the next year. But it never happened. And, as the years have passed, I find that I can never quite put it to the back of my mind."

For Mike Bore, though, the drama of that evening at Trent Bridge was eclipsed three years later by a greater drama still at Taunton.

On the last day of the 1984 season Notts needed 297 for a victory that would give them a second title, and at the start of the last over they were 283 for nine.

And who should be on strike but Mike Bore? 17 to his name and facing the slow left-arm of his fellow Yorkshireman, Steve Booth.

"If he pitches it on the off-stump, I thought, I'll hit it straight. If it's on my legs, I'll sweep it."

They were "calculated slogs", but somehow they brought him ten runs off the first three balls. In *The Times*, he was 'a portly figure with a career batting average of eight' but 'he hit everything off the meat of the bat.'

In mid-pitch he met his partner Andy Pick.

"We had a natter, just to get our breath back."

Five months of cricket had become a simple equation. Three balls, four runs, and the championship was theirs. The next delivery did not suit him, and he blocked it.

"Picky came down. 'What did you do that for?' he asked. 'It wasn't in the right place,' I said."

But the next one was pitched up on his off-stump, and he swung his bat.

"As soon as I hit it, I thought, that's it, we've won."

A boundary, either four or six, would be enough to take them to the top of the championship table, two points ahead of Essex who had completed their campaign the previous day.

The ball sailed high towards the old pavilion. But before the Notts celebrations could begin, the figure of Richard Ollis came into view.

"He must have been one of the tallest people on the county circuit," Mike Bore says, "and he was only fielding as a substitute."

M.K. Bore, ct sub b Booth, 27.

The Notts players packed their bags in silence, and the cheering began in Chelmsford.

"We were stunned. We got in the car, and I don't think we spoke a word till we were well past Gloucester."

It is 18 years ago, but the hand is still there, catching the ball.

"No matter how many times I lie in bed and re-play that ball, I never score those four runs."

"The 'what ifs' are always with you," John Barclay says, "but they don't really help. You have to take satisfaction in what you've done, not what might have been. And somebody else will lead Sussex to the championship one day."

Perhaps it will be Chris Adams.

## Champions at last – the sequel

*In the summer of 2003, a year after 'What might have been' appeared in print, Sussex under Chris Adams did indeed win the county championship.*

TWC, Nov 2003

Sussex have had so many near misses in their history, and nobody got nearer than John Barclay in his first summer as captain in 1981. How fitting then that he should have become their chairman of cricket this year and that he should have been on the ground as the county approached the title.

His was a crucial voice in the decision to engage Mushtaq.

"It was a huge gamble. Sussex cricket has always been based around a seam attack, exploiting the incoming tide and the moisture and green. But I liked Mushtaq, and I thought as an attacking bowler he would give us a chance. Not that in my wildest dreams I thought we'd win."

John was also a source of support as the long season progressed.

"All I did was give them my blessing and cheer them up when things didn't go so well. The championship is a marathon. You're bound to have bad days, but it's so important not to make excuses or blame others. People who can cope with adversity are the ones who come out on top. The bad performances are going to happen. You've just got to keep everything in the right perspective."

So did he join the seven minutes of celebration at the moment of success?

"I waited and waited for it, but my son needed me at school and I had to go. Anything else I would have pushed aside."

As the ball raced away for the last four, he was in his car, listening to the local radio.

"It's been so good for the county championship, and I've had so many congratulations. As if I've done anything!"

## 27. Troubling the scorer

*Ted Lester of Yorkshire* TWC, July 2007

At the breakfast table the Yorkshire players were in earnest conversation when their 41-year-old scorer Ted Lester appeared. It was May 1964, and they were in London to play Middlesex at Lord's in the second year of the Gillette Cup competition. The Cup was just a bit of a fun on the side, and their squad of eleven had been reduced during the night to ten when John Hampshire had been taken to hospital, feverish from the after-effects of a tetanus injection.

Brian Close turned to the scorer. "You'll have to play, Ted."

"Me?" came the reply. "I haven't touched a bat for three years. There's no way I'm going to play."

"I went out for a walk," he recalls, "and I didn't get back till ten minutes before the start. I thought, 'Let them sort it out.' And when I got back, all they'd sorted out was my clothes. I had Brian Close's flannels, somebody's shirt, somebody's sweater – and Donald Carr came in from the MCC with a pair of plimsolls. I had no option but to put them all on."

In no time he was trooping out to field – "and I really enjoyed it. I'd always fielded in boots before, and it was quite pleasant to run around in plimsolls. At one stage Ray Illingworth came over. 'Eh, if you're not careful,' he said, 'you'll be showing us up.' I said, 'I'm sorry, Ray, I'm enjoying this.'"

Back in the golden summer of 1947, when Compton and Edrich lightened the cares of a rationed Britain, Ted Lester had taken a two-month break from his accountancy duties in the Borough Treasurer's Department in Scarborough and had finished in third place in the national averages, behind the Middlesex pair. "Batting was easy," he says. "I thought, 'I can't go wrong.' But I was soon to learn otherwise."

The following summer, turning professional, he became only the second Yorkshireman – after Percy Holmes – to hit two centuries in a Roses match, and there was talk of his being picked for that winter's tour of South Africa. But already he was discovering the harsh truth of words spoken to him by the pre-war player Sandy Jacques: "Once you start getting paid to play, cricket's a different game."

For eight summers Lester was a regular in the Yorkshire side. An attacking batsman, brought up on the lightning fast pitches at Scarborough, he was not a consistent run-maker but – in the words of his captain Norman Yardley – 'he was worth his weight in gold because he could change the course of a game in an hour.'

His last good summer had been in 1954; now ten years on he was being put to the test once more.

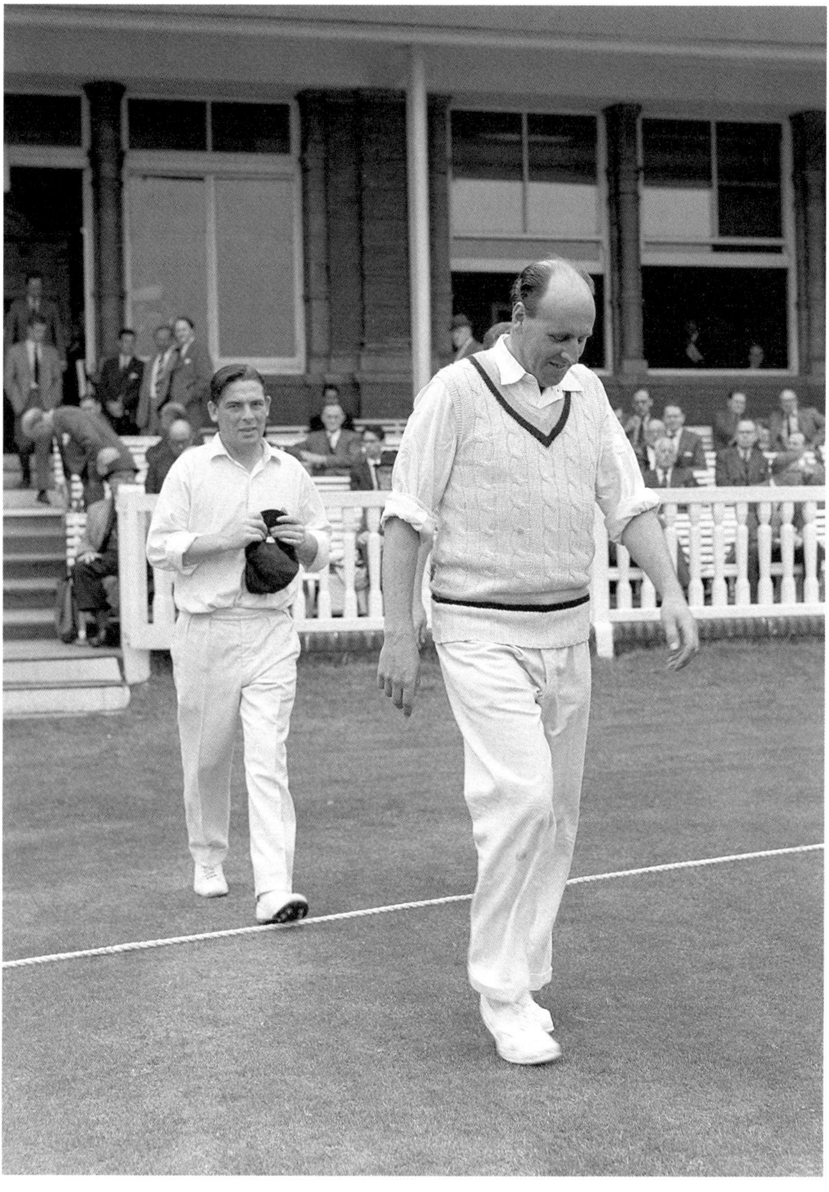

Middlesex were all out for 151 in the 53rd of their 60 overs. "I was down to go in at number nine and I thought, 'That's good, I won't have to bat.' And somebody said, 'You'll be all right for win money now.'"

Nevertheless, still a professional at heart, he headed off to the nets with Mel Ryan and Don Wilson. "I had no idea; I couldn't hit the ball. And we kept hearing this cheering so we knew we were losing one or two wickets."

Back in the pavilion he found the score to be 34 for five, and he bumped into the venerable figure of the *Daily Telegraph* correspondent EW Swanton. "'Watch this fellow Price,' he said. 'He was bowling for MCC against the Australians here earlier this week, and he was as quick as I've seen anybody bowl.' I said, 'Thanks very much, Jim.' That really helped my confidence."

Ray Illingworth and keeper Jimmy Binks led a recovery to 73 for five. Then Illingworth was caught at mid-on and, off the last ball of the same over, Fred Trueman – in the words of *The Times* – 'made a gift of his wicket with an unholy swing.' It was 75 for seven, and the Yorkshire scorer joined Binks with 77 runs to be scored. Was this one last chance for him to change the course of a game?

"The batsmen had crossed so I was on strike for the new over. Fred Titmus, Peter Parfitt and John Price were all together in a huddle, deciding who to put on. And when they saw me, who should come on but John Price? The first ball whistled past off stump, and I never saw it. The second was straight, and that was Goodnight, Nurse."

Or, as *The Times* put it, 'Lester, poor fellow, saluted his first ball and lost his middle stump to the second.'

Middlesex won by 61 runs, and years later Swanton cited the game as evidence of the status of the Cup at that time: 'Yorkshire regarded the competition so lightly that, when someone could not play at the last minute at Lord's, poor Ted Lester, the scorer, had to be pressed into service wearing gym-shoes.'

The great Herbert Sutcliffe, sitting on the Yorkshire committee, was less kind: "He said we'd lost because we had a passenger in the side."

The next summer, when Ted Lester returned to Lord's for the Gillette Cup final, he sat out of the spotlight in the scorebox where he recorded Geoff Boycott's match-winning innings of 146.

"They never travelled with eleven again."

## 28. The end of the drought

*Dennis Brookes of Northamptonshire* WCM, Oct 2002

For four years Northamptonshire went without a victory in the county championship.

They won the first match of 1935. Then nothing till 1939. A sequence of 99 games without success. With a shoestring staff and no second eleven, there were no young players emerging. There was even talk of reverting to Minor County status or amalgamating with Leicestershire.

"We didn't get depressed," survivor Dennis Brookes recalls. "We loved the game, and we enjoyed playing."

Nobody expressed their enduring spirit better than their long-serving scorer, Leo Bullimer. "Bully was a great enthusiast," Dennis tells. "He used to come in the dressing room every morning. 'This is the one,' he'd say. 'We're going to win this.'"

Alas, in 1939, he broke his kneecap getting off a train, and he was missing for the Whit Bank Holiday visit of Leicestershire. The previous Whitsun Northants had lost in two days, collapsing against the left-arm spin of Australian Jack Walsh, making a rare appearances as a Leicestershire amateur.

So it was not surprising that the Leicester players had a spring in their step as they arrived that Saturday in 1939. "When I went through the gates in the morning," Dennis recalls, "Frank Prentice greeted me. 'It'll be all over in two days,' he said. 'We've got Walshy playing.'"

It was a hot day, and Dennis was in no mood for such banter. "I woke up in the morning. I had a sore throat, I had a boil on my neck, and I felt wretched. But I had to play – because in those days, if you didn't play, you didn't get your match money."

Thirty-five minutes later the scoreboard showed five wickets down for eight runs – but this time it was Leicestershire who were batting.

"I think they'd come off a slow wicket somewhere, and they were all playing back when they should have been playing forward."

Among the excited crowd there was even speculation that Northants might finally be rid of the shame of cricket's lowest first-class total: 12 all out at Gloucester in 1907. But the later Leicester batsmen took their total to 134 and, for Dennis, the time in the field brought relief. "I had a scarf round my neck, the boil burst, and it eased the pain."

By close of play, with the Northants reply reaching 280 for two, he had scored 120 not out.

On Whit Monday the town was abuzz. Dennis – 'playing copy-book cricket,' according to the local *Chronicle* – made 187, and Robert Nelson, his captain, declared the innings closed with a lead of 376 runs. Walsh, two for 157.

"Robert Nelson was one of nature's gentlemen," Dennis says. "A good cricketer, not a fancy cap." A schoolmaster, Nelson privately kept a record of every match he had played since the age of 12, but his greatest achievement was his captaincy of Northants. 'He took a disorganised rabble,' wrote WC Brown, the secretary, 'and he imperceptibly moulded them into a team.'

"A disorganised rabble?" Dennis queries. "It could well be. Mind you, WC Brown had been captain previously."

In brilliant weather, with paying spectators alone exceeding 6,000, Leicestershire reached tea at 53 for no wicket, and the Northants twelfth man was busy in the pavilion. "I had to man the pay phone next to the secretary's office," Vince Broderick recalls. "People were ringing up all the time for the score."

The secretary himself had no telephone, and occasionally Broderick had to step aside when committeemen wanted to make calls out. "One was the coroner. He wore a top hat and a frock coat. He was getting on a bit, and he would leave his money in the machine if he didn't get through. We used to press Button B and get his twopence back."

The leg-spinner Bill Merritt set to work, and Broderick's news grew better and better. 60 for one, 100 for two, 121 for six. At 6.30 the last wicket fell, and he looked out on a ground awash with spectators cheering wildly.

"I always remember a lady running from the West Stand and making off with a stump."

An avenue was formed, and three cheers were 'heartily given'. "Robert Nelson had to stand on the balcony and address them," Dennis says. "It was an extraordinary scene."

After four years Northamptonshire had finally won – and in two days. 'The bogey has been disposed of, the stigma removed,' the *Chronicle* declared. 'Now further successes are confidently expected.'

It was not to be. This one victory on Whit Monday lifted them above Leicestershire in the final table, but by the Saturday men were registering under the Military Training Act. Talk of the future grew less confident.

In late August in the Northampton pavilion the Lancashire captain, Lionel Lister, received his call-up papers, unbuckled his pads and quietly left. A week later the Northants team were in Taunton, losing in two days to Somerset, and Robert Nelson slipped away early in his car. "Our New Zealander Frank O'Brien couldn't get on a boat quick enough."

In October 1940 a bomb fell on the Royal Marines barracks where Robert Nelson was stationed, and he was killed.

It was July 1946 before Northamptonshire experienced victory again.

## 29. Cut and dried

*A topsy-turvy match at Eastbourne* WCM, Nov 2002

"Dexter had always got a game cut and dried before it had started," his Sussex team-mate Alan Oakman says, recalling the first morning of the match against Notts in 1962. "He came into the dressing room. 'I've put them in,' he said. 'They'll probably get 300 and declare. We'll get 300 and declare. Then they'll set us a target.' He'd got it all sorted."

It was Eastbourne week, and the Saffrons pitch was at its easy best. The groundsman had tended the square since 1930, his father before him from 1887, and in the run-up to the county week he would arrive at six a.m., rolling the pitch while it was still damp with dew. "It was the best batting wicket in the country," Jim Parks reckons. "If you were out of form, you'd look forward to Eastbourne week."

It was not such fun for the bowlers, of course, and Peter Forman, the amateur who bowled slow left-arm for Notts, remembers the advice he received at the start of the season. "'Don't play at Eastbourne,' Bomber Wells said to me. 'It's a feather-bed down there. They've got Dexter, Parks, Suttle, Oakman, they'll murder you. Say you're busy. Tell them you'll play at Swansea against Glamorgan.'"

He took the advice, travelling down to Swansea and coming up against the unpredictable umpire Harry Baldwin. Twice he wrapped Peter Walker on the pads, and he appealed with great enthusiasm: 'How's that? … How's that then?' And Baldwin took him aside: "Come here, lad. Don't you ever say 'How's that *then*?' And don't shout so loud."

"The next over I had not such a good appeal. 'How's that?' I said quietly. 'That's a lot better,' he said. 'That's out.'"

At Eastbourne Notts were without Peter Forman, and they reached 300 for three just before tea, with Norman Hill nudging his way to 150. The game was unfolding just as Dexter had predicted.

"I can see his thinking," Alan Oakman says. "Put them in, they'll leave us some."

But Notts had other ideas. On and on they batted. The declaration didn't come till 406 for eight, and there was time only for Sussex to make 20 for one by close. "Dexter wasn't best pleased," Oakman recalls.

In the previous four summers Notts had finished last, last, last-but-one, last in the championship. "They were hard years," one young supporter recalls. "I used to run home from school every day for the lunchtime scoreboard on the radio, and it was almost always heart-breaking."

Who could blame Notts for batting on to 400?

The next day Oakman hit 177, Suttle 95 and Dexter 114 not out. Off-spinner Bomber Wells recalls Dexter reaching his fifty. "'Toss them up,' he said to me, 'and I'll have a go at every one.'"

Dexter completed his hundred in 97 minutes. "I was browned off with them for not declaring," he admits, "so I whacked it all over the place."

Wells, nine overs, no wickets for 73.

David Pratt, a slow left-armer playing in place of Peter Forman, 0 for 79.

Sussex declared at four o'clock, with a lead of 17. According to *The Times*, 'the problem was when Nottinghamshire was likely to declare.' In five sessions on the placid pitch, 831 runs had been scored for the loss of just 12 wickets. The game was crying out for a fourth day.

The crowd settled in their deck-chairs for another feast of runs. Sussex's Ian Thomson – who had sunk to his knees in the first innings, raising his hands to the sky for divine help – decided to come round the wicket, and he had Merv Winfield caught for a duck. Maurice Hill followed, another duck, and Billy Rhodes was back in the pavilion with them before the arrears had been cleared. Norman Hill was resolute once more, but wickets continued to fall and Dexter took the ball.

"If Dexter had been a professional," Somerset's Ken Biddulph says, "he'd have been a great bowler. But he'd bowl four or five overs, then he'd lose interest."

That day, though, his interest lasted eight overs – and it was enough. "He'd got the pin with them," Alan Oakman says. "He came in a bit quick and frightened one or two of them."

Dexter took four wickets for 14 runs, and Notts were all out for 57, six of them making ducks. 'All things are credible in cricket,' the *Daily Telegraph* reported, 'but events here stretched credulity to the limits.'

With 15 minutes to spare, Sussex knocked off the 41 runs they needed, and the close-of-play scoreboard on the radio announced its first result.

Back in Nottingham the young supporter tuned in, as ever full of hope. "They were character-forming years," he says now with a sigh. "Heart-breaking is probably not a strong enough word."

But the Notts players were never down-hearted.

"It was National Duck Week," Merv Winfield jokes. "When we got back to Trent Bridge, there were six hampers waiting for us, each with a Cherry Pie duckling. One for each of us who got a duck."

And Peter Forman? At Swansea he took five wickets in the Glamorgan first innings.

## 30. On Broadhalfpenny Down

*Bob Barber's 70th birthday* TWC, Nov 2005

Saturday 17 September 2005. Not since the 1770s, when the great Hambledon club took on and beat an All-England XI, when John Small the elder's batting triumphed over the bowling of the broad-shouldered Lumpy Stevens, has Broadhalfpenny Down seen a gathering like it.

For Bob Barber's 70th birthday, his son-in-law Simon Smith had organised a cricket match between the Gentlemen of RW Barber and those of MJK Smith, and the players arrived from all parts of Bob's life and all corners of the globe. There was his Warwickshire team-mate Lance Gibbs, all the way from Miami: "Man, if Bob Barber invites me to play a game of cricket, I'll be there." His university friend Aizaz Fakir, complete with family, from Karachi: "I couldn't afford it work-wise, but Bob's such a lovely person – and orders are orders." Another Cambridge colleague Ian McLachlan was over from Adelaide, and the Yorkshire keeper Jimmy Binks had flown in from California.

The day was blessed with sunshine, with just a hint of an autumnal chill in the air. The ancient ground proudly sported a marquee alongside its wooden pavilion, with the downland fields of the Meon Valley rolling away in the distance, all harvested and ready for winter.

With match rules that required each batsman to face 18 balls and to be deducted five runs whenever they were out, the day's hardest task was that of the scorers, among them Bob's accountant Robert Godfrey. "They're hoping for a tie," it was explained to me. "So we need somebody who can be creative with figures."

How the years rolled back! With Donald Carr and Jack Bailey the day's first umpires, the new ball was taken by Fred Rumsey and Ian Thomson. It was hard to visualise the menace that the larger-than-life Rumsey had once possessed, but the 76-year-old Thomson still displayed a high arm and a good control of length. "Is that really Tommy?" David Allen – sitting comfortably beyond the boundary - asked, breaking off his reminiscences about MJK Smith as a fine England captain. "I'm sticking to a turn of umpiring," he explained. "I'm afraid my bowling mechanics have completely gone."

First to take strike was Glenn Neil-Dwyer, a friend from Bob's Ruthin School days. The son of a Jamaican airman, he is now an eminent neurosurgeon and, before the first ball was bowled, he turned to the tall figure of Peter Walker standing perilously close to him at backward short leg. "What on earth are you doing there?" Back came the reply from one of cricket's greatest close catchers: "This is where I always field." Behind the stumps, impressively low, crouched Jimmy Binks: "Getting down wasn't the problem," he said. "It was coming up again afterwards."

At the other end Ian McLachlan, a former government minister in Australia, clipped his second ball for four over mid-wicket John Jameson's head. Then, just as Glenn Neil-Dwyer was finding his touch with a four through mid-on, the scorer's voice came over the tannoy: "Come in, number one, you've had your time."

Aizaz Fakir, in his Pakistan top, batted with sweet timing, and several eyes were caught by the confident swing of Harold Rhodes' bat. "They didn't want me to bat at Derby," the one-time fast bowler explained. "They said that, as a tall man, I'd use up too much of my strength." Top score of the day, however, with 31 off his 18 balls, was MCC Secretary Roger Knight but then, at the age of 59, as the watching Alec Bedser put it, "He's a bit young to be playing this sort of stuff."

"I've just had my flu jab," Tom Cartwright said, "and I was looking round the field, wondering if all the others have had theirs. I've never thought about that on a cricket field before."

Aizaz Fakir flighted some lovely leg breaks, and Robert Aiyar offered a hint of the schoolboy pace that meant that, for Bob Barber, "I never had any fear of fast bowling again." But the pick of the bowlers was inevitably Tom Cartwright, immaculately turned out and still leaping, crossing his legs and landing sideways on in his delivery stride. "He doesn't know how to bowl a bad ball," Donald Carr said.

In all his travels with the Old England XI, had Tom ever played here before? "Never, but I did visit here once. I went out on my own into the middle, and I listened to all the ancient voices. And I knew which end I would have bowled. Uphill, into the wind, like Lumpy Stevens used to do."

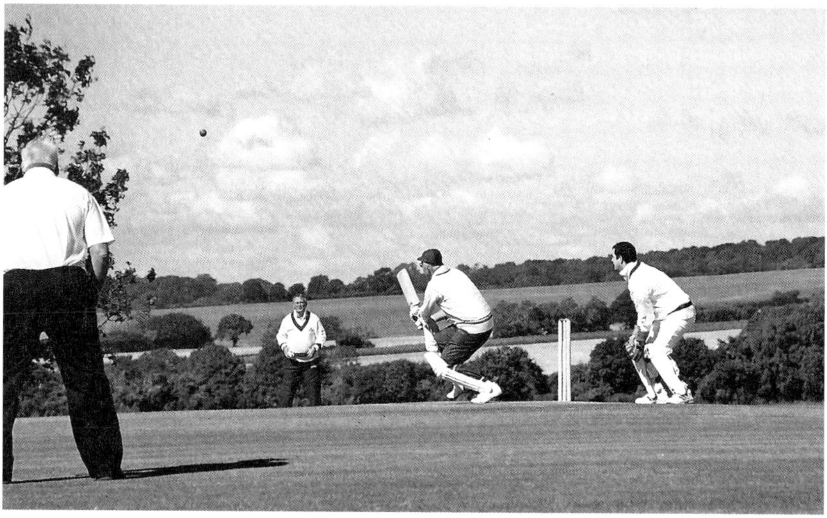

*Bob Barber batting.*

Mike Brearley arrived late. "I looked across the field, at all these old men playing cricket, and I thought it was a very odd sight," he said later in the day, "but now I've been here a few hours, it all seems quite normal." His own day was chequered: a dropped catch, a last ball boundary that saved him from the ignominy of a minus score and a rare wicket, hitting the stumps of Bob's friend Owain Howell. Half an hour later the batsman was still full of delight: "Isn't it wonderful? I've been bowled by Mike Brearley."

The food and drink was plentiful, so too were the memories that flowed from early morning to midnight. The presence of the ever elegant Ted Dexter set off Fred Rumsey: "He was such a fine player. I used to field in the gully, and the way his bat came down, the noise it made, it frightened the living daylights out of me." Then there was Peter Richardson, telling of the encounter between the amateur Walter Robins and the sharp-tongued Roly Jenkins: "'That was a very good article on spin bowling, Jenkins; who wrote it for you?' 'I wrote it myself, sir. Who read it for you?'"

And, in his wheelchair, Gloucester's very own Bomber Wells. "Do come," Bob Barber wrote, "and add a little class to our day." Back in their National Service days, Colin Stansfield Smith told me, a brigadier opened the batting against them, and Private Wells – standing in the gully – produced a red water pistol and squirted it at him. "Only Bomber could get away with that." Then there was the story of how Bob Barber called on Aizaz Fakir's father in Karachi. Under orders not to reveal details of Aizaz's playboy lifestyle at Cambridge, Bob found the old man, a colonel in the Pakistan army, reaching under his bed to produce a bottle of whisky. "Whatever you do," he said, "don't tell Aizaz."

"It is going to take me weeks to get rid of the nostalgia," I overheard one old cricketer saying.

If you wanted to remember how they all used to be, you could sit in the pavilion and watch a film that Simon Smith had compiled of the players' glory days, featuring – above all else – the magnificent 185 that Bob Barber himself had hit on the first day of the Sydney Test in January 1966. It was one of the great Test innings, played by a free spirit – as cricket at its best is always played. As John Woodcock – himself a spectator at Broadhalfpenny Down – had written in *The Times*, 'In every line of Barber's remarkable innings, there showed an independence of character.'

The film was of another age. He reached his hundred with a push into the covers, made one wave of the bat, took his cap off briefly and settled back to his innings. His father had arrived in Sydney that day, and he reported back the words of a man on the Hill: "Why can't we have a batsman like this Barber?"

"Bob hit everything in the middle of the bat," Dennis Silk said. "That innings was sublime. It had the hallmark of real talent."

In later life Bob Barber has settled in Switzerland. Successful in business, he is too private to trumpet his support for various good causes. Among them is the Broadhalfpenny Down Association, who work hard not only to preserve cricket on the historic field but also to provide playing opportunities for children from all sorts of backgrounds.

Batting one last time, Bob was desperately anxious not to fall victim to the bowling of his old Warwickshire keeper Alan Smith, but he struck the ball with freedom.

The final over of the match arrived. RW Barber's Gentlemen had made 155, and in reply MJK Smith's side stood on 144. And who else should bowl the last balls but Bob Barber himself? He tossed up his leg-breaks to his old Lancashire team-mate Roy Collins, and – with a little help from umpire David Allen, who somehow let the over run to 14 balls – the scores finished level and the players departed from the field to much applause. For most, it was a last departure.

The sun dropped down the Meon Valley, and in its absence the chill breeze felt more autumnal. Many of the players drove off to change for the evening meal, MJK Smith led a small posse to the Bat and Ball pub across the road, and a group of wagtails took up occupation of the pitch.

"You've caught the sun," somebody said as I set off for a quiet walk down a country lane.

So much fun, so many friendships. It was a day to live for years in the memory. "This," said Bob Barber, "is the heart and the soul of the real game of cricket."

*Aizaz Fakir and Alec Bedser.*

## 31. A wartime journey

*Stan Cray of Essex* WCM, Dec 2002

On the Imphal plain in Assam, Allied forces were mobilising for an assault on the Japanese in Burma. Among them was Gunner Stan Cray, a radar operator.

The heat was intense, malaria was prevalent, and his half-season in the Essex side of 1939 must have seemed a world away. The 18-year-old boy, whose runs at Sheffield against Hedley Verity and Ellis Robinson had helped set up a famous innings victory, was now nearly 23.

Essex had ended their summer in a glorious fourth place, but the war had been severe on them. Farnes, Eastman and Ashton were all dead, Nichols and O'Connor growing too old, and even their larger-than-life secretary, Brian Castor, was a gaunt prisoner-of-war in Malaya.

"I was young," Stan Cray reflects now. "It's only in the after-years that I've thought about the crucial years I lost."

Then in January 1944 came the telegraphed order, to report to the Brabourne Stadium in Bombay to represent the Services against an Indian XI in a fund-raising match for the Red Cross. "It was a four-day match," he says, "and I'd hardly played since 1939."

But if the match itself was a challenge for him, the journey there was a greater one. First there were five hours in a truck across the mountains to Dimapor. "That was a bit hair-raising. We were 6,000 feet up, and every time we came to a sharp corner our Indian driver just put his foot down. When I looked down the mountain side, I could see all these vehicles that had gone over the edge."

At Dimapor he negotiated a trip by American plane to Calcutta, where there was a long wait before he boarded a train. "It wasn't very pleasant. The seats were wooden, and you had to fend for yourself for food. But I was glad to get away from where I was."

In all, the trip took him twelve days.

His team mate, Captain 'Dickie' Dodds, had only a 60-mile journey from Poona, where he was decoding ciphers and plying his leg-breaks at the local club. But the captain of the Services side, Major Douglas Jardine, had been brought down from Simla in the north. His overbearing manner had discomfited his superiors and, despite his great courage, he had been sidelined into the distribution of provisions.

The new Brabourne stadium provided luxurious accommodation in the pavilion but, unlike the officers, Gunner Cray was billeted in the local YMCA.

According to Dickie Dodds, Jardine called the team together on the first morning. "Gentlemen," he said, "we have got to make this game last four days. Don't forget, batting is simple. All you have to do is put the bat to the ball."

Sixty years on, Stan Cray smiles. "Well, there might be a little more to it than that."

Bombay-born, Jardine had bowed out of top cricket after the MCC tour of India ten years earlier, and his efforts in the nets brought repeated dismissal. But he came out on the first afternoon of the match and he put bat to ball, as he had instructed, before being run out for 43. By contrast, Cray – "it was a bit strange to hold a bat" – scored just 12, Dodds (at number nine) 2.

The Services were all out for 303, and their total was soon looking inadequate as the Indian batsmen delighted the crowded stadium on the second day.

First change, with his leg-breaks, was Captain Dodds, and Mushtaq Ali – who had scored a Test century against England – set about him. "He hit me all over Bombay. I'd never experienced anything like it."

Dodds, 11 overs, one wicket for 73 runs.

After two fours went to an unmanned boundary, he asked Jardine for a field charge. "No," came the brisk reply, and another four followed. When a wicket finally fell, and Dickie Dodds was in the deep, Jardine marched across to him.

"Left, right, left, right," the crowd chanted mockingly as he approached.

"Dodds," he barked. "Now, listen to me. You and I are amateurs. It's only professionals who ask to have their field shifted when they're hit for four."

In the second innings Joe Hardstaff made 129, Cray 18, Dodds 14, and the Indians won on the fourth day by six wickets. After that, it only remained for Gunner Cray to make his way back to Imphal.

"I was very lucky. The day after I went over the mountains through Kohinor, there was a Japanese ambush. There were very few survivors."

The tide soon turned in Burma, and by 1946 Essex were again in business. Stan Cray, though, was still in Rangoon, awaiting a boat, and the vacant opener's spot was improbably taken by a demobbed Dickie Dodds.

Stan Cray did not get back till the winter of 1946/47. Snow lay several feet high, but there followed a golden summer. Dodds hit 2,000 runs, the 26-year-old Cray 1,300, and by August some of the pros were exhausted by the intense heat and the twice-weekly travel.

But not Stan Cray.

"Oh no. After Burma the heat never bothered me."

Nor, after that trek across India, did the train journeys.

## 32. Twice weekly

*The travels of county cricket* TWC, Jan 2005

It fell always to the Surrey Secretary to produce the fixture list, and in the early 1960s that was Commander Babb, sitting with a pencil and rubber, working out a programme for the counties all to play two three-day matches a week from May to August.

From 1960 to 1962 eight counties played a full 32 championship matches. Add in the tourists and universities, and the total could reach 35 or even, in the case of Yorkshire in 1961, 39 matches, all blocked into a 20-week period. The only days off were Sundays when often the same cricketers would be playing benefit games.

Each Tuesday and Friday evening their coaches and cars headed off across country, navigating their ways through the town centres that punctuated the pre-motorway roads. Somerset's Bill Alley loaded the team kit into his Morris 1000 van; Kent's Dave Halfyard squeezed himself into his Messerschmitt bubble car; and all the Yorkshire players tried to avoid Brian Close's passenger seat.

In 2004 Yorkshire's schedule contained 95 days of cricket spread over nearly 24 weeks, with only one occasion – Derby to Southgate – when they played the next day more than 100 miles away. Even then, the Southgate game was a one-dayer, followed by an eight-day break.

Yet in 1961 Yorkshire were programmed to play six days every week from 29 April to 5 September and, with seven home grounds, not once did they stay put from one game to the next. Twenty of their journeys were more than 100 miles, with their season starting at Lord's, then up to Cambridge, back to Bradford, down to Oxford, across to Swansea and up to Hull: nearly 900 miles by the middle of May. Later they would visit Taunton between Chesterfield and Bradford. For Hull-based Jimmy Binks, the ever-present wicket-keeper, even the home games in Bradford and Leeds required a daily round trip of 100 miles for his Beetle.

"It was a game of stamina," Yorkshire's Bryan Stott says. "We weren't as finely tuned as they are now."

"We were fairly fit carthorses," says Gloucestershire's David Allen. "Nowadays they have to be thoroughbreds. And thoroughbreds break down a lot."

In those days it was the cars that broke down. "Our team van, with all the kit, broke down once on the way to Middlesborough," Glamorgan's Don Shepherd remembers. "They got a lorry driver to tow them; he wasn't very happy. The rope broke, and off he went. They arrived next morning on a double-decker bus."

In 1961 Glamorgan found a trip to the Isle of Wight wedged between matches at Neath and Swansea. They went by rail and ferry but, according to Don, "We finished so late that they had to lay on a Vosper power boat to get us across to the mainland for the last train back to Wales."

Northamptonshire went everywhere by coach, and at the end of August they had a journey of 250 miles – with no Severn Bridge – from Swansea to Dover. "We got there about two in the morning," Brian Crump recalls, "and when we reported into the hotel, we found the Secretary had booked us in for the following week. We finished up in Folkestone, with several of us sleeping with blankets on a stage." Inevitably the next day was hot, and they were in the field.

When Geoffrey Howard succeeded Commander Babb as Surrey Secretary, he was offered use of a computer by the Army. "I went down to Warminster to hand everything over, but it was useless. It couldn't cope with all the complications: Kent have to play Sussex at Tunbridge Wells, that sort of detail."

In 1961 Commander Babb had Somerset zig-zagging from Taunton to Westcliff to Taunton to Hull to Dudley. 700 miles in four journeys. Then in August they went from Weston-super-Mare to The Oval via Liverpool. The driver of the van, Bill Alley, hit 3,019 runs, bowled 624 overs, organised a testimonial and worked his way through a healthy ration of black-and-tans, all at the age of 42.

His secret was a bottle of pills, prescribed by a doctor in Portishead as part of an experiment. He took three each day and, he wrote, "I never felt fitter or stronger in my life than I did that year."

He never did find out what the pills contained and, with the doctor's name still on the GMC register, I took it upon myself to ring the surgery. "One moment please," the receptionist said, and I waited eagerly, wondering what I was about to unearth. Then the voice returned: "I'm afraid Doctor Collins passed away recently."

The following year, without the pills, Alley was still in grand form. Now 43, he bet £50 at 10-1 that he would do the double, and he finished with 1,915 runs and 112 wickets. That was a summer when Commander Babb's start-of-season schedule had him driving the Morris 1000 van from Taunton to Lord's to Hull to Peterborough and back to Taunton.

"The legs did get very tired at the end of the season, especially if it was hot," Bryan Stott says. "But that was the routine. It's what we all expected."

## 33. All roads led to The Oval

*The Oval, Weds 19 Aug 1953, with Alec Bedser* The Times, 12 July 2005

There were 30,000 spectators filling The Oval at the start of play that Wednesday. Thousands more were outside: some standing tip-toe on taxi cabs, some perched in trees and on the gasometer. Such was the excitement that BBC television altered its schedule to provide ball-by-ball coverage.

It was Coronation summer. Everest had been climbed, and Stanley Matthews had finally won a Cup-winners' medal. Now, with 132 runs for victory, England stood at 38 for one, and the Ashes – after 19 years with Australia – were within grasp.

'All roads led to the Oval,' Geoffrey Green wrote in *The Times*. 'From early light there was but one topic of conversation. In the quiet countryside, in the bustling cities, the question was whispered: "Can England do it?"'

Nobody had given more in England's cause than the lion-hearted Alec Bedser. "The Australian series was the only one that mattered in those days," he says. "You were measured by your performances against Australia."

The previous Friday, the day before the start of the match, he had been at Loughborough, bowling 21 overs for Surrey. Then on Saturday, with Hutton once more losing the toss, he had bowled another 29, and by teatime he had taken his 39th wicket in the series, a new record in England-Australia Tests.

"I reckon I was getting a bit tired by that stage of the summer, but I can't understand the way the players now are rested so much. To me, they're not match-hardened. It takes them half a day to get used to playing again."

On Monday Hutton, May and Bailey made runs for England. On Tuesday there were wickets for Laker and Lock, working in tandem on a pitch that had turned dusty and 'was full of practical jokes for those able to induce them.'

Fifteen years earlier Len Hutton had stroked a record 364 here – but that was a different Oval pitch and a different Hutton. War had brought an assault course and prisoner-of-war cage to the ground, while an accident had left Hutton's left arm two inches shorter than his right. After eight years of peace, all that remained of war were ration books, bomb sites and memories.

"Although anxious to do well, I was never nervous playing for England," Alec Bedser says. "But I was bloody frightened at Dunkirk. We were on the Belgian border when the German tanks came through, and all I had was a Colt 45 with six rounds of ammunition. We were lucky to get away."

England had escaped with four draws in the Tests. At Lord's Bailey and Watson batted for five hours to save the game; at Headingley, with Hutton slowing the over rate, Bailey bowled down leg to prevent an Australian victory. In its way it revived the Dunkirk spirit: survival in adversity, in hope of better days ahead.

Had that better day finally arrived?

Peter May and Bill Edrich made their way to the middle. May was a young man, playing the tensest match of his life, Edrich a battle-hardened bomber pilot. The excited crowd watched each ball with 'an almost unnatural silence'.

The Australians had only a makeshift spinner, the half-fit left-armer Bill Johnston, and all morning his deliveries sent up puffs of dust. But a wicket did not come till one o'clock, moments after the factory hooters sounded, when May was caught at short leg off Miller.

Now it was Denis Compton, the Brylcreem Boy, joining his Middlesex friend Bill Edrich and, with lunch taken at 101 for two, 'the Ashes were England's, barring some catastrophe.'

Just before three o'clock, Arthur Morris served up an inviting long hop, Compton swept the ball to the gasometer boundary, and 'the magnificent day dreams of a whole summer were reality.' The crowd, throwing off restraint, surged across the outfield; hats were waved and scorecards torn to confetti.

From the balcony Len Hutton paid tribute to the summer-long effort of Alec Bedser, and the champagne corks popped in the dressing room. In the words of Geoffrey Green in *The Times*, 'this happy summer of the Coronation was consummated.'

Yet there was more hard work ahead for Alec Bedser. Surrey had a championship to win, and he still had the duties of his benefit year. In all he bowled 1,253 overs that summer, more than Harmison, Hoggard and Anderson managed between them in all cricket in 2004, and he spent the winter with brother Eric, labouring for their father as they built the house where the two of them still live.

Hard work. Getting out of life what you have put in. It has always been his philosophy, right back to his boyhood when he and Eric worked on local farms. "Digging, mucking out cattle. We'd do it all holidays for fun. Digging the allotment with Dad. If you do that, you don't get a bad back when you're older. We never heard of stress fractures."

He watches today's cricket on television, and he is not impressed by the coverage. "We've overdone it now with adulation. It's nice for kids to aspire to do these things, but not for grown men to get so worked up. Mum wouldn't speak to the press. After I got 14 wickets at Nottingham, some one got through. 'What do you mean, he took a lot of wickets?' she said. 'He's a bowler. I thought that's what he was supposed to do.' And she put the phone down."

But, beneath the refusal to show emotion, there is a pride: pride that he is still the only bowler to have taken 30 Australian wickets in a series both at home and away, pride that he took the wicket of Don Bradman six times in Tests – and pride that his hard work achieved so much when England won back the Ashes in that Coronation summer.

## 34. A lost talent

*Alan Castell of Hampshire* WCM, MAR 2003

"Alan Castell had the greatest potential of any young cricketer I've ever seen," Hampshire's Jimmy Gray says. "He could bat well, he was a terrific catcher, and as a leg-spin bowler he had a lovely orthodox action – like an Australian, getting his left shoulder right round. He was in a different class to someone like Ian Salisbury."

Castell, a car upholsterer's son from Oxford, was 16 when he joined the Hampshire staff in 1960. Two years later, in only his third championship match, he put on 230 for the ninth wicket with Danny Livingstone, a new county record.

The following summer, 1963, his bowling started to grab the headlines. He impressed Denis Compton and Peter May in a charity match at Highclere Castle. Then against Somerset at Bournemouth in July, in his fourth first-team game of the summer, he returned match figures of 54 overs, ten wickets for 102. Bill Alley called him 'the best leg-break bowler I've ever seen, better for his age than Richie Benaud was.'

"It was a wonderful feeling, running in and giving the ball a rip," he recalls. "I was young and carefree, I had reasonable control, and the ball spun and beat the bat. It was a great battle with Bill Alley."

A week later, he took seven wickets at Bristol, his name was in the national bowling averages, and Compton pressed for his inclusion on the winter tour to India. 'Wrist spinners are a rarity,' he wrote, 'and every encouragement should be given to bring them back into the game.'

But it was not to be. Hampshire travelled to Portsmouth where the Middlesex batsmen hit up 409, and he bowled just six overs for 14 runs. The journalist EM Wellings was furious, thinking the pitch ideal for his leg spin and recalling Hampshire's recent release of off-spinner Mervyn Burden: 'Is Castell also to be sacrificed on the black magic altar of the seam fetish? For me, seeing Castell bowl was the attraction of the match.'

"I was bemused," Alan says. "Maybe they were nurturing me. Or were they losing confidence? If only they'd let me carry on bowling."

His regular captain was the Old Etonian Colin Ingleby-Mackenzie: "A natural-born leader, he filled you with confidence." But the following week, when they arrived at a damp Wellingborough ground, the professional Roy Marshall was deputising, and the young spinner found himself returning to Southampton on the train. He was not picked for the next five matches, and suddenly he was in a state of crisis.

"I was doing a bit of ground work and bowling in the nets, and it all went haywire. I just lost confidence."

He had acquired a reputation as a chirpy lad. "I was a bit of a teddy boy," he confesses. "In those days you wore the county tie in a tight Windsor knot. But most of the time mine was down here. And I had these slight drainpipe trousers. One time Harry Altham said he wanted to watch me bowl in the nets, and reputedly I said, 'Oky doky, mate.' Desmond Eagar, the secretary, was standing there. 'Oky what? Oky what? This is the president of the club, the president of the MCC. You don't say 'oky doky, mate.'"

Such carefree chirpiness did nothing to equip him for his crisis.

"I wasn't getting the middle practice," he says, still bewildered by what happened. "If I could have carried on ... I was thinking about it all the time ... I really needed help ... It was a dreadful feeling ... You start to think, 'How did it used to come out? Was it from there, or there?' Before, I just got hold of the ball and gave it a rip ... It got to the point where I could hardly let the ball go."

"It isn't always the most talented who succeed in cricket," Jimmy Gray says. "You've got to make the most of what you're given."

'If Castell had had a good August,' Jim Swanton wrote, 'he might have caught the eye for India. But despite good figures in June and July he has since been kicking his heels, unselected. Such an instance makes one despair sometimes for English cricket: so unadventurous, so stodgy, so short-sighted.'

Essex also had a young leg-spinner, Robin Hobbs, but he was having little success. In 19 championship matches that summer he took 21 wickets at 51.66 each.

"At another county I might have dropped out of the game," he says, "but Trevor Bailey really supported me." The next summer he took 81 wickets in all matches and was selected for England's winter tour of South Africa.

"Perhaps I should have gone to Warwickshire or Northants," Alan Castell says. "Perhaps I was too much of a non-conformist. When I look at what Bill Alley said, I feel I let him down."

He never recaptured the promise of that golden July. He toured Jamaica in the winter with a Cavaliers side, John Arlott reporting that 'he gained more of sunburn and experience than of confidence.' He took one championship wicket in 1964, did not play in '65 and returned in '66 as a seamer.

'Leg-spinners pose problems,' Alan Ross wrote, 'much like love, requiring commitment, the taking of a chance.'

Forty years on, Alan Castell is as chirpy as ever, though he still cannot explain why it all went wrong.

"I've got no axe to grind," he says. "But, as I get older, I do find myself thinking back and imagining what could have been. And I wonder. If I'd been Australian, would this have happened to me?"

## 35. Wet Worthing to dusty Durban

*Ian Thomson of Sussex* TWC, Nov 2006

In the early 1960s Sussex played on three out-grounds: Eastbourne, Hastings and Worthing.

The batsmen enjoyed themselves at Eastbourne. "It was the best batting wicket in the country," Jim Parks reckons. "If you were out of form, you'd look forward to Eastbourne week."

Not so the bowlers. Ian Thomson recalls the delight of his team-mate Don Bates early in 1961. "He liked to do the *Telegraph* crossword, and he used to read the national averages. 'Here, Tommy,' he said one day, 'I'm fifth in the averages, and you're tenth. We're up with Trueman and Statham.' Then the next week we were at Eastbourne, the plumbest pitch of all time. After that our names disappeared."

The Manor Field, Worthing was another story. Ian Thomson, the son of a professional footballer, won his cap there in 1953, taking nine wickets in a match that was all over by lunch on the second day. A council ground, it had been dug up for allotments during the war and the pitches often broke up.

"The crowds weren't particularly big," he recalls, "not like Hastings and Eastbourne, but the county liked to spread the gospel."

In 1963 Sussex made a profit of just £21 from its week there, and the members voted to take the games back to Hove. But Worthing Corporation intervened, and they were still there in June 1964 when Warwickshire were the first visitors.

The month of May was the wettest for sixty years and, with the game set to start on Saturday morning, the council staff mopped 100 gallons of water off the square on Friday. Then, after the visitors had reached 103 for two, the skies opened again.

Ian Thomson was 35 years old, a veteran county seamer on the verge of beating Maurice Tate's Sussex record of taking 100 wickets in 11 successive summers. He was not a fast bowler, not even as fast as he had once been, but he was, in the words of Trevor Bailey, 'a better bowler than he looked, an in-swinger capable of making the ball dance off the seam in bewildering fashion.'

On Monday the sun came out, Thomson set to work, and wickets fell.

"John Snow and Tony Buss were bowling at the other end. They were bowling shorter and hitting people about the body, where I was pitching it up a bit further, making a patch for myself, and some balls would skid, others would lift. I had a leg-cutter, but I didn't bowl it that day. I just plopped it there."

He took the first seven, then the eighth, then the ninth. Then, when

Tom Cartwright hit him for six and was stumped trying to repeat the shot, 'the quiet man of Sussex cricket', as the *Worthing Gazette* described him, left the field to 'a standing ovation and a triumphant fanfare of car horns'. He had taken ten wickets for 49 runs in 34.2 overs.

"Worthing is my lucky ground," he told the *Gazette*. "I like bowling here. In fact, all bowlers do."

He took five more in the second innings, but it was to no avail. The pitch degenerated further and, when Sussex set out with 206 to win, Ian says, 'some balls were hitting the ankles, some the gloves. The batters decided just to swing the bat and hope for the best.'

In less than an hour they slumped to 23 for eight before Tom Cartwright, another who revelled in such conditions, was given the ball. Two deliveries later, it was all over. With the second match of the Worthing week lasting only two days and the receipts down again, that was the end of county cricket at the seaside resort.

Thomson took 23 wickets for 130 runs in 102.2 overs that week and, when Don Bates next showed him the *Telegraph* averages, he was in first place.

Two months later, in the Gillette Cup Final, he again tormented Warwickshire, taking four for 23 on a misty September morning at Lord's and winning the man of the match award.

Mike Smith the Warwickshire captain had been appointed the England captain for the winter tour of South Africa and, when Yorkshire's Tony Nicholson dropped out of the party in early October, he and the selectors surveyed their options. Not the 33-year-old Fred Trueman or the 34-year-old Brian Statham, they were past their best. No, out of the blue came the name of the 35-year-old Sussex seamer Ian Thomson.

"It was quite a surprise," he says with a smile.

When he took the field at Durban for the First Test, he had taken 1,497 first-class wickets, more than any other debutant in Test history.

He bowled whole-heartedly all winter but the pitches bore little resemblance to Worthing or even Lord's. "After Durban, which took spin, the batsmen were always in charge. The bowlers had a real rough time, and I was very tired when I started again the next summer. I think that's why I packed up at the end of that year."

Arthur Gilligan, the Sussex Chairman, approached him about succeeding Dexter as captain, but he returned to his father's garage, then became a teacher. A master craftsman in English conditions, a model of hard work and fitness, he remains modest about his achievements.

"If I was bowling today on covered pitches, I would have to bowl faster. Otherwise I think I might be a little innocuous. I feel proud that I played for England, but I'm well aware of my own limitations."

## 36. The return of the king

*Wally Hammond of Gloucestershire* WCM, JULY 2003

Monday 26 May 2003. A Bank Holiday and a day off for our county cricketers.

How different it was fifty years ago – when every Secretary prayed for Bank Holiday sunshine and traditional rivalries were resumed: from the Roses match in the North to the West Country encounter of Somerset and Gloucestershire.

In 1951, with the post-war attendance boom in decline, Gloucestershire announced that the great Walter Hammond would be returning for the August Bank Holiday match at Bristol. And despite overnight rain, according to the *Bristol Evening World*, the rationed folk of the city 'rolled up to Ashley Down in their thousands, hoping to see the glories of the years between the wars recaptured.'

"Glo'shire are batting, Hammond's number four," went the word down the line.

Five years had passed since Hammond had last stepped out from the Bristol pavilion, scoring 214 against Somerset on another August Bank Holiday Saturday. Now he stood in the dressing room and shook hands with a new generation: Tom Graveney and Arthur Milton, the 18-year-old John Mortimore and the Gloucester new boy 'Bomber' Wells. The generation who had found inspiration in his exploits.

"It was like standing in the presence of God," Bomber Wells says. "You can't describe it, he was such a legend. He was 48 and looking much older because of the way he'd looked after himself – or not looked after himself. He smiled and shook hands. And I realised what large hands he had, and his forearms were huge like legs of pork."

For the crowd the morning passed with no sight of their King. 'The courtiers,' the *Evening World* reported, 'in the form of Emmett and Milton, displayed batsmanship of such quality that they seemed to appreciate that this was a regal occasion and were seeing that the stage was set for the appearance of the Old Master.'

Both made centuries but, after the dismissal of Emmett and Graveney, the moment came and the packed crowd rose to its feet in ovation. For Arthur Milton, the not-out batsman, it was a special moment. "The first cricket I'd watched was in 1946, on my way home from school, and Wally was playing."

Horace Hazell, Somerset's tubby slow left-armer, held the ball, and his first delivery rapped Hammond on the pad. 'There was an agonising split second as Hazell made a very confident appeal.'

In his prime the great man was never dominated. 'If you managed a maiden at him,' Kent's Doug Wright quipped, 'it made your season.' But here, for eighteen minutes, he groped for his first run.

"A lot of people in the pavilion," John Mortimore recalls, "wouldn't watch till he got off the mark."

"I just sat in the dressing room," Tom Graveney tells. "I couldn't watch any of it."

"It was all rather embarrassing," Somerset's Eric Hill says. "There he was. A great giant who had bestridden everything, struggling like a starter. Just struggling. Looking awful."

In later years Hazell liked to tell how he fed him half-volleys outside the off-stump out of sympathy, but this is not how Eric recalls it. "He hit him several times on the pad. They looked unlikely, but Horace screamed at them all."

Hazell had bowled to him here before the War, when Hammond had hit Somerset for centuries four summers running. He had bowled to him in 1946 when he hit 214. "He'd suffered all right," Eric says. "Whenever Hammond missed, Horace appealed – and he wasn't that sort of bloke usually."

"Wally never said a word to me," his partner Arthur Milton recalls.

Arthur was a fleet-footed winger with Arsenal in winter, and without thinking he called a quick single, only to turn in horror to see his ageing partner well short of his ground as the throw came in. "I thought, 'What have I done? I'm going to get lynched.'"

The ball missed the stumps, but the agony continued. "It was terribly sad. I longed to see him do well. But there he was, cursing quietly as he mistimed balls he once hammered."

After fifty minutes, a restless Hammond advanced down the track to the left-arm Hazell and was bowled 'all over the shop'. His comeback was over, with just seven singles recorded in Monty Cranfield's copperplate handwriting in the scorebook.

In the bar that evening Horace Hazell smiled quietly. He had taken eight wickets, but there was only one of them on his mind. Eric Hill still recalls his words: "I owed that bugger that one."

Hammond stood at slip for a while on the Monday, then retired with lumbago. Three months later he emigrated to South Africa.

In June they are celebrating his centenary in Bristol, a month after John Mortimore celebrates his 70th birthday. "Sometimes I tell people I played with Wally, and they look at me. 'God, you've aged well,' they say."

## 37. Not club cricket, you know

*Ian Bedford of Middlesex* WCM, Apr 2003

Ian Bedford played cricket for fun.

In 1947, as a 17-year-old grammar school boy, he broke into Middlesex's championship-winning team, throwing his leg breaks high into the air, dismissing Washbrook with a googly and finishing second in their bowling averages. He was awarded his cap, but the next summer they got him pushing the ball through with a lower trajectory and within two years he had been discarded. Through the 1950s he pursued a career with a construction company and played for Finchley.

"He loved the bonhomie of club cricket," team-mates recall. "He played with a smile. Wherever we went, the first question was always, 'Is Ian playing?'"

Then out of the blue in 1961 Middlesex invited him to be their amateur captain.

"It was a tremendously enjoyable summer," their long-time professional Don Bennett says. "Everything seemed to work. He did the double over Yorkshire, having declared when we all said he was crazy. 'It's not club cricket, you know,' I said to him. 'Just wait and see,' is all he'd say."

Yorkshire, set 300 in nearly four hours, were 128 for one at tea. "He was getting a bit of a wide berth. 'I see I'm not too popular, boys,' he said. And we went back out and bowled them out. He had a wonderful way with him, and he got on so well with all the opposition captains that they all played a game of cricket with us. We didn't have many draws."

At Lord's in June Don Bennett was at the crease, playing out time against Somerset. Then the captain joined him. Seven wickets were down, with 79 wanted in 40 minutes. "Block?" he said. "I can't block." And he hit a half-hour fifty that won them the match.

For the final 36 runs that day his partner was a 19-year-old amateur, Michael Sturt, plucked from Brondesbury club to keep wicket while John Murray was at the first Test. "We'd got a professional keeper in the second eleven," Don Bennett says, "but Ian was quite stubborn. And he was right. Michael kept very well."

"I was with a printing company in North Acton," Sturt recalls. "I'd get to work at 7.30, then go across to Lord's on the tube. As an amateur, I only had to be there at 11 for an 11.30 start. Maybe not till 12 if we were batting."

The Somerset game was the first of six successive victories that took Middlesex to the Wagon Works ground at Gloucester, top of the table for the first time since 1949. The third Test was in progress, and this time Michael Sturt arrived at the crease with nine wickets down, 40 minutes left and 66 runs still wanted.

"The dressing room was awkward," Don Bennett says. "You had to stand on a seat to look out of the window. Titmus was up watching, I was sitting down, and I hadn't to move. He gave me a commentary."

A series of bold hits by Bedford reduced the target to 42 in half an hour. Then, with Sam Cook bowling, he hoisted the ball towards mid-on where the fielder was the home captain Arthur Milton, one of the best catchers in the history of the game.

"That's it," Titmus groaned. "It's all over … No, he's dropped it."

"It must have been too easy for him," Michael Sturt reckons. "It went quite high, but it was a gaper."

"It was a little dolly," Arthur says. "I must have taken my eye off it."

Sturt stayed in for a valiant 4, while Bedford – with 'a majestic exhibition of hard hitting' – struck seven sixes and came off victorious with 75 to his name. They had ten minutes to spare, and their 66 is still the highest tenth wicket partnership to win a first-class match in England.

"Well played, lads," Arthur Milton said, sitting down in the cramped Middlesex dressing room.

"Bloody brave of you to come in here, Art," Don Bennett suggested.

"Oh no, I'm better off in here, Don," replied Milton, painfully aware of the win bonus he had cost his team. "When I go next door, they're going to lynch me."

Middlesex ended the season in third place, and they did not become champions again till 1976 when Mike Brearley solved a mid-season wicket-keeping crisis by summoning a long-forgotten amateur from club cricket: one Michael Sturt of Brondesbury, by now a 35-year-old managing director.

"It was a wonderful summer," Sturt recalls. "It was very dry, the wickets turned and we had Fred Titmus and Philippe Edmonds. Mike was a great captain. A touch unorthodox at times. Somehow he could create results in games. As Ian Bedford could."

Bedford did two summers as Middlesex captain, then he returned to Finchley. In September 1966, batting at Buckhurst Hill, he suffered a massive brain haemorrhage and dropped down dead at the wicket.

The memories are confused. Some clubmates say it was early in the afternoon, others that it was in the last over and that he was preparing to face Essex's Stuart Turner, needing ten runs for another dramatic victory.

At his funeral every first-class county sent a floral tribute in the shape of their emblem.

"He was top of the pops with me," Don Bennett says, "and with a lot of the other boys. That summer of 1961 was the best year I had at Middlesex."

## 38. Wales 2 Australia 0

*Don Shepherd of Glamorgan* TWC, Aug 2004

Forty years ago there were no one-day internationals, no split-summer tours, no televising of cricket in winter, no overseas stars dropping in and out of the English county game. The tourists arrived in April, they stayed for 20 weeks and crowds flocked to see them all round the counties.

Don Bradman's 1948 Australians were the greatest of them all. From Worcester in late April to Aberdeen in mid-September, their schedule took in 109 days of cricket, at the end of which they sailed home undefeated. They won 15 of their 20 matches against the counties, ten by an innings, and attendance records were broken at eight grounds.

For the county player the tourist match was the game above all others to anticipate, and that summer Charles Palmer – a schoolmaster playing only occasionally – was selected for the winter tour of South Africa largely on the strength of his 85 at Worcester against Lindwall and Miller.

Five years later a young Frank Tyson burst upon the nation's consciousness with a sensational first over at Northampton against Lindsay Hassett's Australians. In front of 23,000 spectators, MacDonald was lbw second ball and hobbled slowly back to the pavilion. Then two balls later Hole's middle stump was violently uprooted.

These were not days that the professionals wanted to take off. When the West Indians came to Taunton in 1957, the young fast bowler Ken Biddulph was made twelfth man, and he admitted in later life that he withdrew into a corner to shed a quiet tear.

Nor were they games that the tourists treated lightly. In nine tours from 1921 to 1961 the Australians played 178 county matches and they lost only once: in 1956, when – as a harbinger of greater things to come – Surrey's Jim Laker took all ten wickets in the Australian first innings at The Oval.

But nowhere was the passion for these games greater than in Glamorgan. As the 17th county to join the championship, they were not locked into a traditional Bank Holiday derby so, for many years, they entertained the tourists twice: in Cardiff at Whitsun and in Swansea at the August Bank Holiday. Large crowds gathered, especially in Swansea, and, with the English selectors rarely giving a chance to the county's players, Welsh passion ran high.

"There was always something special about the tourist matches," their long-serving bowler Don Shepherd recalls. "Huge crowds came to enjoy them, and there was applause for a good stop in the field or a good throw, not just clapping for a hundred or five wickets. Everything seemed extra special."

Bobby Simpson's Australians arrived in August 1964, undefeated in all matches, and Glamorgan – under the captaincy of Ossie Wheatley – were struggling near the foot of the table. "We can save the season," Wheatley told his players, "if we do well against Australia."

The National Eisteddfod was in Swansea for the first time for many years and, as the Australian batting sank to 39 for six on the Saturday evening, the crowds at the Eisteddfod peeled away from the performances to watch the cricket on a few black-and-white television sets that had been provided. Then on the Sunday the Glamorgan team took to the stage themselves and received a thunderous ovation. "We were so full of hwyl after that," Don Shepherd recalls, "that there was no way we were going to lose the match."

On a turning wicket Don Shepherd took nine wickets, Jim Pressdee ten and, with a record 50,000 attending over the three days, the Australians were beaten by 36 runs. As the celebrations began, the crowd broke into singing 'Land of my Fathers' and 'Calon Lan'. This was not just a Glamorgan victory. It was a victory for Wales.

"We Australians have very long memories," Bobby Simpson said, "and perhaps in 1968, when we do come to Swansea again, we might remember this day and try to avenge this defeat."

But in 1968, when the Australians returned to Swansea, Glamorgan's Alan Jones hit a match-winning 99 and Don Shepherd, standing in as captain, led his county to a second victory. "And again there was this response from the crowd," Don says. "It was like an amphitheatre. There used to be a huge bank, and all the way round, wherever you looked, there were temporary stands. The whole space was surrounded and packed."

No batsman has scored more runs without playing Test cricket than Alan Jones, no bowler has taken more wickets than Don Shepherd, but they have the satisfaction of knowing that, in the days when such matches mattered, they twice played for their own country Wales and triumphed over the Australians.

"To beat them twice," Don Shepherd says, "was really wonderful. People who were there still come up to me. It happens frequently. They even introduce their sons to tell them. 'I was there the day we beat Australia.' It was of great, great importance all round here."

## 39. Controversy in the Caribbean

*The MCC tour of the West Indies 1953/54* TWC, Mar 2004

Charles Palmer had had remarkable success with Leicestershire. In 1949 they had finished bottom of the table and were close to bankruptcy. The following spring he left schoolmastering in Bromsgrove to take up the reins as both secretary and captain of the little Midland county, and his gentle charm and steely dedication brought a transformation. "They were all good players," he says, "but they had not been a team."

He made himself known to everybody involved with the club – "I went to fifty dinners in the first summer" – and he introduced a football pool that brought in fresh revenue. Such was their progress that for a brief spell in late August 1953 the county stood for the first time in its history at the top of the championship table.

At that moment of glory MCC were sitting down to choose a manager for their winter tour of the West Indies and, with more experienced figures unavailable, Charles Palmer was an obvious candidate. Further, he was a good enough all-round cricketer to double up as the party's sixteenth player.

It was a unique arrangement, a manager submitting his authority to the captain on the field, and it was doubly unique in that the captain of an MCC tour was for the first time a professional cricketer, Len Hutton. With only Bill Ferguson the unobtrusive baggage man and scorer for support, the new manager faced a challenge that would prove even greater than the one he had undertaken at Leicester.

Up to 1950 the leading English players would only tour Australia and South Africa. But the progress of West Indian cricket had been dramatic. In 1947/48 Gubby Allen's second-string side had failed to win even an island match, and the full England team had been beaten at home by three Tests to one in 1950.

So, of the side that won back the Ashes at The Oval, only Alec Bedser and Bill Edrich were missing when the tourists climbed onto the BOAC Stratocruiser in December, the first party ever to fly out for a tour. "There wasn't enough petrol to fly direct," Charles says. "We had to refuel in Ireland. Then we were diverted to Newfoundland."

Landing finally in Bermuda, the manager got his first taste of Caribbean politics. A colour bar. "We were standing round the airport. I was talking about the playing conditions with this Bermudian chap, and I said, 'Let's sort it out at the hotel.' Then I saw people in the background semaphoring: 'Not allowed to fraternise. Black and white.' We had to arrange a special meeting elsewhere."

Much had happened in six years since Gubby Allen's tour. India had won its independence, and in its wake there was an upsurge of Home Rule movements throughout the Empire. The resident white population in the Caribbean was filled with fear for the future of their way of life.

"Every day on the tour we were being invited to social functions, invariably with the white people, and it was difficult to refuse. All the time they would be saying to us, 'For God's sake, beat these people, or our lives won't be worth living.' It became a big millstone round our neck. We were almost afraid to talk to a white person. We knew what they were going to say. We wanted to win, but not for them. After a while it ate into our souls."

Matters were not improved by Len Hutton's decision to play the series as a Yorkshireman would play Lancashire: no fancy stroke play and a minimum of socialising with the opposition. The West Indians had been warmly welcomed in England, they played with a sense of fun, and Hutton's approach upset them. Further, Hutton as captain did not want his players worn down by too many functions, and the manager – recognising the need for them to be ambassadors – found himself pulling the other way. "I could understand Len's point, but the two-fisted structure of authority made it very difficult."

It did not help that, with England now holding the Ashes, many West Indian journalists claimed that the series was for the Championship of the World. Nor that the umpiring was so contentious. In the First Test in Jamaica the local hero JK Holt was adjudged lbw when he was on 94, and the umpire's family was physical assaulted. After that, the mentality developed in the England camp that the officials were frightened to give their fellow countrymen out.

With local men appointed in each island, the eight umpires in the series had stood in only seven previous Tests between them. So alarmed were MCC about the umpiring in the warm-up match in British Guiana that fresh officials had to be appointed for the Test. One of them, Menzies, had to combine his duties with those of head groundsman.

"I would never accuse them of cheating," Charles Palmer says. "Indeed I made a point of this in my report to the MCC. They were just incompetent. They hadn't the experience."

On the fourth evening of the Test the groundsman Menzies put up his finger when his fellow Guianan Clifford McWatt was short of his ground, going for the 100th run of his partnership with Holt, and the decision brought a hail of bottles from the crowd.

Was the riot fuelled by drink, or gambling, or political unrest at the removal from power of their left-wing Prime Minister? Whatever the cause, Len Hutton refused to leave the field. "I want to take these last two wickets this evening," he said, and play resumed with no fielders in the deep and Johnny Wardle defusing the tension by swigging drunkenly from a bottle. A police guard was stationed outside the groundsman's house.

Then there was the matter of Tony Lock's quicker ball. He had been no-balled in one match in England, by Fred Price at The Oval in 1952, and he would eventually – in the aftermath of the 'chucking' controversies of the 1958/59 tour of Australia – have to remodel his action. But in the first Test and again in the match against Barbados he was called, and he had to cut out his deadliest weapon.

'The no-balling caused quite a rumpus,' Jim Laker wrote. 'Yet to my eyes his quickest ball was a genuine throw, and it looked glaring in Barbados.'

To his surprise Charles Palmer recently discovered cine film that he had taken on the tour, and a sequence of frames confirms Laker's judgement. "It certainly shows up Tony Lock's action."

Then there was Freddie Trueman, the young and fiery fast bowler whose bumpers upset the crowd and whose raw personality created incidents both on and off the field. Some, like the debonair southerner Denis Compton, criticised Len Hutton for not talking to him sternly at the outset, but the West Indian Frank Worrell thought Trueman to have been made the scapegoat unfairly, losing his good conduct bonus and not touring again with MCC for five years.

"I like Fred," Charles Palmer says, "but he'd been pulled out of Yorkshire and put in a context which was entirely alien to his upbringing. There was no malice in him, but he spoke as a Yorkshireman would speak in Yorkshire. I remember in a bar one night. This fellow came up. He said he had a friend in Yorkshire and did Fred know him? And instead of Fred saying, 'No, but I'll look out for him' or some such words, he said, 'Never 'eard of the bugger.' They were little things, but they didn't go down very well in a highly sensitive situation."

In each island there were complaints about the English team: from slights supposedly inflicted at social functions to the incident in the final Test at Kingston when Hutton, leaving the field for tea with a marathon double century to his name, did not stop sufficiently to receive the congratulations of a large, flamboyant man in a white tailcoat: Alexander Bustamante, the nationalist leader who had become Jamaica's first Chief Minister.

A few moments later the manager was in the dressing room, being grasped by the lapels and lifted off the floor by a six-foot, five-inch member of the Minister's retinue. "'This is the crowning insult,' he said. 'Your captain has insulted our Prime Minister.' I said, 'Put me down first of all, and we can talk about it.' I was then involved in 48 hours of non-stop diplomatic consultations. Morning, noon and night something was happening. It got to the stage where I didn't know where the next arrow was coming from. All I knew was that it was coming."

The cricket itself, for all the problems, provided a magnificent series. In the first two Tests, the West Indies won easily. Ramadhin and Valentine bowled out England for 170 on a good batting track at Sabina Park, then Clyde Walcott hit a magnificent 220 at Bridgetown where the manager, making his Test debut, found himself admiring the batsman from the covers.

"He'd got tree trunks, not arms. He really did hit the ball hard. Not like Frank Worrell, who stroked it with such grace. The only batsman I can remember hitting the ball harder than Walcott was Wally Hammond, in one of my first matches before the war. I fielded at cover point to him and, oh boy, you really didn't want to field the ball."

Two-nil down after two Tests, it was not what the local white people had expected. "We played like absolute twits in the first two Tests. We were terrible, and of course it put the whites right on the back foot. So they didn't like us at all."

But at Georgetown in the third Test England were victorious. Though he had dropped his instruction to his fellow batsmen to play conservatively, Hutton led from the front with a faultless safety-first innings of 169, and a new-ball burst by Statham destroyed the West Indian top order. At Port-of-Spain, on a matting wicket, the three Ws all made big hundreds, but May and Compton reciprocated and the series went to the final match at Sabina Park with England still 2-1 down.

"The pitch was bone hard like marble," Charles Palmer says. "You could see your reflection in it." The groundsman had told Hutton that the team batting first would make 700, Statham was unfit, and Hutton lost the toss. He threw the new ball to Trevor Bailey. "Three for 100 would have been really good figures on that, and he took seven for 34. Then Len batted nine hours for his 200. He'd got such powers of concentration, and a wonderful technique. But Trevor, somehow he had produced something out of the bag which was quite impossible." The series ended two-all, and there were no world champions.

After four months in the Caribbean heat the tourists sailed out of Kingston. According to *The Times*, it was 'the second most controversial tour in cricket history.' To *Wisden*, the primary intention of the tour, 'to further friendship between man and man, country and country', was not achieved.

"We got out into the Atlantic," Charles Palmer remembers. "We were relaxing on the boat, and we started to feel that we weren't far from home."

The manager returned to an inquest at Lord's, delivering a report that strongly recommended that a player should never again act as manager. He still retains a sheaf of letters congratulating him on his 'splendid performance' at the meeting. One from Gubby Allen speculated how the tour might have avoided much of the trouble: with a slightly different party, a less single-minded captain and Palmer himself 'with a different brief and more power'.

*Wisden* concurred. 'C.H. Palmer won much credit on his first tour as manager but, as a principle, the policy of a player-manager was not to be commended.'

'It was just about the worst decision ever to come out of Lord's,' Jim Swanton wrote with typical forthrightness twenty years later.

Len Hutton was the player of the series, with 677 runs at an average of 96.71. But he missed much of the following summer, exhausted and with back problems. After his 205 at Kingston, he would play just 15 more Test innings and manage only 306 more runs.

"Len reckoned that that tour shortened his career by two years. I'm surprised that he only said two. That innings in the fifth Test, he batted nine hours in the heat. After all the worries of the tour, he was magnificent. He played with a kind of divine inevitability."

Through the following summer speculation grew in the press that the MCC would turn to the amateur David Sheppard to captain in Australia. By then Charles Palmer was back in the calm of Grace Road, Leicester, but he did attend the meeting at Lord's which made the decision.

"At the start of the West Indian tour," he says, "I found Len enigmatical. If you asked him a question, you got another question in reply. But as we were tempered by fire, we got to know each other, and I developed a great respect for him."

Neither Trueman nor Lock boarded the boat to Australia, but Hutton was still in charge, sailing out to secure his place in history with Ashes victory.

"I don't think I could have done very much more than I did," Charles Palmer reflects. "A different man, a Freddie Brown or a Brian Sellers, somebody who could bang the fist, might have made it better. But then they might have made it a damn sight worse."

## 40. A real all-rounder

*Ken Taylor of Yorkshire* TWC, Aug 2004

It could not happen now. In winter Ken Taylor played football for Huddersfield Town. In summer he played cricket for Yorkshire. And all the while he was training as an artist, first at the Huddersfield Art School, then at the Slade in London. His older brother Jeff combined playing football for Fulham with studying for a geography degree at London University; then he went to the Royal Academy of Music and became an opera singer.

Their father worked in the weaving trade, repairing looms, while their maternal grandfather was a ventriloquist who had a punch and judy show on Blackpool beach. They were like many boys in Huddersfield, playing their sport in the ginnels that ran between the houses, and the young Ken was exceptionally fortunate to attend Stile Common School where the headmaster Wally Heap – with no key stage tests and national curriculum to worry about – believed in finding a boy's talent and developing it.

"We played cricket with him in the school yard with a cork ball and no pads, up against a dustbin," Ken remembers. "You batted till you were out. You went in at break, then back at lunchtime. Then in winter we used to play football against the staff at the local recreation ground. We had to mark out the lines with sawdust that we collected from a local cabinet maker. It was a wonderful school. Regardless of what you were good at, Wally Heap nurtured it. There were 120 children, and one term we had 100% attendance."

In 1950, on leaving school, he went on the ground staff at Huddersfield Town: "Cleaning the boots, digging up the pitch on Monday morning." He joined on the same day as Ray Wilson who, 16 years later, would be the left back in England's World Cup winning team. But in those early days Wilson was an inside forward, making little impression, and he was overshadowed by the young Ken Taylor who made his first team debut at 18, marking Billy Liddell in front of 50,000 at Anfield. A year later Ken was called up for the England Under-23s.

"If things had worked out differently," Ray Wilson says, "Ken could even have been playing with me in the World Cup. But cricket called him, too."

The young batsman made his Yorkshire debut at 17, won his cap at 21 and was in the England side at 23, opening the batting against India with Arthur Milton. These were times when many county cricketers could be found on the football field in winter, and both Milton and Willie Watson were double internationals. Mike Smith played rugby union for England, and Ted Dexter was only prevented by his cricketing commitments from playing golf for Great Britain in the Walker Cup.

"Playing two sports," Ken thinks, "was quite tiring physically, especially after I got to my mid-twenties, but mentally it was less demanding. If I didn't get any runs, I would think, 'I'll be back playing football soon,' and that made it easier for me."

But his father was a hard-working Yorkshireman, and he wanted his son to have a career. "You can't play games for ever," he would say, and Ken became a full-time art student, his football limited to three nights' training and a match on Saturday afternoon. Then in 1956, when he was 21, he gained a place at the Slade, accepted by Sir William Coldstream.

In winter he combined an art student's life in London with two nights on the Brentford Town training ground with his brother Jeff. Then on Friday evenings he would catch the train to wherever Huddersfield were playing and join up with the team, amongst them Denis Law. Their manager was the tough-talking Scotsman, Bill Shankly. What did he think of Ken studying art? "He couldn't even understand my playing cricket. He called it a lassie's game."

But Ken was a tough footballer, a centre half who gave no quarter, unlucky not to play for England where Walter Winterbottom's 2-3-5 formation was very different from the fluid man-to-man marking that Shankly adopted. Not that Ken was ever briefed about the opposing centre-forward. "Shankly told us never to read the programme. He said we'd be marking the name, not the player on the field. "'Don't worry about them,' he used to say. 'They're not fit to be on the park with you.'"

Ken also had a short spell as a centre-forward, scoring four goals against West Ham, but his most dramatic match was at Charlton. "Derek Ufton the Kent wicket-keeper dislocated his shoulder, and they were down to ten men for most of the game. We were 5-1 up at half-time, and we lost 7-6. They had this left-winger, and every time he hit the ball, it went in the net. Shankly didn't speak to us for a week afterwards."

As a cricketer Ken was a good enough batsman to play three times for England: twice in 1959 against India, then in 1964 when a superb 160 at Sheffield against the touring Australians brought him a recall. But he broke a finger in the Test, and his chance passed again. According to Jim Swanton, he had the potential to be a good Test cricketer – but not the luck. 'His cricket,' Swanton wrote, 'suffered from his career as a footballer giving him a shortened season and possibly somewhat diluting his ambition.'

His straight drives owed much to the narrowness of the ginnels where he batted as a child and, unlike most Yorkshiremen, he could play wrist spin, as a result of the hours in front of the school dustbin when he faced his teacher Colin Garthwaite, the old Cleckheaton pro. He was one of the great cover fielders of his generation, and for some years his seam bowling was a valuable option for Yorkshire. "Then Closey became captain. Whenever Ray Illingworth said to him, 'Why don't you put Ken on?', he'd say, 'I'll have a go.' I hardly bowled."

He was a key member of the Yorkshire side that won seven championships between 1959 and 1968, when he retired after taking a benefit. It was in that last year that he reported back to Headingley, sporting an artist's beard. Brian Sellers the chairman was not impressed. "Take that bloody thing off," he barked, "or you're not playing for Yorkshire again."

There followed a lifetime of art teaching and cricket coaching, briefly in South Africa, then for over thirty years in North Norfolk. Now he is only teaching part-time, and there is more opportunity to engage in his own art work: ranging from large pastel portraits of sportsmen, that somehow capture their movement, to evocative drawings of buildings and landscapes, from the mills of his childhood to the village churches and grand houses of Norfolk.

'He goes about his job without fuss or mannerism,' they said of him when he was an England footballer in the making.

'His fault,' Michael Parkinson wrote, 'was that he shrugged off the gifts he was granted as if perturbed by their abundance. He had it in him to be a permanent fixture in the England cricket side.'

But Ken has no great regrets. "I might have done better if I hadn't done so many things. But I've been a very lucky man. I've had to work hard, but I've always enjoyed what I've done. So it's never felt like work."

*The ginnel, drawn by Ken.*

## 41. Know yourself

*Tom Cartwright of Warwickshire* TWC, Apr 2007

"Know yourself, be in control at your end," the veteran Warwickshire leg-spinner Eric Hollies would tell the young Tom Cartwright. "When you can come off the field, whether you've got wickets or not, and you can put your hand on your heart and say truthfully, 'I bowled well again today,' that's when you become a bowler, when that happens every day. And the only way you can do that is by being in control at your end."

They were words that the youngster had little opportunity to put into practice in his early years at Edgbaston. He made his debut as a batsman in 1952, and by the end of 1957 he had played 53 first-class matches and taken just three wickets in 71 overs. He was an in-swinging medium-pacer at a county that was brimful of such bowlers. In some years he did not even bowl in the second eleven.

He had one golden day at Scarborough in September 1957 when, playing for Warwickshire Seconds in the Minor Counties Challenge Match, he was brought on for an over, to switch the ends of the opening bowlers. He so exploited the damp, misty conditions that he finished with seven for 19 in 26 overs.

But in June 1959, approaching his 24th birthday, he was still a batsman who bowled only occasionally. Then came the moment at Dudley that changed the whole course of his cricketing life.

"As a kid at school I'd bowled all out-swingers. Then when I came to Edgbaston I didn't bowl much, only in the nets, and I went in the army, grew a bit, and by the end of it all I could only bowl in-swing. But that day at Dudley it was sultry. I was in the middle of an over, I just ran up and the ball swung away. It was the first time I'd done it since I'd left school.

"The miracle was that I knew exactly what I'd done. I didn't want anybody to talk to me as I walked back. I just wanted the ball, and I did it a second and a third time."

"Be in control," Hollies had told him. "Know yourself."

"I knew the shape of my hand when I let the ball go. I could see it in my mind's eye. And I retained the shape after I'd delivered the ball."

For two overs he bowled only out-swing. Then, as his confidence grew, he mixed in his in-swing. In 22.3 overs that day he took five wickets for 36 runs.

Suddenly he was a front-line bowler, in time one of the outstanding bowlers of English cricket. In 1967, when an experimental law prohibited any polishing of the ball, he took 147 wickets at an average of 15.52.

"Tom was a wonderful bowler," Brian Close says. "Under English conditions there wasn't a finer one at that time."

"He was the man you could never hit off the square," says Mike Brearley. "He became a sort of myth in county cricket."

"The ball moved two ways," Peter Roebuck explains. "That was the problem. It might swing a bit away, not violently, then come back off the seam, or it might come in and go away. Only two or three inches, but it meant that you couldn't line him up. That's why great attacking players like Sobers and Kanhai couldn't take him on."

In 1970 Tom Cartwright moved to Somerset where for four more summers he tormented county batsmen, a master craftsman still good enough at the age of 38 to top the national averages.

Then, appointed county coach, he worked with a young Ian Botham. Botham had been on the ground staff at Lord's where they thought his bowling a joke, but Tom changed all that.

"Do you want to bowl?" he asked him.

"Well, yes, of course I want to bowl."

"Well, if you want to bowl, I'll work with you because I think you could bowl."

"I can honestly say Ian was one of the most receptive people I've ever worked with. He learned to swing the ball both ways in a very short time, literally in weeks, and to have control in doing it."

"Tom always had time, always had faith in me," Botham says. "I couldn't have had a better man to teach me the art of bowling."

In his heyday, in all forms of cricket, Tom Cartwright averaged 1,000 overs a summer where none of the current England seamers average even 400.

"I feel sorry for the young bowlers today," he says. "Success comes with repetition. There are no short cuts or easy ways. They need to be bowling, out in the middle in matches."

For many observers it is a tragedy that he was never appointed England's bowling coach, but perhaps his thinking is uncomfortably out of synch with current orthodoxies.

"There's so much emphasis on speed now. I think it came from the great West Indian team of the 1980s. We became obsessed with finding fast bowlers. Also from this flaming machine that measures speed. You've got bowlers all trying to bowl at 90, 95 miles an hour. If you watch them, they're hurling the ball; they're not getting up there and bowling it. Every bowler has an optimum speed; once you go above that, you lose control. And it was only because I had control at Dudley that I knew what I had done. I had the peripheral awareness, and I could repeat it."

## 42. Stepping up to three-day cricket

*Norman Gifford of Worcestershire* TWC, JAN 2006

"It was my first experience of a three-day game," Norman Gifford says, recalling the day in June 1960 that he made his first-class debut.

Three summers earlier, as a 17-year-old apprentice decorator, he had been bowling his slow left-arm spinners for Ulverston second eleven in the North Lancashire League. "I had no idea what my standard was," he says. Then an older club member spotted an advert in *The Cricketer* Winter Annual: 'Worcestershire County Cricket Club require top-class spin bowler.' The man approached Norman's father. "If I can get my boy a trial, would Norman want to go with him for company?" The following April, after three days at the Worcester ground, Gifford was astonished to be offered terms.

"People say that, when you start in cricket, you dream of playing for England. I think that's crackers. For me, just to get on the Worcester staff and be paid was way beyond what I'd dreamt of."

The next big step came in 1960. Playing a second eleven match at Maidstone, he received a call to join the county side at Tunbridge Wells.

"I'd played one-day games for the Club and Ground and two-day games for the second eleven, but I'd never played the longer game. And I suppose I was thinking, 'Can I hold my own at this level?'"

The senior players went out to inspect the pitch while he unloaded the bags from the Worcester coach. "When they came off, I said to Dick Richardson, 'What's the wicket like?' He said, 'You don't want to know.' It was just a rolled piece of mud, like a strip of plasticene. Had it been dull and overcast, it might have stayed like that. But the sun was out, the moisture went out of it, and the ball started to break through the surface."

Kent won the toss and batted, reaching 41 before debutant Gifford, with his third ball, bowled Arthur Phebey. "If we get 200 on that," the batsman said when he returned to the dressing room, "we'll win by an innings."

The Nevill ground was owned by the council, with a new groundsman with no knowledge of cricket pitches. In unsettled weather he had somehow managed to remove all the grass, and his late addition of marl was a disaster.

"Even in club cricket," Norman says, "I'd never seen anything like it. At first there were indentations where the ball pitched. Then the whole wicket disintegrated. It just collapsed."

Kent's Peter Jones took his life in his hands. Dropped at long-on by the young Norman, 'he mixed good strokes with bad,' according to the *Worcester Evening News*, and his 73 took Kent to a total of 187. They were all out at 3.40 pm and by this stage 'the pitch had broken up into a gravelly bed, more in keeping with a seaside beach.'

Norman Gifford, with four for 63 in 17 overs, was happy – "I'd got four first-class wickets" – but, with hindsight, he realises that his figures were not what was required.

"In those days I bowled four or five good balls an over, but one you could do without would creep in. If I'd had those figures a few years later, I'd have been mortified. But you need to play a lot of cricket, and to bowl a lot of overs, to eliminate that one average ball."

In fact, his figures were looking indifferent within half an hour – by which time the scoreboard read 9 for six and he was padding up. They needed to reach 38 to avoid the follow-on, but – despite two fours by Doug Slade – they were all out for 25 and batting again at 5.35.

Dave Halfyard, a master of seam and cut, had taken four wickets for seven runs while Alan Brown, just by dropping the ball onto the broken surface, out-bowled him with six for 12. "In the end," Norman remembers, "Halfyard was complaining. 'I've developed the skill of bowling cutters, and he just runs up and does more than me."

"Dave was a great complainer," Alan Brown confirms. "One day he came back to the dressing room without a wicket. 'I'm doing so much with the ball,' he said, 'that they're playing up the wrong line and middling it.'"

The Worcester second innings soon reached 18 for five, with pairs for Ron Headley and George Dews. "Dick Richardson used to have a cigarette before batting," Norman says. "He put it down and said, 'Don't put that out. I'll have it when I come back.' And he did. There was that sort of feeling in the team."

Back in 1954, on a treacherous Oval pitch, Worcestershire had been bowled out for 25 and 40, a two-innings aggregate of 65 that was the lowest in England since 1908. Somehow at Tunbridge Wells, thanks to a gutsy 22 by Bob Broadbent, they managed to pass that mark – with a final total of 61 that included a wide from Halfyard that had pitched in line with off stump.

At 7.15 they were all out, the last occasion on which a first-class match has finished in one day.

Roy Booth, the Worcester keeper, nursed a black eye, 'a brute of a ball' having reared up to have him caught off bat and cheekbone, and he recalls going across to the Lady Mayor's marquee for close-of-play drinks.

"As we arrived, we heard her saying, 'Here come the Worcester side. Of course, they've ruined the Festival.' I don't think we stopped long."

Back in Worcester the next afternoon they were summoned for net practice, and Norman Gifford returned to the second team. He would have to wait a little longer for another taste of three-day cricket.

## 43. You play the way you think

*Colin Griffiths of Essex* WCM, June 2003

Brighter Cricket was the order for 1952. The previous summer had seen damp weather, falling attendances and a county championship in which a record-breaking 53% of matches failed to produce a result. Colonel Rait Kerr, the MCC Secretary, called for more enterprise and for cricket that was 'eager, quick and full of action' while Neville Cardus wondered if the safety-first culture reflected the condition of England: 'Life in this country is rationed. The times we live in are against the bold extravagant gesture. Our first-class cricketers seldom are allowed to play for fun.'

To reverse the trend, the *News Chronicle* initiated a Brighter Cricket Trophy, to be awarded to the county that scored its runs fastest, and the winners – ahead of Surrey and Yorkshire – were Essex. Across the whole summer, on uncovered pitches, they maintained a rate of over a run a minute.

With a weak bowling attack, they preferred to bat last and chase. At Brentwood they hit 195 in 97 minutes to beat Leicestershire by two wickets, then they hit 231 in 140 minutes for a thrilling tie with Lancashire.

Their opener Dickie Dodds, a convert to Moral Re-Armament, sought to 'play beautiful shots for a creator who loves beautiful things', and he began the run chase against Lancashire by hitting the ever-accurate Brian Statham's first two balls for four and six. Called 'an anachronism' by the *Playfair* annual, he scored 1,801 runs that summer at a rate of 40 an hour, the second fastest in the country.

"You play the way you think," he said. "You'll never hit the first ball for six if you've never thought of it." Forty-five years later, when two little-known West Indian openers took the same approach to Fraser and Caddick, he sent me a postcard: 'Three cheers for Lambert and Wallace!'

Doug Insole the Essex captain was almost as quick, averaging 37 an hour. "I could get on with it when the spirit moved me," he says, and he found similar support from Dick Horsfall and the all-rounder Ray Smith. "Ray got out as often as he got runs," Doug recalls, "but he was a tremendous entertainer. He ate off-spinners for breakfast." Of Smith's eight first-class centuries, three won him the accolade of Fastest of the Summer.

But the fastest century of 1952 and the fastest run-scorer in the country – at 48 runs an hour – was the young Essex amateur Colin Griffiths in his only season as a county player. Unable to defy his father's edict that he enter the family's demolition business – "I wasn't brought up, I was ruled" – he was granted one summer of county cricket as a compromise. Essex, knowing his position, employed him as a hitter.

"I was never developed as a player. They used me to throw the bat. I went in at number nine in the first innings, then at three or four in the run chase. My average was of no importance. I wasn't put in ahead of the professionals in the first innings, and I didn't have to justify my place. I was cheap labour."

He too hit Statham for a six and a four, but his top score in his first nine matches was only 31. Then at Tunbridge Wells, batting at number nine, he hit 105 in 90 minutes, completing his maiden century – 'with no question of jitters' – 6, 4, 1, 6. 'It was champagne cricket for the crowd,' the *Daily Express* declared.

That was on Wednesday and, after close of play on Saturday at Edgbaston, he flew to Paris to celebrate with his girl friend. "I do remember the club complaining at all the phone calls to France that I was putting on my expenses sheets."

At Colchester the following Saturday, still batting at number nine, he hit a vigorous 89 against Middlesex, and the thinking changed.

"Doug and Trevor Bailey said to me, 'You're proving yourself. It's time we gave you a better chance in the first innings.' Unfortunately in the second innings I was going great guns, I got to 25 off two or three overs, I was hitting Jack Young over his head, and I tore this muscle in my back. It was agony. And I had to go up to Old Trafford to play the next game. I said, 'I'll be a passenger. I'll only be able to throw the ball in under-arm.' But they said, 'That doesn't matter.' That was the state of Essex in those days; they didn't have anyone else."

He played a few matches at the start of the following summer. "They rang me at work one morning, wanted me to play that day, and I hadn't even cleaned off my kit from the previous year."

Ten years later he played a summer of club cricket at Wimbledon, where the older members still recall the day he repeatedly hit the former Notts leg-spinner Gamini Goonesena out of the ground. But, apart from that, he never played cricket again, turning instead to mountaineering, rock climbing and now scuba diving.

His only century for Essex was the fastest in England that summer, and he still possesses a *News Chronicle* Brighter Cricket tankard with his name inscribed on it. Essex's enterprise raised the membership above 5,000 for the first time. "But it didn't do us any favours. Some of the counties, knowing how we batted, wouldn't give us a fair chance with their declarations."

The Brighter Cricket campaign was declared a success. Draws in the championship fell that summer from 53 to 37%, with every county bar one achieving a result in at least half of their matches.

Essex were 'eager, quick and full of action', but in the cruellest irony they were the exception, managing only 13 results out of 28.

## 44. Quick on his feet

*Alan Rayment of Hampshire* TWC, March 2007

'He's got dancing feet,' the headlines would say when Hampshire's Alan Rayment scored runs.

On a broken pitch at Weston-super-Mare in 1955, with the ball 'turning at strange angles', Somerset were bowled out for 37 and 98 and between their two innings Alan Rayment hit a free-scoring century. "I danced up and down the wicket a bit," he recalls. "Punchy McMahon got the main stick. I got him really mad."

In ten years with Hampshire he did not score the consistent runs his talent promised, but he was an outstanding cover-point fielder and, in the words of John Arlott, he was 'almost incapable of playing a dull innings.'

"I played my first cricket at Finchley," he says. "We played to enjoy it and we came off with a smile, whether we'd got 0 or 100."

It was not an approach that was appreciated when he arrived in Southampton. "After one match I was called in to see Desmond Eagar, who was captain and secretary. 'Some of the senior players,' he said, 'have commented that you're coming off with not many runs and you're smiling. That sort of thing doesn't go down well in Hampshire, you know.'"

In that summer of 1949 he was on five pounds a week and by October, when his wife Betty gave birth, he was so poor that he could only buy her flowers by selling the wind-up gramophone he had had since he was three years old.

Back at Finchley in 1944 the club president, noticing his nimble footwork, had encouraged him to take up ballroom dancing. "It will help you when you chassé up the wicket." So in Southampton he and Betty, both qualified dancing teachers, advertised classes, first in church halls, then – as the business developed – in the Hamtum Hill Hotel next to the Hampshire ground. Often, within an hour of close of play, he was on the dance floor.

He even persuaded some of his team-mates to come along on Sundays. "Peter Sainsbury was the only one who stuck with it. He got his Bronze, but he wouldn't do the Silver. He thought the tango was a bit too sexy."

Inevitably Alan started to observe his fellow cricketers through the eyes of a dancing instructor. "It's a trained response. If Marilyn Monroe were to come past me, the first thing I'd take in was how she walked. And movement is beautiful in cricket."

Derek Shackleton was Hampshire's leading bowler: "He was wonderfully balanced like Fred Astaire, very up, where Fred Trueman was lower down like Gene Kelly."

Roy Marshall, the white West Indian, opened the batting: "He was wonderfully co-ordinated and very relaxed, but there was also a Caucasian stiffness in him."

Recently he has watched *Celebrity Come Dancing*. "I'm still in awe of how those teachers raised them to that standard in such a short time – and how hard the celebrities worked."

Does he think that other cricketers could follow in the footsteps of Gough and Ramprakash?

"Ian Bell could be good … but not dear old Harmy. Hoggy could; he's more loose-limbed. Not Flinty, though. He's too big, too much of a yeoman build like Peter Schmeichel. … Pietersen would be a very good Latin American dancer, but he wouldn't have the discipline to learn the foxtrot and the waltz. It would take him too long; he'd get bored. … Michael Vaughan could be very good physiologically, but he'd have to let his innate reservations go."

Shane Warne? "He'd fit the razzamatazz of the American version, but I don't see him doing it on British television." He pauses for breath. "I'm just thinking on my feet, you know. … Monty, he's got it. There's no doubt about that. But he would have to stand up straight.

"David Gower would be the very best. He had the beautiful co-ordination, the grace, the timing, the nonchalance, the sophistication, and he wouldn't be embarrassed. He would be the tops." Botham? "No. Not Botham. I don't think he'd even begin. I don't think he'd want to."

On a rainy day in Nottingham in August 1956, Alan went to the cinema to see *Rock Around The Clock*. "They stopped the film because people were dancing in the aisles. I rang Betty straightaway: 'We've got to do this.' We went up to Kingston to the top Latin American dancers, and we learnt all the throws."

That autumn they converted an old building in the town centre, and The Alan and Betty Rayment School of Dancing became The Grosvenor – Southampton's Gayest Ballroom, with an 11-piece band on Saturday nights.

"Thursday was always the dead night, the night before people were paid, so we advertised a Rock'n'Roll class. The first night we had 185 people, queuing all down the road."

He was rich beyond the scale of a professional cricketer, able to buy a five-bedroom house from the chief engineer at Cunard, but by 1958 marital problems and a mystical experience led him to give it all up. He spent a summer at Lord's, where he turned down the job of Head Coach, and his later life has seen him a wandering spirit, at different times estate agent, property developer, social worker, mature student and psychotherapist.

"I've always had a curiosity about life and people," he says, "and curiosity is the key to learning."

The money has long gone, but he is still smiling.

## 45. A frustrated wrist-spinner

*Johnny Wardle of Yorkshire and England* TWC, Dec 2004

Cape Town, New Year 1957. England, fresh from victory in the First Test, set South Africa 385 to win and dismissed them for 72. Bowling chinamen and googlies, Johnny Wardle had match figures of 12 wickets for 89 runs. They remain the best ever by an England wrist spinner.

'The pitch didn't break up,' England captain Peter May said, 'but he turned the ball huge amounts and, apart from Roy McLean, no one had much idea how to play him.'

'His control was astonishing,' Alan Ross wrote. 'Against any other bowler in the world, South Africa could have been expected to save the match.'

Vice-captain Doug Insole, off the field with an upset stomach, sat on the balcony with the South Africans: "They were all trying to work him out. I watched as one by one he diddled them, the ball going one way and the bat the other."

In all matches on that tour Johnny Wardle took 105 wickets at an average of 11.88. Twenty years later, Jim Swanton called it 'the best performance overseas by a slow bowler in my time.' It was the more remarkable in that, for most of his career, Wardle rarely bowled wrist spin.

Establishing his Yorkshire place in 1947, he had to maintain the great tradition of slow left-armers that stretched back through Verity and Rhodes to the Victorians Peel and Peate. Even in 1946, following Verity's wartime death, the 43-year-old Arthur Booth, 'Grandad' to his team-mates, topped the national averages in his only full season. With Yorkshire winning their eighth championship in ten, Wardle had much to live up to.

Bob Appleyard recalls the atmosphere: "So much was ingrained into us about the way Yorkshire played. Hedley Verity had set the standard, and Johnny had to measure up to that." It was not enough that the youngster was selected to tour the West Indies after his first summer nor that the next year he took 150 wickets. As far as captain Norman Yardley was concerned, 'He has not yet got proper Yorkshire control of length.'

By 1952 Wardle had matured into a fine orthodox left-armer. With Trueman on National Service and Appleyard in a TB sanatorium, he carried the county's bowling that summer, sending down 1,847 overs, a total only ever surpassed by Kent's 'Tich' Freeman, and his control was such that his 810 maidens remain an all-time record.

"He never complained about bowling," his contemporary Ted Lester says. "We used to have a few set-tos when he thought he was at the wrong end, but he never turned it in."

Playing on uncovered pitches and carrying so much responsibility, he was not often allowed to experiment with his chinamen, as Lester remembers: "Yorkshire had never had an unorthodox left-armer. Wilfred Rhodes, Hedley Verity, they bowled the orthodox stuff, and Yorkshire saw no reason why it should change. It upset Johnny an awful lot. He'd slip one in occasionally, but it was very rare that he could set a field to bowl it."

In Trevor Bailey's view, Wardle the orthodox bowler was "better than Tufnell, better than Edmonds, not as good as Underwood." And he would have played regularly for England if it had not been for Surrey's Tony Lock. But, while Wardle bowled with a perfect action, Lock's lethal quicker ball had a decided jerk to it. "Tony Lock was throwing, and Wardle was bowling," Trevor says. "We all knew it."

"Johnny used to go on all the time about Locky throwing," Bob Appleyard recalls. "It really upset him."

Ted Lester remembers a match at The Oval: "Locky was bowling at Vic Wilson, and he let this one go. Vic hadn't even finished his back lift when it knocked middle out. So Wardle and Closey decided that they were going to sort Locky out when he batted. They both tried to throw. You've never seen anything like it. They got to the wicket with the proper action, and they just stood there like baseball pitchers. They didn't know what to do."

In Australia in 1954/55 Wardle's role in Len Hutton's side was to keep the game tight while Tyson and Statham rested. Then, with the Ashes won and the last Test ruined by rain, he was allowed to bowl his chinamen, taking seven Australian wickets on the final day. "He often fiddled about with them in the nets," Bob Appleyard says. "And gradually he got to bowl them more in matches."

One batsman to whom he did bowl them was Cyril Washbrook, the England opener: "He didn't know if it was Christmas or Easter," Yorkshire's Ken Taylor says. "He was playing down the line and missing; he was padding away, and the ball was coming back and hitting him on his behind. All sorts. Johnny was brilliant."

Ted Lester recalls what Norman Yardley once said to him: "I wish we could find a good orthodox left-arm bowler. Then Johnny could bowl this stuff all the time."

By 1956, with Yardley and Hutton having retired and Yorkshire's new captain Billy Sutcliffe lacking the authority to stop him, Wardle was bowling as he wanted. "He perfected his chinamen," Bob Appleyard reckons, "because he enjoyed bowling them. He was a competitor, and he loved nothing better than beating the batsmen. A good wrist spinner can beat the best batsmen when other bowlers can't."

The fruits were yielded in Cape Town, though the next Test at Durban followed a different script. South Africa, chasing 190 to win, were 60 for four, and Wardle – with five for 61 in the first innings – had already removed Goddard and McLean. The reporter Eric Hill recalls watching the crucial moment. "Funston came in. He was a good attacking player, but he had no idea how to play Wardle. He had a whack and hit him for 11 in an over. So PBH told Wardle to go back to the normal stuff."

According to England's Peter Richardson, "Wardle nearly went berserk. We were winning the match. The rest of us knew it was wrong."

"Wardle knew exactly knew when to bowl his chinamen and when not," Eric Hill says. "He knew who could play them and who couldn't. When we only drew the match, I remember thinking, 'If we don't win the series, I wonder if anybody will look back at that moment.'"

It was a prophetic thought. South Africa won a close-fought fourth Test and, with Wardle out of action with a knee crocked while playing snooker, they levelled the series at Port Elizabeth.

Wardle was now, according to Trevor Bailey, "the best wrist spinner in the world". He was a fine orthodox bowler, a useful batsman capable of hitting the ball hard and high, and a safe catcher close to the wicket.

He was also, to the delight of the crowd, a wonderful comedian: rubbing his thigh after a painful blow on the elbow, miming a sensational running catch when the ball had flown past him for six. When the bottles flew in the 1954 Georgetown Test, he picked one up, affected a long swig and staggered drunkenly around. 'To say I was scared is putting it mildly,' he wrote, 'but I seemed to amuse them and it made me feel a bit safer.'

In AA Thomson's words, 'Rarely has any player stepped on to the turf who can so instantly banish the encircling gloom.' The title of Wardle's 1957 autobiography was *'Happy Go Johnny'*.

Yet his team-mates knew a less happy Johnny: a harsh, sarcastic man, a stickler for discipline who set himself the highest standards and had no tolerance for anything less in others, a bowler with a selfish edge. He was not the life and soul of a tour, taking the strictest view of his marriage vows and preferring to send his earnings home than to spend them in the bar. He could also be jealous of the success of others though there was little occasion for this in South Africa.

"I'd heard that he wasn't a very good tourist," Doug Insole says, "but I found him very pleasant company, always supportive of his colleagues and never averse to paying his whack. Perhaps it helped that there were no other Yorkshiremen on the trip so he had no 'local' rivals – and that he was selected ahead of Tony Lock. At Johannesburg he even volunteered to act as nightwatchman against Heine and Adcock. Somewhere I've got a letter he sent me after the tour, paying tribute to the camaraderie of the party and saying that the cricket had been the most enjoyable he'd ever experienced."

Wardle had learned his cricket in a harsh environment. When he took five wickets in only his second bowl for Yorkshire, there was little congratulation: "Anybody can take wickets if the batsmen get themselves out like that," was one old pro's verdict. "Beginner's luck," said another. You were cut down to size at Yorkshire and, when in turn he became a senior player, he maintained the tradition.

"He put a lot of us on edge," recalls Bryan Stott, one of a younger generation who did not relish fielding to Wardle's bowling. When Mick Cowan missed a gully catch, Wardle descended on him: "Don't worry, lad. It's my own bloody fault for putting you there."

Ken Taylor's attempt to run out a tail-ender met with disapproval: "You don't run out nine, ten, jack," Wardle told him before adding the wicket to his own tally. Trueman even alleges that Wardle deliberately dropped a catch when Fred threatened to overtake him to the £100 prize for the season's best bowling figures.

Wardle was a frustrated genius. After his triumph in South Africa, he played only one home Test before losing out again to Lock. Then, when he hoped to become Yorkshire's first professional captain, he found himself taking orders from Ronnie Burnet, a 39-year-old engineer who had never played a first-class match. Burnet decided to crack the whip, sparks flew and in mid-match in July 1958 Wardle was summoned to the committee room and dismissed.

For some, citing Yorkshire's seven titles in the next ten years, his departure was the making of a better team spirit. "Ronnie got every one playing for each other," Ray Illingworth reckons. For others like Appleyard, it was a tragedy: "It never should have happened. It was bad man management."

"I could see both sides," Ted Lester says, "but it was very sad, really. Johnny was at his peak then, especially as he was bowling what he wanted to bowl."

Wardle put his name to a series of intemperate articles in the *Daily Mail*, and his invitation to tour Australia was withdrawn. "Peter May was distraught," Bob Appleyard remembers.

In Wardle's absence Australia won 4-0, with Lock returning Test figures of five for 376.

Thereafter Wardle took his wickets in the Lancashire League and for Cambridgeshire.

'Doesn't tha think tha's been a fool, Johnny?' he was asked when he addressed a meeting of miners.

'Aye,' he replied. 'Aye, I have.'

He died in 1985 and has become an almost forgotten figure in English cricket. Yet, when the *Wisden Cricketer* recently invited 25 experts to choose their greatest post-war England side, Derek Underwood – with almost three times as many Test wickets – pipped him by just one vote.

"Johnny was different," Bob Appleyard says. "He had that extra dimension. And his value would be far higher today with covered pitches."

The great Wally Hammond was among the spectators who witnessed Wardle's triumph at Cape Town. 'That was the finest piece of spin bowling I've ever seen,' he said. 'I've never seen anyone with such control as a wrist-spinner.'

*Bob Appleyard, Brian Close, Johnny Wardle, Fred Trueman*
*Headingley, 1955*

## 46. Faith, hope and charity

*The Somerset rebellion of 1953* PREVIOUSLY UNPUBLISHED

"They were sound blokes in their own fields," Eric Hill says of the Somerset committee of 1953, "but they reckoned they knew about cricket when they didn't. They were the sort of men who liked to say they were on so many committees – the Conservatives, the British Legion, that sort of thing: 'giving up my time when I could be at home doing the crossword or listening to the wireless.' They were extremely good at passing votes of thanks at the end of the year."

It was a pre-war set-up at a time when other counties were starting to change. Somerset had finished fourth in 1946, but their team that year had an average age of 38 and, as it broke up, little was done to find suitable replacements. "The club let things drift," Eric says, and by 1952 they were at the foot of the table for the first time in their history.

Captains came and went, seven in eight years, all of them amateur, and for 1953 they turned to the Berkshire farmer Ben Brocklehurst. "He wasn't really a good enough player, but by then there weren't the amateurs available. Later on, we found out that, because he'd had to leave his farm, he was being paid to employ a manager in his absence – and paid, I may add, rather more than the professionals were earning."

Again the county finished last. In two years they had won only four matches, and three of them had been after winning the toss on the notorious Bath wicket.

They advertised for players in *The Cricketer*, and other counties were scouted. But, when good players were interested, Tom Clark of Surrey or the Middlesbrough footballer Harry Bell, they never materialised, and the best of the trialists – Devon's Len Coldwell, later of Worcestershire and England – was deemed 'not to be up to standard'.

Discontent grew among the members, and in the press box the seeds of an organised rebellion were sown. Hill, an opening bat with the county from 1947 to 1951, was now sports editor of the *Somerset County Gazette*, "earning the princely sum of five pounds a week", and together with two colleagues Ron Roberts and Bob Moore he petitioned for a special members' meeting.

Fifty years on, he recalls the atmosphere at the Corfield Hall, Taunton, as 350 members from all over the county arrived. "We were astonished. The room was packed, and the committee obviously hadn't prepared for it. None of us had ever spoken in public before, but Bob made a brilliant speech and we carried the vote by a considerable majority."

Their main demand, that former cricketers should be involved on the team committee, was mild enough, but the exchanges were spirited. The committee defended itself, citing a flurry of recent activity. One speaker threatened to arrange the sacking of the three journalists while, on a lighter note, an old man attacked modern batting techniques: "They don't do this any more," he said, demonstrating shots with his umbrella.

When the rebels put down a vote of no confidence to be taken at a second meeting, the committee out-flanked them by switching the venue to Weston-super-Mare. "At 5.30 on a Friday evening, in late November, when people didn't have motor cars." They sent out a postal voting form, with a full defence of their own conduct and no statement from their opponents.

"It was a beautifully produced document, all about the things they had done since they had been elected in April and saying how the fault lay with their predecessors – regardless of the fact that most of them had been on the committee for years."

The rebels set to work with an out-of-date members' list, sending out a reply. "It cost us eighteen quid, but a lot of people came up and gave us money."

The trio worked from the offices of the *County Gazette*, and they were joined by the Somerset professional Maurice Tremlett and his fiancée Lee. "Maurice was being paid two and six an hour by the county to fill their envelopes. Then he came over to us and did the same for nothing."

Ben Brocklehurst had encouraged them. "More than once he'd said to us that the committee was 'a complete dead loss'." But at the Weston meeting he took a different tack, lampooning the three leading rebels as 'Faith, Hope and Charity'. "Let's close ranks," he argued. "It will be all right next year."

With Bob Moore unable to repeat his earlier oratory, the committee won the day, though the outcome was a very English one. All three journalists were co-opted onto the committee, and Eric Hill became captain of a newly-formed second eleven, joining the team committee with former players Bill Greswell and Bill Andrews.

Ben Brocklehurst's second summer in charge again brought only two victories, and they were last for a fourth time in 1955. But slowly the county began to move forward. The Guianese Peter Wight added sparkle to the batting, and for the summer of 1956 Ron Roberts recruited the Australian Test player Colin McCool. They also appointed their first professional captain: Maurice Tremlett.

Many of the same faces remained on the committee. Ken Biddulph, recruited in 1954, remembers one man, a poor club cricketer in his time, giving McCool a lecture on how to bat in English conditions: 'You've got to play forward. Play forward.' "Colin went out and got a hundred. And he deliberately hit everything off the back foot."

In 1958 the Australian Bill Alley arrived and, under Tremlett's leadership, they rose for the first time in their history to third place in the championship.

## 47. From Zorro to hero

*Melbourne, Fri 26 Dec 1986, with Gladstone Small* THE TIMES, 26 DEC 2006

Boxing Day 1986. The Melbourne Cricket Ground. 58,203 spectators, and the Ashes at stake. "It doesn't get much bigger than that," Gladstone Small says.

Four years earlier, a promising 21-year-old, he had spent his winter playing club cricket in Melbourne. There he had met his fiancée Lois, and during that winter's Melbourne Test England had asked him to train with them.

"The dressing room is down in the bottom of the pavilion. You can't hear or see anything down there. I remember the openers Geoff Cook and 'Foxy' Fowler going out to bat. They walked up the stairs, opened the door and suddenly they were hit by this great roar. There's nothing else like it in cricket. They almost had to be pushed out."

Now he was in the dressing room again, this time one of the tourists though he had not played in the first three Tests. England were 1-0 up, and the first-choice fast bowlers were DeFreitas, 'Picca' Dilley and Botham. While they finished their net, he prepared the pre-match drinks.

"You're disappointed," he admits, "but you're part of a team set-up. You've still got a role to play. And it was a tremendously happy tour."

The previous day they had had a champagne breakfast with the press, a grand Christmas meal and a fancy dress party.

"Gower was in charge of the social side, just the man for that, and he handed us all letters of the alphabet. I got Z. I mean, what on earth do you do with Z?"

In the dressing room Mike Gatting appeared at his side.

"You can leave the drinks, Stony," he said. "Picca's hurt his knee. You're playing."

Gatting won the toss and opted to field, and it seemed only moments later that they were emerging into the roar of the stadium. He was no longer Zorro of the fancy dress party, with cloak, mask and rapier. He was GC Small, England's opening bowler, and he began the match with a ghastly wide. A two and a four were struck before the over was out. It was clear that the Australians were in aggressive mood.

"I went down to the boundary. The crowd were all shouting, calling me a Pommie, and I think that spurred me on. It was an overcast day, and there was a bit of moisture in the pitch."

In his third over he swung the ball away from David Boon, caught the edge of his bat and saw Botham at second slip clutch a chest-high catch. Then Botham himself took over from DeFreitas. Recovering from a rib injury, he ran in off what John Woodcock in *The Times* said 'they call in Somerset his Sunday run' and kept a fullish length – though his two morning wickets, Marsh and Border, both came from long hops.

By early afternoon it was 108 for three. Jones and the young Steve Waugh looked settled, and the game was in the balance. Then in quick succession Gladstone Small removed them both and by teatime Australia were 141 all out. Botham and his young stand-in partner, with five wickets each, left the field arm in arm.

"Beefy, being the great sportsman he is, pushed me through the gate first."

The great roar of Melbourne had long been stilled, and the crowd 'were leaving in droves long before the end' as Chris Broad, with centuries in the previous two Tests, led England to 95 for one at close of play.

That evening Gladstone and Lois left the team for a quiet meal.

"When we walked into the restaurant, everybody stood up and applauded. It was a very special moment. Mind you, we still had to pay for our meal."

The next day Broad completed his hundred. "He was in wonderful form that tour, but that innings was his best. The pitch had something in it, and nobody else scored fifty."

Gladstone's part was not done. He hit an enterprising 21 as England's first-innings lead passed 200, then he took two second innings wickets including that of Border – "that was the crucial wicket" – and he held the winning catch.

"Edmonds was bowling, and he liked to move his fielders around. One pace this way, three paces up. Mark your position with a cross. Most of it was just for his own humour. Merv Hughes swept him and the ball came down into my hands. Right where I was standing on the cross. I didn't have to move an inch. I threw it in the air and ran off. And the party started."

Across town, at the Kooyong Tennis Club, Australia were beating Sweden in the Davis Cup Final, and Lois was there with Lindsay Lamb. "I think their party got under way before ours."

England had beaten the Australians in three days for the first time since 1934, for the first time in Australia since 1901. For the fifth time in six series England had won the Ashes.

Was it really twenty years ago? Gladstone, Lois and their three children will be in Melbourne on Boxing Day this year, and Gladstone will be sitting among the roaring crowd when the teams appear.

"It will be a hard task for them," he thinks. "The Australians are a great side, and they won't be as complacent as they were over here. But having broken the hoodoo, our boys will have the confidence to beat them again. We've certainly got the talent in the team."

## 48. Training on pints and pies

*Pre-season training* WCM, May 2003

Fifty years ago Keith Andrew was a newcomer at Northampton. The county was run on a shoestring by its secretary Colonel Coldwell, and after a week in the nets Keith turned to one of his colleagues.

"Who's the old bloke behind the net with the trilby on?"

"He was a smart man," Keith remembers, "with a raincoat and a brown trilby. I knew he was a bit deaf because, when you spoke, he never answered."

"That's the coach, Jack Mercer," came the reply. "He doesn't do much coaching, but he gives the Colonel some great tips."

Mercer was a fount of cricketing knowledge, but it was not the role of the coach to organise the established players. After April he worked with the youngsters outside the first eleven.

Three weeks of pre-season training were followed by four months of six-day-a-week cricket. So the first-team players had to make their own adjustments.

"We used to rely on the senior batsmen and bowlers," Worcester's Martin Horton says. "Or the umpires. You'd edge one through the slips and, when you got down to the other end, there would be Jack Crapp or Emrys Davies. 'Do you realise you're lifting your head?'"

In April they worked mainly in the nets. "Two hours or so in the morning, another two in the afternoon, and at lunch we'd walk up to the pub and have a couple of pints and a pie. If it was too wet, we might go to Edgbaston – though I remember Reg Perks, when he was captain, taking us up on the Malvern Hills, smoking his inevitable cigarette all the way."

Perks, a fast bowler, was 43 years old by then. "He stopped off for a cup of tea at St Ann's Well while we went on up."

"If it was raining," Essex's Robin Hobbs says, "we went home."

Essex did not own a ground so they gathered at the Old Blues rugby ground at Fairlop. "Frank Rist was the coach. We'd get there in the morning, and he'd have this great urn on the boil. There were a couple of nets, right by a chicken farm and, of course, there was no top on them. So, if somebody like Gordon Barker was batting, a compulsive hooker, we'd be climbing over to get the balls from among all the chicken.

"Trevor Bailey would turn up, a stone or two overweight, he'd wrap himself up in all sorts of plastic, and he'd sweat it all off, bowling. Then he'd go up to Fenner's, take six wickets, and we'd all be happy."

You got cricket fit by playing cricket. The fitness training started to appear in the '60s.

"I went out running early every morning from January," Worcester's Ron

Headley says, "and I don't think any of the others did that. I remember Stewart Storey running round The Oval one day, and Don Kenyon saying, 'Look at that silly so-and-so. What the hell's he doing?'"

"We had Brian King, the West Brom goalkeeper, come to train us one year," Robin Hobbs recalls. "He nearly killed us. Ray East and I had to stop behind the sight screen."

David Allen recalls that it was 1969 before Gloucestershire ventured out of the ground – for a hill run around Failand that proved too much for the burly David Shepherd. "He got a lift on a milk float and came sailing past us, giving us this royal wave."

"Being fit and being cricket fit are different," Martin Horton says. "Jim Standen played for West Ham, and he came back straight into the team one year. He bowled twenty overs, and he couldn't take the field, he was so stiff."

"When I started in 1960," Worcester's Bob Carter says, "if it was raining on the first day, you put your overcoat on, had your photograph taken and went home. But by the time I finished in 1972, you took your track suit and you were tearing about, whatever the weather. Pressure fielding was starting to come in."

Gone were the days when captains reprimanded their bowlers for diving about in the outfield. "Forget the two runs," Somerset's Maurice Tremlett used to say. "I want you fit to bowl."

Gone now are the older men and the overweight figures like David Shepherd and Colin Milburn.

"The fielding is much better," everybody agrees.

But what about the skills of batting and bowling?

"It's good to be fit," Martin Horton says, "but I always remember what Dennis Lillee wrote. Fitness can never replace skill."

And the entertainment of watching the big men?

"It's difficult to imagine somebody of my build playing today," David Shepherd reckons.

## 49. Studious and playful

*Hedley Verity of Yorkshire and England* TWC, Apr 2005

He took 14 wickets in a day. Against Australia. In a Test match at Lord's. On Monday 25 June 1934. It remains the only occasion since 1896 when England have beaten Australia at Lord's.

Hedley Verity was born on 18 May 1905, a coal merchant's son who grew up in Rawdon, north of Leeds. He started out in cricket as a fast bowler but, by the time he made his Yorkshire debut in 1930, he was a slow left-armer, stepping into the shoes of the 52-year-old Wilfred Rhodes. Both were great craftsman, studiously observing every batsman for signs of weakness but, where his legendary predecessor relied on flight and spin, Verity – a taller man – was faster through the air and could make the ball pop awkwardly.

His first-class career began in 1930 and ended in 1939 at the outbreak of war – a war in which he was killed in action in Italy. In an era in which conditions generally favoured batsmen, he took 1,956 wickets at an average – 14.90 – lower than any other bowler since the Victorian age. He took a world-record 17 in a day against Essex at Leyton, and twice he took all ten in an innings, including the best figures – ten for 10 against Nottinghamshire at Headingley – ever returned in a first-class match.

But his greatest day was at Lord's that Monday in June 1934. On the Saturday evening, on a pitch that was playing easily, he had caught and bowled Bradman when the Don was in full flow. Then, after rain on Sunday, he returned to a pitch that was wet on top of a hard base, and he bowled all day, mostly from the pavilion end. It was not quite a 'sticky wicket', but the Australians had spent all tour on hard, fast tracks and they failed to save the follow-on. In the second innings he frustrated Bradman into a wild swipe –'the worst stroke he has made in his life,' *The Times* called it – and by ten to six it was all over. In 58.3 overs in the match, he had taken 15 wickets for 104 runs.

'All day he bowled with only short rests,' Neville Cardus wrote, 'and nobody was his equal. Beautiful left-handed spin, there is nothing like it. The click of the finger, the spit of venom on the ground. The record-hunters will revel in his figures. And the gods of the game, who sit up aloft and watch, will remember the loveliness of it all, the style, the poise on light toes, the swing of the arm from noon to evening.'

More than seventy years have passed, and his son Douglas – a one-year-old infant at the time – watches once more the film of his father that day, the father who was taken from him when he was only ten years old.

"His run-up is so smooth, isn't it?"

Douglas was a promising young cricketer himself but, rather than try to follow in his father's footsteps, he took up golf and worked as a professional in North Wales.

"I've taught myself to play several games," he says. "And I've come to the conclusion that, whether you're kicking a ball or bowling it or hitting it with a club or a racquet, the key to them all is to be balanced, with your weight distributed right. When my dad releases the ball, he's perfectly balanced."

A wicket falls on the film.

"It's amazing, isn't it? There's nobody bothering with my dad at all. No congratulations or anything. He just stands there at one end and talks to the umpire. It's all changed so much. Sometimes, when I'm sitting here watching cricket on television, I wonder what my dad would say if he walked in and saw it. I think he'd be surprised how crude it is, how it's all bash and crash, how the finesse seems to have gone from the game."

As a young man in post-war Yorkshire Douglas struggled to shake off the expectations that came with his name. "I hated the fact that I was always my dad's son, I wasn't me. If you did any good, so you should. And if you didn't, you'd only got there because of your father. I know Billy Sutcliffe felt the same. And Richard Hutton. People used to say to Richard, 'You'll never be as good as your father.' And he'd say, 'Neither was anybody else.' I wish I'd thought of that. In the end I never told anybody my name. But later, once I'd made an identity for myself, I became very interested in finding out about my father. And thinking back to my early childhood memories of him.

"He was a mixture, really. He was a very serious man. A great student of the game. Bill Bowes would come round, and they'd sit and talk cricket for hours, planning somebody's downfall. He was a strict tee-totaller, a member of the Band of Hope, and he gave talks at religious gatherings. I think he would have stayed in the Army after the war. He liked the life, the discipline.

"He was a happy man, always singing and laughing, playing tricks on people. He loved to play games, especially if you'd got to think about them. We had Monopoly soon after it came out, and he'd set up games like Kim, where you have to memorise a tray full of things. I once asked Len Hutton if my dad laughed when he was playing cricket. 'Not on the field,' he said, 'but he laughed a lot off it.'

"He used to walk my brother and me up onto the featureless moors, by devious routes. And without warning he'd say, 'Right, you've got to find your way back to the car. And I'm not going to help you.' It was his way of making us notice things, find our way from nature, know that the green on a rock is on the northern side."

Douglas became an expert mountaineer, climbing every rock face from Skye down to the Cornish coast, and his first pair of climbing boots

were converted from his father's skating boots. "We used to go skating on the frozen tarns. The cars would come, with their headlights on, and we'd be on the ice all evening. He was very keen on the outdoor life."

Douglas was born in June 1933, two months after his father returned victorious from the Bodyline tour, and was named after Douglas Jardine. "My dad didn't really agree with Bodyline, but he admired Jardine greatly. On the boat going out to Australia, the two of them sat up all night, talking about my dad's role on the tour. He was to curtail their scoring between the bouts of Larwood."

In the crucial Tests at Adelaide and Brisbane, when the series swung decisively England's way, Verity bowled 82 overs for only 126 runs. Then, in the final match at Sydney, when Larwood was injured and the pitch took turn, he took eight wickets for 95. "Somewhere I've got a letter from Jardine to my grandfather, saying what a great job my father did on that tour."

Bradman compared him favourably with the great Australian spinner Grimmett: 'I think I know all about Clarrie, but with Hedley I am never sure. You see, there's no breaking point with him.' Later, after Verity's death, he wrote, 'I could never claim to have completely fathomed him.'

In his early years with Yorkshire Verity often bowled in tandem with the fiery George Macaulay who, according to team-mate Bill Bowes, 'was always filled with a devilish energy; when he saw the ball turning after pitching, we used to tell him that his ears flapped and his eyes darted fire.' Verity, by contrast, 'never altered his expression. If you saw nothing but his poker face, it would be impossible to tell whether his ball had been knocked for six or spread-eagled the stumps.'

At Sheffield in 1935 South Africa's Jock Cameron hit Verity for 30 in an over, and they say that Arthur Wood the Yorkshire keeper quipped, "You've got him in two minds, Hedley; he doesn't know whether to hit you for four or six." But Douglas repeats what Bill Bowes told him. "He could have stopped it if he'd wanted, but he thought that Cameron would miss one soon enough."

But against Nottinghamshire at Headingley in July 1932 Verity was in complete control. Before lunch, when the pitch was wet, he opened up with nine maidens. Then, after the break, as it started to dry, he pulled the fielders round the bat and the wickets began to tumble: a hat-trick, seven in 15 balls and final figures of ten for 10. At one point Notts were 44 for none; then they were 67 all out. Frank Shipston, joint top scorer with 21, is still alive to tell the tale: "He was a tall man, his arm came right over the top and, on a wicket like that, he was almost unplayable."

Yorkshire won seven championships in the nine summers before the war, and Shipston recalls them as a team always arguing with each other. "But not Verity. To me, he never seemed like the rest of the Yorkshire team."

"The thing about my dad," Douglas says, "is that he wouldn't reckon that ten for 10 as being as good as one for 60 in 40 overs on a batters' wicket. He only valued things which were difficult."

At Hove, on the last day of the 1939 season, with Yorkshire champions and Verity once more top of the bowling averages, he bowled the last six overs of his first-class career, taking seven Sussex wickets for nine runs.

Four years later, as a Captain in the Green Howards, he was shot in Sicily, leading his men through heavy German fire. When English cricket reassembled in 1946, he was not there to pass on his knowledge and his skills to another generation.

Douglas preserves what he can. "My dad said, 'The best length is the shortest you can bowl and still get them playing forward.' With slow bowling particularly, you set your field and you try to get them driving at you. Then you try to deceive them with flight, or change of pace, or spin. I don't know what he'd say about the modern game when, as soon as someone hits you for six, you start darting it in just short of a length. I sometimes think that people have forgotten the art of slow bowling."

For Robertson-Glasgow, Hedley Verity was 'the nearly perfect bowling machine, directed by one of the acutest brains that the game can have known, and kept in motion by an indomitable purpose' – while for Cardus, he was 'lovely to see, grace concealing his deadliness.'

On Wednesday 25 May at Headingley Yorkshire County Cricket Club, together with the Green Howards, will mark his centenary. The man who bowled England to victory at Lord's in 1934.

## 50. Gentlemen's cricket

*The Wimbledon Club in Surrey* TWC, June 2004

150 years ago, on 20 May 1854, a group of gentlemen formed an exclusive club to play cricket on Wimbledon Common. On a previously untended area they had a pitch cut and erected tents for a match with Surbiton in late July. No reports survive, but the scores give some idea of the game: Surbiton 84 and 87, Wimbledon 26 and 45 for 4, with extras easily the leading scorer on both sides.

They were an amateur club, and they employed professionals to bowl to them on practice afternoons. When one of these men, George Brockwell of the Surrey Club, made up their eleven against Price's Candle Company in Vauxhall, they called themselves 'The Wimbledon Club (with Brockwell)'. James Southerton, later to play in England's first Test side, worked on their square for a while, but he was not invited to play.

Travel to the games was eventful. Both Wimbledon's opening bowlers were tipped out of a dog cart on the way to Richmond and arrived limping. 'Both sprained their feet,' the match report records, 'Mister Oliver badly; they nevertheless bowled throughout the match without a change.'

On another occasion Southgate, making the long trip from north of London, arrived three hours late and encountered a volley of abuse from the Wimbledon captain. "There's still time to finish the game," they insisted and, with two of the Walker brothers taking all the wickets, they dismissed their hosts for 32 and 42.

Each year Wimbledon staged a match with the great wandering side I Zingari, who loved the setting: 'There is not a prettier spot for a cricket match than the green on Wimbledon Common on a fine summer's day.' But there were problems when the 1858 match was won on first innings by Wimbledon. A full four years later Wimbledon was forced to alter its records, with the note that 'I Zingari did not accept the universal custom of deciding one-day matches by first innings.'

The new Waterloo-to-Southampton railway line was opened, allowing journeys to Hampshire and even a tour of the Isle of Wight in 1865. Eight days of cricket were played, with only Sunday off, with nine of the fourteen tourists playing every day. Their only defeat occurred at Shanklin where 'in consequence of the roughness of the ground, an agreement was made not to bowl fast on either side.'

Club rules were passed, with five-shilling fines handed out to members who agreed to play and failed to turn up, also to 'any player in a match who shall smoke in the field, after having been requested not to smoke by an Officer of the Club.'

It was gentlemen's cricket. Few of the Wimbledon Club played with any regularity, but their matches attracted enough notice for their specialist wicket-keeper John Oliphant to be selected to play in the Gentlemen-Players match at Lord's in 1861.

Long stop was a vital fielding position, under-arm bowling was a common sight, and one summer three hats – costing ten shillings and sixpence each – were awarded to members who took three wickets with consecutive balls.

The Wimbledon Club today is comprised of cricket, tennis, hockey and squash sections. But hockey did not start in Wimbledon till the 1880s, and lawn tennis only gained popularity when the All England Croquet Club, down by the railway line in Wimbledon, decided to stage a tennis tournament in July 1877. Twenty-two competitors entered, and the final was held over to the following week, 'on account of its being the Eton and Harrow Cricket Match at Lord's.'

The first All England champion was a Wimbledon Cricket Club member, Spencer Gore, an Old Harrovian who cycled each day from Wandsworth and introduced the new tactic of running forward and playing the ball on the volley. Nine days later he was back on the Common, scoring 58 for I Zingari.

"Anyone who really plays well at cricket," he said, "will never give attention to lawn tennis. The monotony of the game will choke him off."

By the 1880s cricket had become more sophisticated. 'Dressing and taking lunch in tents was considered no hardship in the sixties and seventies,' WG Grace wrote in 1899, 'though we should regard it differently now. I sometimes think that the modern conditions of cricket are too luxurious.'

The best clubs no longer wished to play on the Common so the Wimbledon Club found a new home in Church Road, opposite the site where the tennis championships are now played, and they are still there 104 years and three clubhouses later.

In that time their membership has included five Test captains, not to mention Jim Swanton, Ian MacLaurin and Willie Rushton, and they have won the Surrey Championship five times in the last twelve years. As at all times in their history there is still a strong public school air about the place, though the rule book no longer contains a fine for smoking in the field.

## 51. One gentleman, one player

*Michael Spurway of Somerset and Frank Shipston of Notts* TWC, Nov 2004

Michael Spurway was born in January 1909, the youngest son of the Reverend Edward Spurway, founder of the amateur club, the Somerset Stragglers. Frank Shipston was born in July 1906, his father working at the Bullcroft Main Colliery outside Doncaster where he had been taken on as a pit surveyor in order to strengthen the cricket team. Michael Spurway kept wicket three times for Somerset while he was at university; Frank Shipston was on the staff at Trent Bridge for nine years. They belonged to different worlds; now their longevity links them as the only men left who played county cricket in the 1920s.

Michael Spurway made his debut for Somerset in July 1929. An Oxford undergraduate, he cycled into the Taunton ground with his kit strapped to his bicycle. On the river side, the only building was a little white hut which housed the pony that pulled the roller. His fellow amateurs, men like Reggie Ingle and Bunty Longrigg, parked their smart Bentleys and walked to the pavilion. Meanwhile the four professionals in the side changed in the groundsman's quarters, among the mowers. In the winter they painted the pavilion and the boundary pickets.

"It was sort of master and servant," he says. "If you found yourself two short, playing for the Stragglers, you'd go round to the groundsman and find two of the professionals. 'Be good chaps. Put on a pair of boots and come and play, will you?' They didn't come to the lunch, but the actual relationships were all very happy – as they were in the countryside. My late gardener and I were for many years the closest of friends."

Somerset had the smallest professional staff of the 17 counties, and in 1929 they used nine different wicket-keepers. "I don't think I'd played much that summer and John Daniell the chairman said, 'You'd better have a game for the county.'"

The Taunton ground was little developed in those days. "It was surrounded by trees. At the river end, where the Botham stand is, there was a rusting corrugated iron fence, about ten foot high, with one or two loose sheets in it. If anybody hit the ball out of the ground, they'd move a sheet and try to retrieve a ball – if it hadn't gone into the river."

The match was against Leicestershire, and he went to the wicket at 98 for nine. "Astill bowled me my first ball, about 18 inches outside off stump. I cut it down into the corner, and we ran four. Eddie Dawson was captaining Leicestershire, and he came into the pavilion afterwards. 'I thought they put the batting order upside down,' he said. I always remember that."

His keeping was more challenging. "In club cricket the wicket-keeper stood up to all the bowlers, but Arthur Wellard was too quick for that. So I had to stand back, and that was quite a different game."

Nevertheless the young debutant did well enough for Daniell to say, 'Come and play in the Bath Festival.' "I had my first ever first-class train journey, and I stayed at the Grand Pump Room Hotel with Jack MacBryan and his wife."

The local paper records that he kept 'competently' against Sussex and, when he batted, he survived the bowling of Maurice Tate: "He was quite slow through the air, but he came like lightning off the pitch. He was the greatest bowler I ever played against."

But the next match against Derbyshire was a disaster. "Jack MacBryan was much older than me, and one night he gave me more whiskies than I'd ever had in my life. I was absolutely thrown. I had the most frightful hangover the next morning. I went to the thermal baths, hoping that the atmosphere there would make me feel better, but it didn't. I really played very badly. I dropped two catches, and one of the guys went on to a hundred."

After that, his cricket was far afield and very occasional. In the Colonial Service in Northern Nigeria, he played the annual 'Test' against the Gold Coast in front of a large crowd on the Lagos polo ground. "Twenty-two Europeans surrounded by a thousand Africans. At that time they had hardly embraced football, let alone cricket." In 1945 he led a Desert Air Force side, with two South African Test players, on a short tour of England. "The best team I ever captained." Then he was posted to the East, and he represented Singapore against Malaya.

"I never played very much cricket in my life. It was just a bit of fun."

By contrast, Frank Shipston spent many years in the game. He first caught the eye playing with his father for the Bullcroft Colliery side, going for a trial at Trent Bridge in the Spring of 1925. "I went there as green as grass. 'Put your pads on, young man,' the coach Jim Iremonger said. 'And your box.' 'Box?' I said. 'What's that?' And the next thing I'm in the net, facing Harold Larwood. 'Be on your feet. He's a bit quick.' The ball hit me on the thigh, and I turned round. 'You're right,' I said. 'He *is* quick.'

"I never saw a quicker bowler. My father said that, when he sat behind Tyson, he could see the ball. But he couldn't see it with Larwood."

A three-year contract followed, and by the end of the summer he was making his debut at Swansea. The captain Arthur Carr came from a family that owned racehorses. "A big, burly man. He always used to scare me. You never knew what he was going to do next."

The rest were all professionals, mostly from the Nottinghamshire pits where he, too, found work. "You left Trent Bridge at the end of August, and you spent the winter looking forward to April."

In those days the counties arranged their own fixtures, and Notts did not agree to play Somerset till 1928. And, with Larwood and Voce, they were much too strong for the West Countrymen.

"The Northern counties were the hard nuts," Michael Spurway recalls. "Somerset never expected to beat any of them. Our cricket was all great fun, not much different from a Stragglers match, and Kent was by far the jolliest game. Tich Freeman used to throw up the ball and, if he didn't get the length right, you had to get another ball."

"Somerset had an amateur, CCC Case," Frank Shipston chuckles.

"Box Case," Michael Spurway says. "He really was the dullest cricketer ever. Such an inelegant batsman."

"One day at Taunton he came out to bat," Frank continues, "and Carr said to Bill Voce, 'He says he's going to get after you today.' Bill wasn't as quick as 'Lol' Larwood, but he could be just as dangerous and you could rile him. And he hit Case in the groin. Case fell back onto the stumps, his bat went off to point and, as he went off, in his confusion he picked up one of the stumps. He had to walk back past the bowler, and Bill thought for a moment that he was going to get the stump around his head."

The bravest batsmen against Larwood and Voce, Frank reckons, were Andrew Sandham of Surrey – "He was only a slight man" – and Duleepsinhji: "He had eyes like a hawk."

The greatest bowler Frank Shipston ever saw was in Minor Counties cricket, Staffordshire's Sydney Barnes. By 1929, Barnes was 56 but he took seven for 29 against Notts 2nds at Stoke – "He still had a very high arm, nearly brushing his ear" – and Frank remembers with pride his 49 in the second innings. "I hit him for six over mid-off."

In 1932, at the age of 25, he established himself with two centuries, even top-scoring with 21 in the innings in which Yorkshire's Hedley Verity took ten for 10. In the same match Arthur Carr, the captain, was dismissed for a pair, caught Barber bowled Verity both times. "I finished up with his green batting gloves. When he was out in the second innings, he came in and threw them down. And they happened to drop near me. 'You can bloody well have them,' he said."

Frank Shipston married the following year, and he decided to opt for the security of a career in the Nottingham Police, whose Chief Constable wanted nothing so much as a strong cricket team.

"But there was something about me that was not suitable to be a policeman. I was in the centre of town, and they had these 20-minute waits before you got a parking ticket. And I used to think, '20 minutes when a chap's trying to earn a living.' It didn't sit very well with me."

He bought a newsagents, became a first-class umpire and in 1957 – after taking the coaching courses at Lilleshall – started ten years back at Trent Bridge as coach. By this time the players were no longer coming out of the pits, and the county regularly nestled near the foot of the table. "They were just a minor county side at that time."

The world was changing – "The players were beginning to look more to their futures" – but the cricket itself was still played much as it had been played forty years earlier. But how it has changed in the forty years since! The helmets and arm guards: "Frank Ryan of Glamorgan once came out to face Larwood with four towels down him. 'He's not bloody well hitting me,' he said. But that was unusual." The pressurising of the umpires: "We used to get told off if we appealed in the slips for leg before." And the diving stops in the field: "The fielding these days is out of this world. I never did a slide in my life. It was half a crown for a pair of flannels at the laundry."

"One wouldn't have considered greening one's creams just to save a few runs," Michael Spurway adds. "Half a crown would have bought five pints of best bitter." He, like Frank Shipston, still watches with interest on television. "The greatest change," he says, "is in the emotional side of the game. If somebody was out, there was a smattering of applause, that's all. And if somebody got five wickets, you'd say, 'You've had a good day, haven't you?' There was no clapping the bowler on the back."

The world in which these two men grew up has changed utterly. The Somerset Stragglers no longer provide cricketers for the county side, playing fewer than 20 matches a summer, while Bullcroft Main Colliery has long closed, its once-mighty cricket club now in the middle reaches of the Doncaster and District League.

Their memories are all that remain.

"You look back," Frank Shipston says, "and you wonder where it has all gone."

*Since this article appeared, both men have died: Frank Shipston on 6 July 2005, three weeks short of his 99th birthday, and Michael Spurway on 7 July 2007, at the age of 98.*

## 52. Concentration is everything

*Keith Andrew of Northamptonshire* WCM, Aug 2003

It has been a world record for almost forty years – but it does not appear in *Wisden*. Wicket-keepers are the invisible men of cricket. Their skills and achievements are rarely chronicled.

It began on 12 June 1965 at the United Services Ground, Portsmouth. A fast, seamer's track. Keith Andrew, captain of the unfancied Northants side, was returning from a fortnight out with a finger injury, and he kept wicket to cricket's unlikeliest new ball pair: the six-foot-seven David Larter and the five-foot-five Brian Crump. One was fast, bouncy and at times wayward, with his keeper way back; the other skidded the ball through with nagging accuracy and liked Keith up to the stumps.

In the next match at Northampton rain transformed a slow pitch into a spiteful one and Larter destroyed Somerset with 'venomous pace bowling' while his captain, behind the stumps, masterminded a series of bowling changes.

"You didn't know he was captain," Brian Crump says. "He just spoke to people nice and quiet, and everybody got on. People had their moans and groans, but Keith would switch off."

"He was a greatly under-rated captain," the late Colin Milburn reckoned. "He had a way with every member of the side, and he could read a match as well as any skipper I played under."

At Headingley they beat Yorkshire, Larter again to the fore on another testing pitch. Then at Kettering it was the turn of the spinners, with Peter Watts breaking the back of the Leicestershire first innings.

"Leg-breaks, flippers, googlies, he bowled the lot," Keith Andrew recalls. "He'd even fire a fast one down the leg side. 'What the hell do you think I am?' I'd tell him. 'A coconut shy?'"

Then at Northampton Surrey's John Edrich hit 188. "He made us look ordinary. The ball would be swinging or turning, and he'd still be hitting it with the middle of his bat. I thought he was a great player."

Keeping on such a day was not so much about taking the ball but about retaining concentration.

Bob Taylor, of Derbyshire and England, explains: "Even as the batsman is playing his shot, you have to imagine yourself taking the ball. You might have been in the field for five hours 55 minutes, and it's the last over. And you're in India, and there's 90 degrees of heat. The wicket's flat, and maybe you've got Delhi Belly. That catch or stumping in the last over, that's what it's all about."

"Concentration is everything," Keith tells young keepers. "Even concentrate on concentration."

"Alan Knott and Godfrey Evans gave England great service," the old Warwickshire and England keeper Tiger Smith said. "Yet neither had the class of Keith Andrew or Bob Taylor behind the stumps."

"Keith was my inspiration," Bob Taylor says. "You never heard the ball drop into Keith's hands; he was so deft and unspectacular."

"He was a master craftsman," Surrey's Micky Stewart says, "like a silvery, smooth, slinky shadow behind the stumps."

"You didn't notice him," Northants' Dennis Brookes says, "and that's the hallmark of a good wicket-keeper."

But Frank Tyson, reflecting a more modern view, saw it differently. "I'd rather have Godfrey," he told a team-mate once. "He does drop more, but the way he makes catches puts me right on top of the world as a bowler. Keith is so methodical and easy, you hardly realise you've taken a wicket."

Keith's next match in 1965 was against the touring New Zealanders, when he kept for only the third time to the Pakistani leg-spinner Mushtaq Mohammad. Then came a trip to Trent Bridge, where Malcolm Scott's drifting slow left-arm brought an innings victory on a beautiful batting track.

Since his return from injury, Keith had played on a variety of surfaces, keeping wicket to a range of bowlers and captaining his side into championship contention. It was a happy side, with no great stars, least of all their unobtrusive skipper.

"If you bowled badly," Malcolm Scott says, "some of the captains would be at you, and it would make you worse. But Keith would come up quietly. 'Malcolm, take your sweater, have a rest. I'm going to try Fred.' You didn't feel rubbished. He managed everybody superbly."

Then Jack Mercer their enigmatic scorer looked through his book. "You know, Keith hasn't conceded a bye for several matches."

On uncovered pitches. Captaining the side. Standing up to the wicket much of the time. And wearing old-fashioned, pouch-free gloves. It was a display of traditional keeping at its best.

He had kept wicket for seven matches. Nearly 900 overs. 40-odd hours in the field. And 2,094 runs. The total had reached 2,132 before a Crump delivery flew over his left shoulder at Leicester.

"I never thought about byes," Keith says now, as unassuming as when he played. "They didn't bother me. In fact, sometimes, when I wanted to gee up the bowlers, I used to say to them, 'No wonder I don't give any byes away. You guys can't get past the bat.'"

## 53. Getting away with it

*Michael Barton of Surrey* TWC, Oct 2003

"I think Nigel Bennett made a great mistake accepting the Surrey captaincy," Michael Barton says. "I think I made a great mistake, too, but it turned out all right."

In the aftermath of the second world war the counties struggled to find available amateurs to captain them. In 1946 Surrey appointed Major Nigel Bennett; he had never played first-class cricket and was not remotely good enough. Alf Gover always swore that they had meant to appoint the better-known Leo Bennett, also a Major, and had got confused when Nigel arrived to renew his membership. The county's eleventh place that summer was as low as they had ever sunk.

In 1947 they turned back to a pre-war captain, the 41-year-old Errol Holmes – but only after they had found a benefactor who could pay him to play as an amateur.

In 1948 Holmes retained the captaincy, though he was only available for a few matches, and he recruited Michael Barton, who had impressed him when they had played together for the Free Foresters. Barton had been in the Oxford University side in the mid-1930s and had a career with Dunlop.

"It's extraordinary really," he says. "I was only playing occasional club cricket, and I'd never captained a side in my life."

The professionals were easily won round by his quiet charm and his three centuries in May. But the crowd took longer to settle. "One chap, whenever I misfielded, used to shout out 'What a captain!' but he gave up after a year or so." And the irascible secretary Brian Castor never did stop bombarding him with criticism. "He used to write these letters to me. One day I went in his office, and he had this huge sheet of paper on his desk. It was headed 'Barton' and had eight items on it: 'Didn't do as I said when … Mucked the whole thing up at …' On and on. I insisted on raising it all at the cricket committee, but he just crumpled it up and threw it in the waste paper basket. 'Never mind all that; there's something else I want to raise with you.'"

Surrey, for all the greatness of their inter-war batting, had not won the championship since 1914, but they almost won it in that summer of 1948. One more victory would have taken them above Glamorgan, and at the end of the season they looked back with anguish on the third day at Cheltenham when rain stopped play with only one wicket left to take and on the return catch that Laker dropped at The Oval. Middlesex's Sims was at the wicket, ten to make and the last man in, and he went on to hit the winning runs.

"On the surface Jim Laker was a dour Yorkshireman, but he was quite sensitive underneath. He was very upset, but no one said a thing. Then the next year he caught Jim Sims, a brilliant one-handed caught-and-bowled, and all he said was, 'One year too late.' It was the only time anybody ever mentioned it."

For all Brian Castor's criticisms, the record of the two captains that summer told a revealing story: Holmes, won 3, lost 5. Barton, won 10, lost 4.

Jim Laker was emerging as a world-class off-spinner, Alec Bedser was in his prime, and the batting depended on Fishlock, Parker and Squires. But by 1950 Stan Squires had died of leukaemia, and the Oval pitch was becoming more testing. They needed new batsmen, and in mid-July the Cambridge undergraduate Peter May arrived. He went in at number three and made seven runs in his first four innings. "Herbert Strudwick, our scorer, said to me, 'Why don't you put him down a bit?' But I said no. He was obviously going to be a world-beater. The next day he got a hundred on a bad wicket at Worcester and won us the match."

It started a winning sequence that saw them reach The Oval in late August, needing to beat Leicestershire to share the championship with Lancashire. Alec Bedser had already bowled nearly 1,200 overs in a long summer, and he was summoned before play to the captain's room.

"He'd been rather overbowled in our ascent, and he'd lost his fire. I said to him, 'I know you've been over-bowled, Alec, but I really must ask you for one last supreme effort.'"

The great-hearted Alec Bedser looked upset. "I've never been told that I'm not trying before," he said.

Rain threatened to deny them but, between the delays, Alec Bedser bowled 54 overs and took 12 wickets. The last Leicestershire wicket fell with an hour remaining, and Surrey were left with just two runs to score. "You go in first and I'll bowl," Leicester's captain Charles Palmer told his counterpart.

"He took a run all the way from the pavilion and bowled a slow full-pitch to leg."

It was only a shared title, but it was the first Surrey had won for 36 years.

In 1952 Stuart Surridge took over the captaincy. His aggression galvanised the developing team, and they became the greatest of all county sides, champions for seven successive summers. Peter May left university, Tony Lock learnt to spin the ball, and Peter Loader, Micky Stewart and Ken Barrington all emerged. Amid the celebrations everybody forgot the name of Michael Barton.

"I was lucky," he says today, 88 years old and modest to the last. "I think, if I was asked to do it now in the same circumstances, I would say no, but I got away with it. And I became a part of the cricket community, which has given me such pleasure in my life."

## 54. Beside the red smoke

*The Margam ground in Wales* TWC, Feb 2004

"That summer," Gloucestershire's John Mortimore remembers, "there was a prize for the side who reached 200 the fastest."

It was August 1962. The county was set to play at an unfamiliar venue: Margam. The ground of the Steel Company of Wales.

"On the way down we suggested to the batsmen that Margam might be the sort of small ground to go for the prize."

They arrived to find an open, windswept field beside the steel works, a sulphurous smell of rotten eggs in the air and smoke billowing out of the chimneys. "I have this vision," he says, "of red smoke, and everybody coughing their hearts out. We got there, the pitch was soft and we were struggling to score at one run an over."

There were 17,500 employees at the works, and their cricket team had risen rapidly to the first division of the South Wales League. "We used to pay a shilling a week to the Sports Club," former Secretary Colin Davies says. "It was deducted at source." Facilities were established for 17 sports: from angling and sailing to archery, rugby and golf.

In 1953 they hosted a friendly fixture between Glamorgan and the Gentlemen of Ireland. Seating was brought in, marquees erected and a new scoreboard built by works apprentices. "They wouldn't let us put the scoreboard by the ground," another veteran Ken Hopkins says. "There was a football pitch next to it so it had to be beyond that. A two-storey building, with the numbers high up. Big numbers, too. Otherwise you couldn't have seen them from the middle."

Rain ruined a low-scoring game, and it was 1960 before the county returned. "The sun never shone in the three days we were there," says Sussex's Les Lenham, who carried his bat for a four-hour 51. "Don Shepherd bowled superbly, and after every ball I had to go down the pitch and slam back down these great chunks of earth. It was an extraordinary place. You had to walk about 75 yards from the pavilion before you reached the boundary."

"It was so far away," Glamorgan's Peter Walker adds, "that you had to leave two balls before the bloke was out in order not to be timed out under the two-minute rule. In that Sussex game I used a bat that was made four inches longer. The wicket was so slow and low, it was perfect."

The next year Leicestershire came. Set 274 to win, they reached 63 for one when 'Ginger' Evans took six for eight and they were all out for 95.

"We didn't get a chance to watch the county games," Colin Davies says. "We had to work. The only time I went was the last day of that Leicester match. In the time I took to walk from the manager's office to the boundary, and stop for a couple of chats, seven or eight wickets fell and it was all over. They were coming off."

But a total of 95 was more than any of the four innings when Gloucestershire visited. The first day saw 20 wickets fall: Gloucester 88, Glamorgan 62, then Gloucester 34 for no wicket. 'On a spongy pitch,' *The Times* reported, 'few batsmen could play any sort of scoring shot.'

"Martin Young hit a six right at the end," Gloucestershire's Tony Brown recalls. "Even when you hit the ball, it slowed up in the outfield. That six was just about the only boundary of the day."

Worse was to follow. After a washed-out second day, Gloucester slumped on the final morning to 92 all out, scored off 70 overs. At one stage Tom Pugh, the visiting captain, grew so frustrated that, when he went out to bat, he flailed wildly for 15 minutes before returning: bowled Shepherd, 3.

"Sam Cook was watching from the dressing room," Tony Brown recalls. "The windows were very high, and he was standing on a wooden, slatted bench. Tom Pugh took his pads off, and Sam said to him, 'Skipper, it looks as if that swarm of bees has gone now.' 'What swarm of bees?' 'The ones you were trying to swat out there.'"

Glamorgan had more than three hours left to make 119, but such was the state of the pitch that they finished up playing for the draw. 'Those who succeeded in staying for a time,' said *The Times*, 'survived perilously with five and sometimes seven fielders clustered only a few yards from the bat.'

"All the close fielders were in there," Tony Brown says. "Tom Pugh tried to come up, too, and we had to send him out. 'There's not really room for you.'"

The end came with nine minutes remaining. In the 67th over Glamorgan were all out for 49. Mortimore, 26.4 overs, five wickets for ten runs.

"We came off the field," David Allen says, "and we were all covered in this red tinge from the steel works."

'The game was farcical,' the Gloucestershire handbook recorded, 'but the hospitality of our hosts will be remembered by all those who took part.'

On only one other occasion in England since 1906 has a game of four completed innings produced fewer runs, and that too was on a works pitch: the Ind Coope ground at Burton-on-Trent where on one damp 1958 day 39 wickets fell. At least on that occasion the runs came at 2.34 an over. At Margam the rate was 1.23.

The next year Margam was only given the Cambridge University fixture, with the students batting through the third day for a draw: 105 overs for 157. There was not one paying spectator all day, and near the end the players came off for a while for bad light.

"There wasn't a cloud in the sky," Peter Walker says, "but this orange smoke came over and obliterated any possibility of seeing."

For all the hospitality, county cricket did not return. Then over the years the work force declined to 3,500. The square was moved to make way for a rugby pitch, the scoreboard got taken over by the golfers, and the club sank down the league.

"Glamorgan were trying to take the cricket out," Alan Jones says. "We always got a good crowd at Llanelli, and Neath was a good ground. It was trial and error, I suppose."

Now there is no such effort. Half the 1962 fixtures were in the West, now there are just a few days at the historic St Helen's ground in Swansea. The county side no longer draws most of its members from the West.

"It bothers me," says Tom Cartwright, for many years the national coach. "All the folklore was in the West. Now there's getting to be a disconnection with the first-class game."

"It's like taking cricket off terrestrial television," says his son Jeremy, Development Officer for South-West Wales. "It gets less and less likely that children will chance upon cricket."

"It's so important for kids to see their heroes," Alan Jones says. "I queued up for hours to see the West Indians at St Helen's in 1950. Just to have Everton Weekes walk by, three or four yards away, it was such a thrill."

Several of the works grounds have gone – to car factories, soccer

pitches, housing – but the Margam one has survived, and in recent years there are signs of revival. No longer does the Works, Corus now, subsidise the Sports Club, but the members have raised money to improve the square with help from groundsman Wayne Duggan; they have bought covers, and now their Saturday scores are rising.

"We've had the Wales Under-15s down here," Paul Donovan says proudly, "and we're hoping for the Under-17s and the Glamorgan second eleven."

There is still a smell of sulphur in the air, but the pollution controls mean that the yellow smoke is never as dense as it once was.

"It should never have been a venue for county games," Colin Davies says. "It didn't have the pitch preparation or the atmosphere. But the players would have been well looked after."

So is it the grimmest ground on which county cricket has been played?

"Oh no," Leicestershire's Jack Birkenshaw says. "That has to be the Snibston Pit ground at Coalville. There was a slag heap alongside and, if the wind blew the wrong way, you were in trouble."

"Among the dreadful grounds," Peter Walker says, "Margam was Premier League. But Coalville was worse. If you fielded at short leg and the batsman started patting down the pitch, you'd come off at the end of the day looking like one of the Black and White Minstrels."

## 55. Taken by surprise

*Adelaide, Weds 2 Feb 1955, with Bob Appleyard* THE TIMES, 18 NOV 2006

In his bed in the Pier Hotel outside Adelaide Bob Appleyard lay awake.

"My mind was racing with the excitement of the day," he says, "and I couldn't stop bowling. All through that night, as I lay there, I was running in and bowling."

Two years earlier he had lain in a Yorkshire sanatorium, recovering from the removal of a TB-infected upper left lung. Beneath the bedclothes he had secretly worked his spinning finger against a cricket ball, trying to retain the hardness of the skin. His chance of playing for Yorkshire again seemed small, yet now he was the man on whom England's Ashes hopes seemed to rest.

It was the fourth Test. England were leading 2-1, pressing for a victory that would win a series in Australia for the first time since the Bodyline tour of 1932/33, and Bob Appleyard's mind ran over and over the start of the Australian second innings. As tea had approached, their openers had taken the score to 26, for an overall lead of eight runs, when, to the surprise of everybody, England's captain Len Hutton had removed Brian Statham from the Cathedral End after only two overs and had thrown the ball to Bob.

His success in England had been as a medium-paced off-spinner relying on spin and bounce, but he had realised in the early weeks of the tour that this was not what was needed Down Under.

"Because the pitches didn't take much spin, I'd had to work hard to perfect my control of flight, my changes of pace and direction, and by Adelaide I really felt in control. In fact, in my whole career, it was the closest I came to 100% control."

"He was easy to play at the start of the tour," Richie Benaud says. "By Adelaide he was a different bowler altogether. The ball was never there where you expected it to be."

"The dip was the most remarkable thing," says Trevor Bailey. "I'd never seen a bowler of his pace with that dip before, and I've never seen one since."

Morris, playing a fraction early, was caught and bowled. Burke was beaten by spin and bowled, then Harvey was frustrated into an ungainly hoick and left the field, according to EW Swanton, 'hanging his head in dejection'. In ten eight-ball overs that evening Bob Appleyard took three wickets for 13 runs, Australia's 69 for three left the match in the balance, and the journalists were of one mind: England's chances of victory rested with Appleyard.

He barely slept.

In intense heat they took the field at twelve o'clock the next day, but

Bob's moment did not arrive. Once more defying expectation, Hutton turned to Frank Tyson and Brian Statham, the fast-bowling heroes of the tour. "Brian had a badly damaged toe nail," Bob recalls, "and he was bowling with a hole in his boot." Tyson, meanwhile, developed a niggling groin strain as he persevered in the heat.

Stuart Harris, deputising for John Woodcock on *The Times*, called them 'two great hearts summoning all their strength and skill'. After ninety minutes, when lunch was called, they were still bowling, and the scoreboard in the shadow of the cathedral had moved from 69 for three to 103 for nine.

The Yorkshire off-spinner's contribution was two maiden overs after lunch. Then he watched as the England batsmen set out to score the 94 runs that would win the Ashes.

By the time they had hit 18 of them, Edrich, Hutton and Cowdrey were back in the pavilion, all sent there by Keith Miller. 'What a man is Miller,' declared Harris. 'Four meteor jets flew over at 200 feet. They looked and sounded quite tame beside this wild man bowling.'

Len Hutton was distraught. A long winter had taken its toll of him, and he plunged into despair.

"It meant such a lot to Len. For years he'd been the backbone of the batting. Sometimes he'd fought the Australians almost single-handed. He was the first professional to captain England, putting up with a lot of criticism. And he had such a high regard for Keith Miller that he really thought he could beat us."

Denis Compton had other ideas. He strode out full of purpose but, when Miller caught May in the covers to make it 49 for four at tea, the tension became unbearable.

"We got to the stage where we couldn't watch," Bob recalls. "Len and I spent some time in the back of the pavilion."

They heard the cheers as Compton drove Benaud for four, then as Bailey hooked Johnston clear of the legside field, and run by run the pressure eased. With four wanted, Bailey was lbw but Evans was soon striking the winning hit.

"Pray God no professional may ever captain England," Yorkshire's Lord Hawke had famously said, and Hutton had carried that burden around Australia. As the cheers rang out, he smiled. "I wish Lord Bloody Hawke were here," he said.

"It was a great turning point in English cricket," says Bob Appleyard, who has followed in Hutton's footsteps as only the second professional cricketer to become President of Yorkshire. "Len was a magnificent captain. Everybody had expected me to bowl that morning, and he caught them by surprise. It was the happiest of tours. We won in Australia – and that's the height of every English cricketer's ambition."

## 56. The twelfth man's tale

*Michael Hall of Nottinghamshire* TWC, Feb 2008

Nottinghamshire was one of the wealthier county clubs in the 1950s, paying better wages than most and having a large pool of players. "Some years," Mike Hall remembers, "there were 27, even 28, on the staff."

Mike Hall joined their number in April 1953, a promising 17-year-old batsman, but it took him till his sixth summer at Trent Bridge to make his first-class debut. They were summers of second-team cricket, of bowling to the members in the nets, of pushing the heavy roller – and of doing twelfth-man duties.

"I was a good fielder and I could catch," he says, "so I was twelfth man an enormous number of times."

Twelfth man was a general dogsbody. He brought in all the bags on the first morning, in some of the larger pavilions heaving them up several flights of stairs. At lunch he carried trays of food into the dressing room for the not-out batsmen, and at tea he collected the close-of-play drinks orders.

He had to watch the match at all times: "New gloves, extra sweaters, broken shoelaces, a message to somebody in one of the stands. Joe Hardstaff was my great hero, but woe betide you if you missed a signal from him."

In the pavilion, too, he was a general errand boy, as often as not to the Cambridge undergraduate Gamini Goonesena, one of the last of the true amateurs. Goonesena would drive into the ground in an old Lagonda, with gas lights on the side, and he would issue his instructions in a cut-glass accent. "Michael, would you be good enough to run down to the office and fetch me a stamp?"

On the last day it was the twelfth man's job to take his own team's autograph books into the opposition dressing room. "There would be twenty or so books, and I found myself in with all the great players of that era. To be talking with Godfrey Evans or Colin Cowdrey, it was a wonderful education."

All the players signed willingly, with one exception – at Scarborough. "I'm not here to sign autographs," Fred Trueman told him. "I'm here to take wickets." Trueman then took seven for 23, and the twelfth man returned with the books. "Every Nottinghamshire player instantly looked for the one signature, and it wasn't there. I was not a very popular chappie."

At the end of the game he had to load the bags into the van, and often he would find himself where no senior player would ever be: a passenger in his captain Reg Simpson's car. "We did normally stop at traffic lights but, if there were three lanes, Reg would make a fourth."

Twelfth men were required to field less often in those years, but two occasions stand out in his memory, the first in his first summer at Trent Bridge when Frank Tyson was making his championship debut for Northants.

"There was a team meeting beforehand," he recalls. "Joe Hardstaff said, 'They've got a young fast bowler, he's come down from Durham. I don't want you to be frightened of him. He's just a piddler.'"

Within minutes the Northants keeper Brian Reynolds had been hit behind the ear by a throw-in. He was carried off and, being too poor to have brought more than eleven, they borrowed the Notts twelfth man. "I found myself fielding at slip, and we were standing further back from the wicket than the length of the pitch."

Joe Hardstaff battled his way to 64, and at lunch he revised his opinion of Tyson. "I'm holding my hands up, lads. He ain't no piddler."

"That was a good game for me," Mike says. "I caught Bruce Dooland at extra cover. It came quick to my left, knee high. 'Well caught,' he said. I got my £6 off Notts, and Dennis Brookes the Northants captain paid me £6 as well."

Two years later Middlesex were the visitors, and on the final morning Denis Compton, surrounded by autograph-hunting boys, managed to trap his finger in his car door and departed for hospital. In the Middlesex innings he did not bat till number eight, coming in at the fall of Don Bennett's wicket. At that moment Johnny Clay, fielding at slip, ran off for a pee, and Arthur Jepson, the stand-in Notts captain, summoned his twelfth man.

"So I walked out to field, through the members, with Denis Compton at my side. 'Have you played yet?' he asked me. I said, 'No, I haven't, Mr Compton.' He said, 'It's Denis.' I went to the bowler's end where Bruce Dooland was standing, and Arthur said to me, in his gruff voice, 'Get thee bloody sen where Johnny was.' So I went into the slips."

Dooland's fourth ball to Compton was a leg-break. "Denis played forward and got a wafer-thin edge that came through to me just above waist high. It was an absolute nob-ender to catch."

Compton, caught sub, bowled Dooland, 0.

Then Clay reappeared. The twelfth man walked off, as he had walked on, alongside the great Compton.

Mike Hall's greatest cricketing achievements were for the Retford club where he was a prolific run-scorer and nurtured the young Derek Randall. Despite some scepticism, he got him taken onto the county staff when Garry Sobers was captain.

Mike had left his mark as a reliable twelfth man, and now his protégé followed in his footsteps. "I was Garry's favourite twelfth man," Randall says. "I was the one who could run fastest across the Bridgford Road to the bookmakers."

## 57. A professional experiment

*Warwickshire in 1951* TWC, July 2008

Friday 17 August 1951. All Warwickshire was waiting for news of Yorkshire's match at Scarborough.

'I rang up the newspaper offices in Birmingham and the county ground,' leg-spinner Eric Hollies recalled, 'but the lines were all engaged. Everybody, it seemed, was on the same quest.'

The previous day at Coventry Warwickshire's bowlers had sent down 145 overs to dismiss Northants twice, their sixth two-day win since the start of July. Only a Yorkshire victory over Worcestershire could prevent them sealing their first championship since 1911.

"We were ordinary county cricketers," Alan Townsend says. "That's how we classed ourselves. But we knitted together as a team. When we batted we didn't bother about averages, we had a go for each other, and we were able to bowl sides out."

They came from far and wide, only Charlie Grove and Fred Gardner born in the county. "The older players like Jimmy Ord and Eric Hollies made us all so welcome," Durham-born Alan Townsend says. "I couldn't have gone to a better side. And Tom Dollery was such a good tactician. He knew all the players on the circuit; when a new man came in, he'd often change the bowling straightaway."

They had won 16 of their 25 games. With nobody in the England side, they had called on only 13 players and, unlike all the other counties, every one of them was a professional – including Dollery, who was in his third full summer as captain. The amateur dressing room at Edgbaston was now labelled Home Team.

'Tom thrived on the responsibility,' Hollies wrote. 'He knew that he was on trial. Professional captaincy was something of an experiment, and its future might depend on the events at Edgbaston.'

Post-war England no longer had an amateur class with time to spare for cricket. Even for the previous winter's tour of Australia, with George Mann and Norman Yardley unavailable, MCC had only been able to appoint their third-choice captain. 'It cannot be long,' Dollery wrote early in 1952, 'before a professional has to be considered seriously for the post.'

Friday 17 August 1951. Yorkshire, chasing 250 to win, had reached 232 for five, and Hollies in desperation set off for the office of his local evening paper. There he found a man with the result in his hand, waiting for the outcome of the 4 o'clock at Newbury before stamping it into the Stop Press.

'It was one of the most frustrating moments in my life,' Hollies wrote. Here he was, Warwickshire's greatest bowler, the man who had bowled

Bradman for nought in his last Test innings, offering to buy six advance copies, but all to no avail. 'He could not tell me, even if I was Eric Hollies – which he said in a way that clearly implied he thought I wasn't.'

"I was at home," Alan Townsend recalls, "and this telegram arrived from the ground. We had to go to The Plough on Stratford Road for a celebration that evening."

Yorkshire's last five wickets had fallen for nine runs, and Warwickshire were champions.

17 August 1951. Only once since the First World War – Yorkshire, on the same date in 1923 – had a county won the championship so early. And only once since: Surrey, on 16 August 1957.

The next day at Edgbaston money was flowing into a members' fund for the triumphant players, enough for Alan to buy a Pye radiogram to listen to his Richard Tauber records. "It had a lovely tone. I could even pick up the trawlers out at sea." But the county capped the donations to the players, diverting the later money into ground improvements. "Bert Wolton and I spent a whole winter laying down concrete steps for the Rae Stand. For five pounds a week. Oh, that was a cold job. We were absolutely frozen."

He parted company with the radiogram only two or three years ago, but he still treasures the inscribed watch. "There were only thirteen of them made. The more I look at it, the more I feel proud. It reminds you that you've achieved something in your life."

According to the *Cricketer* magazine, the county 'enjoyed a reputation throughout the country as one of the happiest playing in championship cricket today.'

"Eric and Tom Dollery, to my mind they were the real strength of the side," Alan Townsend says. "Possibly Charlie Grove and Tom Pritchard, the new-ball bowlers. And, of course, Tiger Smith the coach. The rest of us, we all had to do our bit."

Alan Townsend's bit was as a free-scoring batsman, effective change bowler and brilliant slip fielder, his 41 catches breaking the county record.

*The Times* commented on the quality of his close catching, but it emphasised above all 'the popularity, the skill and the knowledge of Dollery's captaincy. The whole side have pulled together with him and for him.'

The next June England were led onto the field by a professional, Len Hutton.

## 58. It can't be beaten

*A Sunday League match at Yeovil* WCM, July 2002

When the 40-over Sunday League was launched in 1969, *Wisden* labelled it 'Instant Cricket': 'The batsmen have to sharpen up their strokes, the fielders to be on their toes. It has a feverish tempo. Every ball counts.'

The idea was to bring back the crowds. County cricket was in the doldrums, with Essex down to a playing staff of twelve and Somerset abandoning its second eleven. Bankruptcies were close.

John Player & Sons were the first sponsors, their prize money including a pool of £1,000 to be shared by every batsman who hit a six. Essex's Barbadian Keith Boyce led the way with 16 and netted £44 11s 4d. He also won the £250 that the BBC put up for the fastest televised fifty.

Somerset decided to take their matches out and about. Bath, Glastonbury, Brislington, even Torquay. In 1970 they packed up on Saturday night at Clarence Park, Weston, and moved the stands to the larger club ground half a mile away. Cricket was working hard to find a new audience.

On Sunday 27 July 1969 Somerset and Essex broke off their three-day game at Taunton to convene at Johnson Park, Yeovil. It was a large field with good parking space, but the clubhouse was not a proper pavilion, the ground suffered from drainage problems and the pitch did not encourage free stroke play. "The ball was turning square," Somerset's Peter Robinson recalls.

Essex were struggling to raise an eleven. Keith Fletcher was playing for England at Lord's, and Gordon Barker, their senior batsman, was out of action with heavy bruising. "He'd probably gone up to his allotment in Darlington," his team-mate Robin Hobbs says.

So, as a last resort, they sent for the long-retired Doug Insole, who left home at seven o'clock on Sunday morning and travelled down by train. "It was full of sailors from the Royal Tournament, all desperately hung over. I had to stand all the way."

"He came down with his old leather kit-bag," Robin Hobbs recalls. "He even had to walk from the station."

Essex batted first, and after eight overs of medium pace the score had reached 15 for one.

There were no fielding circles, no pinch-hitters, nothing as unorthodox as a reverse sweep. 'The first few overs are spent ensuring not too many wickets are lost,' Somerset's Roy Virgin explained in the local paper.

The spinners came on. Peter Robinson, the slow left-armer, took two quick wickets to bring in Keith Boyce. Meanwhile the off-spinner Brian

Langford, the Somerset captain, bowled to the Essex opener Brian Ward.

"I went round the wicket and bowled a very tight line," he remembers. "I kept the ball well up."

For five overs he bowled almost entirely to Ward, and the batsman just played him back. "Boyce was tearing his hair out," Robin Hobbs says, while Peter Robinson recalls Brian Taylor, the Essex captain. "He was on the edge. 'Get on with it,' he was shouting."

"I wasn't the greatest batsman in the world," Doug Insole says, "but I could play off-spinners. I was sitting there, waiting to go in, hoping to belt Langford all round the ground."

Boyce hit two fours and a big six over extra cover, all off Robinson, but he did not face Langford till the first ball of his sixth over, off which they ran a single. "It may have caught a glove," Peter thinks, "but John Langridge the umpire signalled a leg bye." Then Ward blocked the last five balls.

"I thought Langford was the danger man," he explained afterwards. "I thought I'd play him out."

And play him out he did. When the Somerset captain took the ball for his last over, John Langridge turned to him: "You do realise they haven't scored off you, don't you?" But Brian Langford, like most captains, was struggling with the mathematics of this new game. "I had no idea till he said that. I was more worried about who was going to bowl the overs."

Another maiden followed, and his ration was complete. Eight overs, eight maidens, no wickets for no runs. 24 overs had been bowled, and Essex were 43 for three.

"There's not much point in my going in now," Doug Insole said.

"No, old son, you get in," Brian Taylor replied. "You'll be marvellous."

So at 69 for four Doug replaced Brian Ward. He blocked two balls. "Then I hit the third ball to square leg, called Boycey for a run, he sent me back and Langford hit one stump. I was run out for nought."

Essex were all out for 126. Somerset – 82 for eight at one stage – crept home in the final over. Sunday League cricket may have had 'a feverish tempo' to *Wisden*, with 'every ball counting', but only nine times that summer did a side chase and make more than 160. Compare that with 1997, when it was still a 40-over game and it was done 50 times. But then today's cricketers don't play at places like Johnson Park.

Eight overs, no runs. "One of the most wonderful records of all time," Robin Hobbs calls it. "It can't be beaten, can it?"

Doug Insole has other memories. "The train back was full of people returning from the seaside. I put my bag down in the corridor, and one of them said, 'My son's very tired. Do you mind if he sits on your bag?' And he wee-ed all over it. I got home at about one in the morning – and, as I keep telling the club, I still haven't had my expenses."

## 59. A hint of paradise

*Reg Simpson of Nottinghamshire and England* TWC, Dec 2006

Australia had not lost a Test match since the war. In 1946/47 they had beaten Wally Hammond's ageing England side 3-0. In 1948 it was 4-0, their team becoming known as the Invincibles, the greatest of all Test sides. Now, as the final match of the 1950/51 series approached, they were 4-0 up again and Freddie Brown, England's captain, was facing the prospect of returning home as Johnny Douglas had done in 1921, with a 5-0 whitewash against his name.

Brown was MCC's third choice to captain the tour, with Norman Yardley and George Mann both unavailable, and he had sailed from England in September with the strangest of parties. Six of the seven specialist batsmen were openers, and no fewer than six of the tourists were under the age of 25: Berry, Close, Dewes, Parkhouse, Sheppard and Warr. The six had nine Tests between them, and neither of the two young extras who flew out in January – Statham and Tattersall – added to that total.

"It was the worst selected side I've ever seen," Alec Bedser says. "Freddie Brown had this idea that you had to be 21 to beat Australia. Some of them were only kids."

"We had Bill Edrich stuck at home," says Reg Simpson, "and good batsmen like Jack Robertson and Dennis Brookes. And Les Jackson of Derbyshire. All the opening batsmen in England thought he was the most difficult opening bowler in the country. But Gubby Allen thought his arm was too low, he wouldn't do any good in Australia. Just stupid theory – instead of going on what the chap does with the ball. It was all very sad."

None of the youngsters made an impression on the series and, with Compton and Washbrook in the worst form of their long Test careers, the batting had a fatal fragility, not only against the pace of Lindwall and Miller but against the spin of 'Big Jack' Iverson, the 35-year-old newcomer with a strange action.

"He was a mystery," Reg Simpson says. "He had the ball wrapped in his fingers, and he flicked it. His leg-spinner hardly moved, it just straightened up, but his off-spinner really turned a lot and he was pretty accurate. He had little idea of cricket. Lindsay Hassett fielded at forward short leg to him, and he had to keep telling him where to bowl. In the last Test I went outside leg stick a bit to fox him."

As a player of spin Reg Simpson was poor in his early years with Notts, but on the 1948/49 tour of South Africa he learnt from Gloucestershire's Jack Crapp the method that the great Wally Hammond had applied. "He didn't watch the hand. He concentrated on the flight, direction and length of the ball, and he'd see it spinning. And if he couldn't see it, wherever it pitched, he'd play for it to hit his wickets. The funny thing was, when you concentrated on the ball, you actually spotted when the action of the hand was different. Before then, I'd had terrible difficulty with spinners like Jack Walsh. And the next summer I got two hundreds in a match against him."

Reg Simpson was a free-scoring batsman – "one of the greatest stroke-players I've seen," wrote the Australian Jack Fingleton – and in the summers of 1949 and 1950 he was the outstanding batsman in county cricket. Yet he had not cemented his place in the England Test team and, despite hitting 259 against New South Wales, he started the final Test at Melbourne as another who had not lived up to expectation on the tour.

Brown lost the toss once more and found himself leading his team into the field. Alec Bedser was his main bowler, but his partner Trevor Bailey had fractured a thumb in the third Test, missed the fourth and now during the morning twisted his ankle. So Brown himself, aged 41, his shoulder still sore from a car crash a fortnight earlier, took over and with typical wholeheartedness he and Bedser put out Australia for 217.

"Freddie just bowled very accurate medium pace, but he worked jolly hard at his bowling."

Brown was a big man in every way, a ruddy-faced, hard-living extrovert who ten years earlier had captained an English Services side against Lindsay Hassett's Australians when they had both been in Egypt, fighting on the same side against General Rommel. With such men at the helm, it was impossible that the 1950/51 series would be unfriendly. "Freddie was such a marvellous captain, always attacking, never rattled, never down at all. He was a tough competitor, like an Australian, and they loved him out there."

"Lettuces only a shilling," called out a quay-side barrow-boy in Sydney, "and 'earts as big as Freddie Brown's."

Saturday's play was washed out, but on Monday in hot, humid conditions England took control. Some time after tea they reached 204 for two, with Simpson unbeaten on 77. Then came a fresh burst of Lindwall and Miller – "Keith wasn't always interested in his bowling, but that evening he was really quick" – and, within an hour of the start on Tuesday, the England innings had crumbled to 246 for nine. Reg Simpson, on his 31st birthday, was still eight short of his hundred.

Roy Tattersall was England's number eleven and, in the words of EM Wellings, 'Iverson had eight men packed like a bandage round him.' Somehow he survived the over so that his partner, facing Miller, could hit a four, two and three to complete his century.

"You want to pack it in now, Reg," chirped the fast bowler. "Have a nice not out."

"Rubbish," came the reply, and Reg farmed the bowling. 'Looking like a master showing strokes to the boys,' wrote *The Times*, 'he pierced the field almost at will.'

Reg Simpson was known as a great player of fast bowling, as good as any in his generation, and his secret was a back-foot technique that he had adopted as a young man playing for the Nottingham Police against the menacing left-arm pace of Bill Voce. "He made me look a bit of an idiot," he recalls. "Then I saw that Frank Shipston at the other end seemed to be playing him all right. And I suddenly realised that he was going right back and waiting for it. From that moment I always went back and across, stood up, waited for the ball and had no problem at all. I've never forgotten Bill Voce at the end of that over, with his hands on his hips, wondering what the hell had happened."

It was a technique he passed on to Dennis Amiss when the Warwickshire opener was struggling against the West Indian pacemen in 1976, and Amiss made 203 with it at The Oval. "What happens if the ball is pitched up?" Amiss asked, and Reg laughs as he repeats his reply: "Well, Dennis, if it's pitched up from a fast bowler, once you see it in the air, you can close your eyes and hit it."

Simpson was not a Hutton, crafting long, chanceless innings. He was a natural shot-maker, who had grown up admiring the elegance of Duleepsinhji: "He was an artistic batsman with lovely strokes. I used to play games of cricket with myself, and Duleep was always one of my favourites."

Now he was at the top of his game, playing Australia at Melbourne, and he could express himself freely. "The situation really suited me. I could take some calculated risks and play my shots."

With eight-ball overs, he could face five or six before giving the strike to Tattersall, and in 50 minutes the pair added a match-turning 74 runs, all but ten of them from the flowing bat of Reg Simpson, whose strokeplay and running between the wickets – according to Fingleton – 'had the fieldsmen upset and the bowlers withering under his rapid fire.'

"He made Lindwall and Miller look very ordinary," his team-mate David Sheppard thought.

At the end, Reg Simpson's 'nice not out' sat next to a score of 156.

With Alec Bedser taking five more wickets in the Australian second innings, England needed only 95 for victory and on Wednesday evening, with rain in the air, the unmovable Hutton hit the winning single.

England had finally broken Australia's winning streak.

In front of the pavilion the cry went up from one and all: "We want Brown. We want Brown."

The telegrams flooded in, one from the barrow-boy: 'Well done,' it read. 'Lettuces will go up to eighteen pence.'

Amid the celebrations Reg Simpson felt that he had established himself at last. In the first Test next summer, against South Africa, he made 137 – though, early in the innings, his new-found freedom did not meet with the approval of his partner Hutton. "I hit Athol Rowan over the top to the pavilion for a near-six and, as we crossed, he said to me, 'This is a Test match, you know.'"

By the fourth Test he was out of the side. "All the time I was playing Test cricket, I had the feeling I was fighting for my place, and it does make you over-cautious. If somebody had said to me, 'You're in for five matches,' I could have attacked in my own way as I did at Notts."

'All Simpson lacks is confidence,' was the verdict of Fingleton at the end of that Australian tour. 'He could be one of our great modern players.'

It was not to be. Yet, in that one innings at Melbourne, he touched the heights of cricketing success. In the words of EW Swanton, 'he brought a hint of paradise to English eyes', setting up a victory that, Godfrey Evans reckoned, 'marked the turning point in English post-war cricket.'

The next three Ashes series were all won by England.

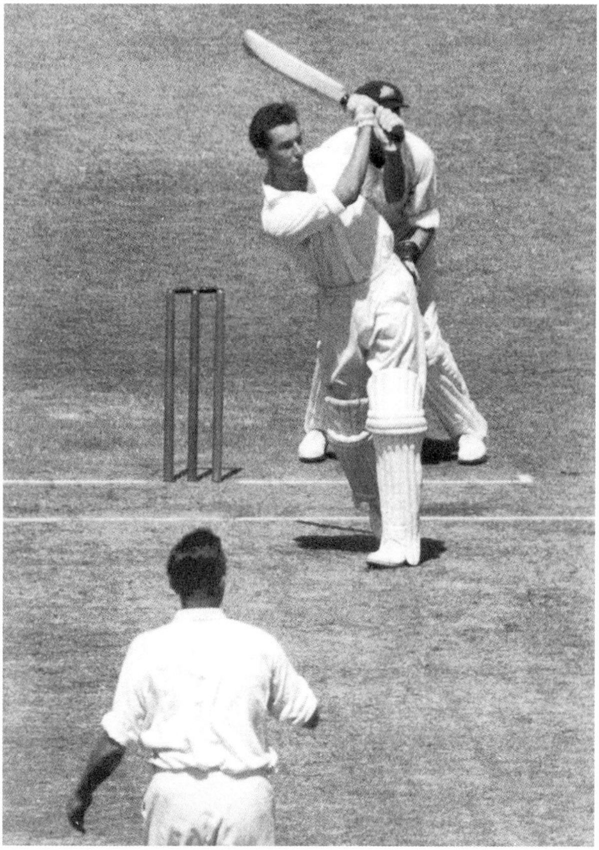

*Reg Simpson batting against Jack Iverson at Melbourne.*

## 60. Close to giving up

*David Allen of Gloucestershire* TWC, Feb 2007

"Where am I going?" the young David Allen asked the Gloucestershire committee in the winter of 1958/59. "I'm 23 years old, I'm engaged to be married, I've got no prospects in the office where I'm working, and my cricket is getting nowhere."

How long ago seemed the summer of 1953 when, as a 17-year-old, he had stood in for the county's two off-spinners, John Mortimore and Bomber Wells, while they were away on National Service. At Bristol, in only his fourth championship match, he had conjured an improbable last-over victory against the mighty Surrey, taking six for 13 in 12.4 overs, and he had been chaired from the field by a large group of excited boys, many of them from his old school, Cotham Grammar. 'He bowled with the experience and coolness of a veteran,' reported the *Western Daily Press.*

"The secretary Colonel Henson came up to me afterwards," he recalls. "'Well done, Allen. Very well played. I'm afraid you're not in the side tomorrow. Wells has got three days' leave.'"

Five years later, he was still the third-choice off-spinner, and that was in addition to the slow left-armer Sam Cook. "In those days, they thought, if people had the ability, you had to give them four or five years to see if they had the character. But Morty and Bomber were such good bowlers that I never got the opportunities."

In the wet summer of 1958 he played in seven championship matches; he batted at number ten, bowled 29 overs and took two wickets.

"I'd had enough. Maybe I should have gone to another county, but Gloucestershire were greedy, they wouldn't release me and I'd have had to spend a year or two qualifying."

The county made him an offer: 'Play next summer, and we'll secure you a reasonable winter job.' But, as things worked out, they were not required to keep their promise.

In May he got a late call-up for the first championship match, replacing the injured batsman Arthur Milton. He went in at 35 for seven, top-scored with 62 and, when he added a second top-scoring fifty, the new captain Tom Graveney awarded him his county cap.

The county's batting was prone to bad days. One newcomer Richard Bernard found himself walking out to bat at 31 for five in each innings of his debut match at The Oval. "Don't worry, it's not normally like this," the senior players reassured him, and at Bristol the next day he went out at 16 for five. With such top-order fragility, David Allen in place of the rustic hitter Bomber Wells – career average, seven – seemed a sensible switch, even if the young David was nursing a split spinning finger and could hardly bowl.

By mid-June he had played nine matches, bowled 40 overs and taken one wicket. Four weeks later, thanks to a long bowl against Cambridge University and an outstanding week at the Wagon Works ground in Gloucester – "the best wicket in the county at that time" – he had 44 wickets and was second in the national averages. The selectors were looking to fill the gap left by Jim Laker, and the bus driver's son from Bristol was suddenly attracting attention.

He proved an elusive figure. The chairman of selectors Gubby Allen turned up at Bristol when the seamers bowled out Somerset for 61, then again at Leyton just as his spinning finger split once more. Nevertheless they decided to play him at The Oval and, within minutes of receiving the news, he dislocated a knuckle in a Sunday friendly and had to be replaced by the leg-spinner Tommy Greenhough. He was still something of an unknown when he boarded the boat to the Caribbean.

"RWV Robins was the manager. 'You're not going to be playing much cricket on the tour,' he told me. 'And I'll have a lot of speeches to make. So I'd like you to look after my briefcase. That'll keep you busy.'"

There were only 15 in the party, including two keepers. Statham was unfit for the first Test, and Greenhough bowled badly against Barbados. "You could see the sweat dripping off his fingers in the heat. Fred would take the ball: 'You've dipped this in the bloody river, haven't you, lad?'"

So, after one wicket in a two-day match against Barbados Colts, David Allen, nursing a sore finger from some hard work in the nets, found himself in the side for the first Test. 'He is a lucky young man to be given a Test match on what he has done,' EW Swanton wrote.

He took no wickets in a high-scoring draw, but he got another lucky break in Trinidad. His rival off-spinner Ray Illingworth was allocated the warm-up match at Port-of-Spain while he found himself in action on a 'raging turner' at Point-a-Pierre, down among the oilfields. Illingworth's 35 overs brought him match figures of three for 82 while David Allen sent down 49 overs and took ten for 63. "Illy wasn't very happy, as you can imagine."

In less than a year Gloucestershire's third-choice off-spinner had become England's premier slow bowler, one who would go on to take 122 wickets in 39 Tests.

"My game was better suited to Test cricket," he says, "and I loved the pomp and ceremony of it. You do need luck in cricket, don't you? If they hadn't said they'd find me a better job, I'd have packed up the previous winter."

## 61. The calm destroyer

*Jim Laker of Surrey and England* TWC, Aug 2006

Nineteen wickets for 90 runs. In a Test match against Australia. To settle the destination of the Ashes. Fifty years on, Jim Laker's triumph at Old Trafford still stands as the Everest that towers over every other bowling performance in cricket's long history.

The drama began at four o'clock on Friday 27 July 1956. England, thanks to centuries from Peter Richardson and David Sheppard, had scored 459, and in reply Australia were 48 for no wicket. Then Laker, who had been switched to the Stretford Road end, had Colin McDonald caught by Tony Lock at short leg, and in the same over he pitched a ball on the line of left-hander Neil Harvey's leg stump, spun it past his outstretched bat and clipped the off. "It was the ball that won the Test series," Laker reckoned.

In that one over the mood of the Australians altered irrevocably. In May Laker had taken all ten in their first innings when Surrey had become the first county to beat them since 1912. Then at Headingley, in the third Test, they had found themselves on a pitch that was taking sharp turn by the second day, and Laker's eleven wickets had sent them to an innings defeat. Now another surface was starting to break up and, according to their captain Ian Johnson, they were 'trapped on a stinker, the fellows were angry and the batting blew up.' Lock had Burke caught with the first ball after tea, then Laker struck seven more times as they slumped to 84 all out – with Jim Laker taking nine wickets for 37 runs.

According to the England captain Peter May, "The pitch was not that bad. Jim just dripped away at their nerves, realising that they had got a little obsessional about him and the wickets."

Alan Oakman was fielding at forward short leg. "Most of the Australians were back-foot players. They tended to push at the ball when they went forward. I was standing very close and, when Keith Miller came in, he said, 'If you don't look out, I'll hit you in the bollocks.' I thought, 'He's kidding me.' I wasn't wearing a box or anything. Then I thought, 'Is he?' But he just stabbed at it, and that helped it on its way to me."

Ken Mackay tried pad play, resembling in his own words 'an elephant on ice'. Richie Benaud was more adventurous, but his first big hit was caught by a solitary deep fielder.

"Jim always wanted a fielder at cow-shot corner," says his Surrey team-mate Micky Stewart, recalling the disagreements with their captain Stuart Surridge. "Sometimes, when nine, ten, eleven came in, Stuart would try to bring the fielder in. And Jim would put the ball down. 'If you want him up,' he'd say, 'somebody else can bowl.'" Thirty years later, it fell to Micky

Stewart to accompany the Laker family to The Oval with Jim's ashes. "I was coming down the steps, and I hadn't thought about where I was going to scatter them. I couldn't put them on the square – so I put them down at cow corner."

Jim Laker's name is forever bracketed with that of Tony Lock, but they were wholly different characters. Lock, excitable and demonstrative, was an aggressive cricketer while Laker, sensitive and thoughtful, was a quiet, philosophical man.

'He moved to his bowling mark with a constabular stroll,' John Arlott wrote. 'In the moment before he turned, he looked up into the sky, often with half a smile.'

"He told me how he once talked to Bobby Locke the South African golfer," Micky Stewart recalls. "Locke trained himself never to do anything in a hurry. Everything was in the same slow way: walking on the fairway, addressing the ball. 'By nature I'm quite excitable,' he said. 'I've schooled myself so that I've got total control, so I've got repetitive rhythm.' And Jim did the same. He didn't rush about."

Colin Cowdrey, writing of Laker's performance at Old Trafford, called him 'the calm destroyer': 'He was in perfect rhythm. The batsmen played and missed so often, yet you couldn't tell from his expression.'

It was a wet summer. Pitches were not covered, and there was no limit to the fielders who could stand in close on the leg side. Of the 23 bowlers who took 100 wickets, 17 were spinners, eight of them off-spinners. Apart from Jim Laker, there were Bob Appleyard, Ray Illingworth, Robin Marlar, Don Shepherd, Roy Tattersall, Fred Titmus and Bomber Wells.

It was a golden age of off-spin, but who was the greatest of them?

Ray Illingworth plumps for Bob Appleyard in his brief period of greatness. "Bob would bowl on anything and never know when he was beaten."

"Tattersall was a very good bowler," Gloucestershire's Arthur Milton says. "He had a flatter trajectory, and I couldn't use my feet to him so easily."

What about Bomber Wells, with his broad girth and one-pace run-up? Does he think Jim Laker was the best? "Well," he says, a twinkle in his eye. "It was either him or me."

"Jim was in a class of his own," Trevor Bailey says emphatically. "He was surely the finest off-spinner in the history of the game."

"Jim was a great bowler," Tom Graveney agrees. "He had a fantastic action. Beautifully balanced. And he read the batter so well. In his early days he used to lose it a bit if someone got after him. George Emmett used to say, 'Have a go at him. He won't bowl so well.' But he soon got over that."

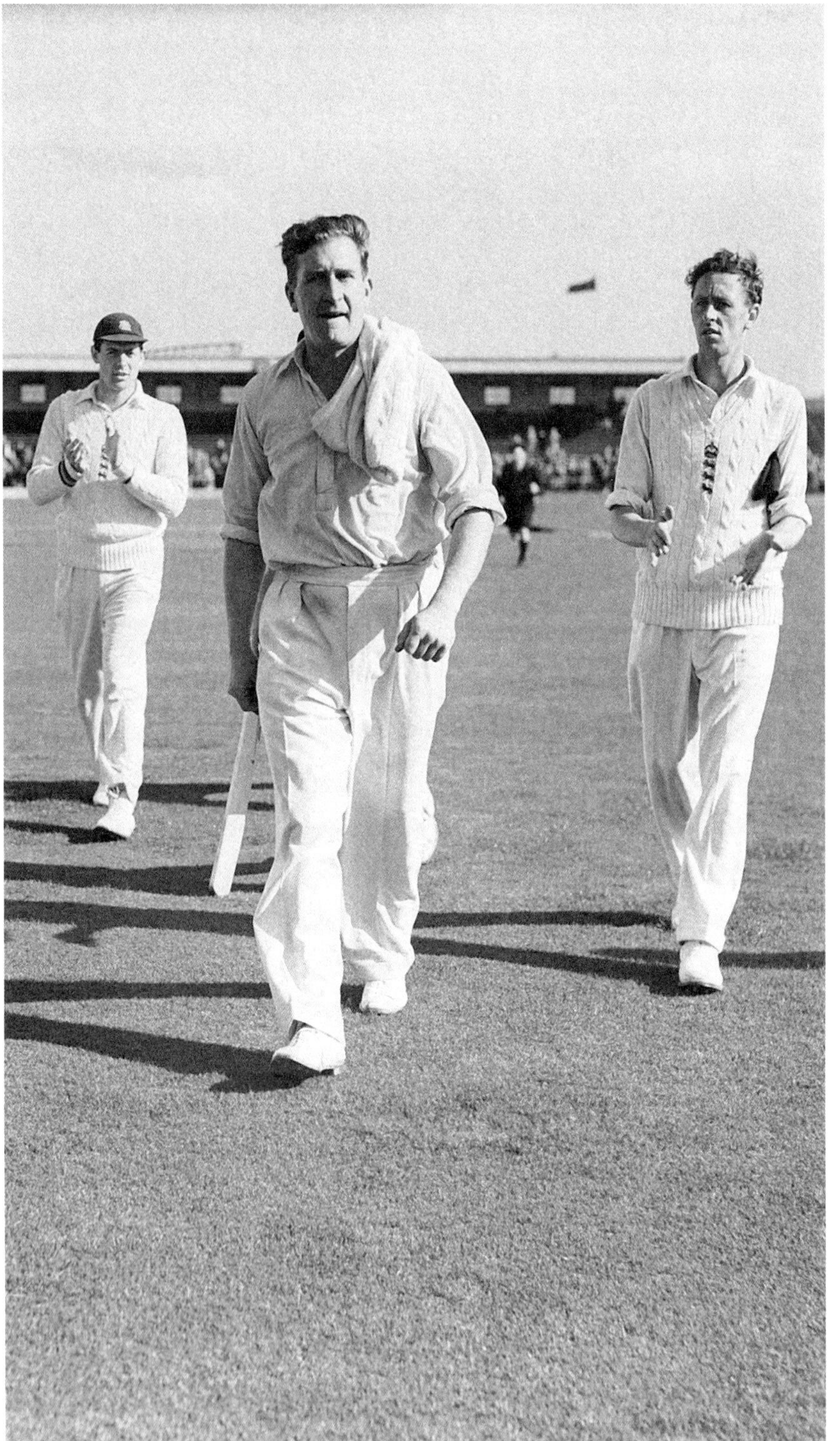

'Throughout my career,' Laker wrote, 'I never ran up to bowl without some plan in my mind.'

"I was the sacrificial lamb at forward short leg," Micky Stewart recalls. "He was so accurate that I never felt in any danger. He was the biggest spinner of the ball at that time, too. You could hear the snap of his fingers when he spun it, and on many days you could hear the whirr of the ball as it came down."

For a big spinner he was not blessed with outsize fingers, suffering throughout his career from soreness, corns and split skin that he tried to prevent by applying liberal quantities of friar's balsam.

By close on Friday at Old Trafford he had dismissed Harvey for a second duck, within two hours of the first. Then came the torrential storms. One wicket fell in nine overs on Saturday, none in 22 on Monday when EW Swanton described the ground as 'a blasted heath'. More heavy rain fell through Monday night but, against all the odds, play started only ten minutes late on the final day. On a pitch that *The Times* reckoned to be 'too saturated to be of use to anyone', McDonald and Craig survived till lunch.

Then the sun came out and wickets fell quickly, all to Jim Laker. When he had Lindwall caught in the leg trap, he became the first man to take 18 wickets in a first-class match. Then, when he trapped Maddocks lbw, he became the first to take all ten in a Test.

He slung his jersey over his shoulder and walked, as leisurely as ever, towards the pavilion.

His 19 for 90 had passed the Test record of 17 for 159, set in South Africa in 1913 by the great Sydney Barnes, who was in the Old Trafford crowd. "No beggar got all ten when I was bowling at the other end," was the old man's gruff comment as he left the ground.

Lock had bowled 69 overs in the match to Laker's 68. They had switched ends several times, and Lock had beaten the bat repeatedly. Yet he had taken only one wicket. "At the start," Alan Oakman says, "he'd been applauding Jim's wickets, but by the end you could see him just folding his arms."

To add to the indignity, Lock had been in line for a £100 prize for the season's best bowling, with ten for 54 against Kent at Blackheath, and now Laker had pipped him with ten for 53.

"Tony tried too hard," Trevor Bailey reckons. "He was closer in temperament to a fast bowler, and he bowled quicker and quicker. If Johnny Wardle had been bowling at the other end, Jim would never have got 19 wickets."

It was a match that would always haunt Lock. "We used to say to him," Glamorgan's Don Shepherd recalls with a chuckle, "'Tell us about that match at Old Trafford when you and Jim shared all those wickets.'"

Some years later, when Lock spoke to Lilly, Jim's wife, he had acquired a different perspective. "I wish I hadn't taken that one wicket," he said.

Laker was a no-fuss Yorkshireman, devoted to his wife and two girls, and he drove home that evening from Manchester to Putney, stopping in Lichfield for a sandwich and a beer. The whole pub was talking about the cricket, and the publican broke away to serve him. "Are you going far?" he asked, without much interest in the reply, then turned back to the conversation about the Test. Jim sat alone with his pint.

Next day he was at The Oval, playing for Surrey against the Australians. By the end of that match he had taken 103 wickets, of which 56 were Australians. He added seven more in the final Test.

Three winters later the Australians got their revenge, preparing pitches of no use to Laker and Lock, but even in such unhelpful conditions the off-spinner showed his class, topping the England averages.

Laker had started his working life with Barclays Bank and, after a bad day, he would occasionally say to Lilly, "I could be sitting in my own office as a bank manager." But he never meant it and, when he retired as a player, he was delighted to stay in the game as a commentator, his long silences and distinctive pronunciation (bowlin', fieldin', innin's) part of the charm of television cricket in the 1970s. One day he received a letter full of gs that the writer had cut out of the paper specially for him. On another occasion he received two letters on the same day, one full of praise, the other highly critical. "He changed them over," Lilly recalls, "put them in envelopes and sent them back."

By this time spin bowling was no longer at the centre of the English game. "I retired in 1972," Micky Stewart says, "and I came back as Surrey manager in 1979. And, when I came back, I noticed a huge difference in the knowledge of spin: the bowling, teaching, captaining and coaching of it. And every year that's gone by since, there's been a further decline."

That Old Trafford Test was the high point of English spin and, to commemorate its 50th anniversary, a foundation is being established to encourage young spinners – with an annual award, the Laker Spin Scholarship. In honour of a master craftsman – a thinking cricketer who, in his own words, got "more satisfaction out of seeing a bail drop off than a fast bowler blasting the stumps out of the ground."

"Jim had everything you look for in an off-spinner," Don Shepherd reckons. "He was a big lad. He had a lovely action. He spun it, he had flight, he had change of pace and he could bowl round the wicket, too. If you're going to be an off-spinner, you'd want to be like Jim Laker."

## 62. Football's strangest match

*Charlton Athletic versus Huddersfield Town* THE TIMES, 17 DEC 2007

Saturday 21 December 1957. There was drizzle in the cold London air as Huddersfield Town prepared to take the field at Charlton's Valley ground. The Yorkshire side, like their London hosts, had not long been relegated from Division One and, under their ambitious manager Bill Shankly, they were keen to return to the top flight.

Shankly's dressing-room talk was simple, as the Town right-half, Yorkshire cricketer Ken Taylor, recalls. "Bill just walked around the table, telling us how good we were. 'Charlton? They're not fit to be on the same park.' He was a great motivator. That was his greatest quality."

The 17-year-old Denis Law, resting a thigh injury, watched the match alongside Shankly. After 17 minutes his replacement, Stan Howard, challenged strongly for a loose ball, and Charlton centre-half Derek Ufton dislocated his problem shoulder. With no substitutes allowed, his team-mates were left to play with ten men. By half-time they were 2-0 down.

Charlton regrouped in their dressing room. Their left-winger Johnny Summers, a left-footed goal-scorer going through a lean patch, was switched to centre-forward. He put on a new pair of boots, not fully broken in, and after three minutes he mis-hit a close-range shot with his weaker right foot and made it 2-1.

Gaps opened up, the pitch was muddy and, by the time the second half was 17 minutes old, the score had become 5-1. According to Law, "Shanks was full of what a bad side they were and how we were going to rub it in."

Ray Wilson, the World Cup winner, was at left back for Huddersfield. "Later, when I moved to Everton, if we were ever two or three in front, the other side might as well have gone off, because we just used to keep the ball. But at Charlton we were 5-1 up, and we were still having a go! That was Shankly for you."

Within two minutes it was 5-3. First, Buck Ryan scored. Then Summers, again with his right foot, this time off a post. Ten minutes later he completed his hat-trick, blasting a right-footed shot past the diving Town goalkeeper Sandy Kennon. 5-4.

"Sandy was a showman," Ken Taylor remembers. "A great lad, but he liked to turn easy saves into slightly more difficult ones by moving to one side and diving at the ball."

Five minutes later Summers drove in the equaliser. Then in the 81st minute, with the Town defence slithering in the mud and the Charlton spectators in pandemonium, Summers hit the ball once more towards goal. It took a deflection and rolled through Kennon's outstretched legs. Summers had scored five goals, all with his weaker foot.

Bewildered, he told reporters, "I'll keep these boots for the rest of my life." Alas, falling victim to leukaemia, he was dead within five years.

"He was an easy-going, happy-go-lucky sort of boy," his team-mate John Hewie recalls. "When the game finished, they put him in a car and rushed him up to the BBC."

Ten-man Charlton, from 5-1 down, had scored five goals in 19 minutes.

"If you wrote a book about that match," Ray Wilson reckons, "you'd get halfway through and you'd say, 'What a load of bollocks!'"

Yet it was not over. In the 86th minute the ball was punted towards the Charlton goal and, with Howard running towards it, Hewie attempted to side-foot it out of his path. "The ball skidded, I stretched and I could only toe-poke it. And it went into the net." 6-6.

The match neared its end. A throw-in was taken just inside the Huddersfield half.

"For pity's sake, referee," a spectator called out. "Blow the whistle!"

The ball travelled across the field. The Town right-back Conwell moved through the mud to intercept it. "He had it all nicely covered," Ken Taylor sighs, "and he just slipped. He fell. BANG! And that was it."

Kennon came out, Ryan shot and the keeper's attempt to divert the ball merely sent it up in the air, over his head and into the net.

Charlton 7 Huddersfield 6. The crowd would not leave, chanting Summers' name as if he had won them the FA Cup.

No team in the history of the league, before or since, has scored six goals and lost.

"Shankly was pacing up and down in the train," Ray Wilson recalls. "He was muttering to himself, 'It's just one of those things .... It's history ...' He was trying to sort it out in his mind, how it had happened."

"He didn't speak to anybody for days afterwards," Ken Taylor says. "We had a good side. But when you played in muddy conditions like that, all sorts of things could happen. In many ways football wasn't as skilful a game as it is now, but it could be more exciting."

**Teams**

*Charlton Athletic:* Duff; Edwards, Townsend; Hewie, Ufton, Kiernan; White, Lucas, Ryan, Leary, Summers.
*Huddersfield Town:* Kennon; Conwell, Wilson; Taylor, Connor, McGarry; Ledger, Howard, Bain, Massie, Simpson.

*Sandy Kennon catches a cross*
*The Valley, December 1957*

*The cricketer in winter.*

## 63. Called

*Derek Pearson of Worcestershire* TWC, Sept 2008

It was a sunny morning in late April 1959. Worcester Cathedral looked down on the traditional season-opener: the county against the summer's tourists. In deck chairs and on seats 2,500 spectators watched quietly as the Indian openers, Roy and Contractor, grafted 34 runs in 70 minutes. Then suddenly at 12.40 the calm was shattered.

The 22-year-old fast bowler Derek Pearson, running in 15 paces, sent down the third ball of his third over, and from umpire Syd Buller at square leg came the cry, "No ball."

Derek Pearson's action had been questioned on his championship debut five years earlier, when the umpires had removed him after three overs, but he had spent time at Alf Gover's school in South London and there had been no further problems. "I knew I had an unusual action," he says now. "But people said it was OK. I certainly never thought I threw."

By the start of 1959 his prospects were bright. He was genuinely quick according to the Worcester keeper Roy Booth: "We had Jack Flavell who was among the fastest in the country, and Derek was a little quicker than Jack when he let himself go."

"I wasn't as accurate," Derek admits, "but I loved bowling fast. I took great pleasure from the energy of it." He was a quiet, thoughtful man, the church-goer in the side, but he had no inhibitions when he bowled. "I knocked Bernie Constable's hat off once, and I turned the South African Roy McLean's metal box inside out. He had to retire for a while. There's something unique about a fast bowler tearing up and sending the wickets flying. Or getting the batsman ducking. It's exciting; it's a bit of theatre. If I'd managed to get the control, I'd have stood a good chance of playing for England."

That aspiration died in an instant as Buller raised his right arm. The previous winter a strong England side had lost 4-0 in Australia, a tour bedevilled by controversy about 'chucking'. Unknown to the young Derek Pearson, MCC had drawn up a list of 'bowlers with doubtful actions' and instructed the umpires to show extra vigilance. 'If the umpire be not entirely satisfied,' the law read, and Buller was not satisfied.

"There were some umpires you could have a chat and a giggle with. Others you wouldn't, and Syd was one you wouldn't. He was a nice man. But he was very reserved, very serious."

When the hubbub died down, Derek Pearson ran in again. This time there was no cry from square leg, the ball lifted sharply and Contractor – also unsettled by the fuss – nibbled a catch to Booth. Another no ball followed before the over was out, and in his next over Derek trapped

Pankaj Roy lbw. In all there were five calls of no ball, the fourth of which hit Manjrekar's stumps and ran away to the boundary.

After lunch he was switched to Buller's end and, with a photographer capturing stills of his action, the gentler Emrys Davies remained silent at square leg.

'A respected Army cricketer,' *The Times* reported, 'held that Pearson's arm was as straight as if he had been launching a grenade.'

That summer Derek took 79 wickets and won his county cap, but he never recovered from that morning. He was no-balled on another two occasions, and he tried once more to reconstruct his action. "I could see that, if I was very careful, I could muscle through – but the bit I loved so much, the real pace, was finished. I started to be so conscious of my arm, and I cut my run-up to seven paces. Being a professional cricketer had a lot of kudos, but in the end I bought out my contract."

The purge of bowling actions continued. Between 1909 and 1951 not one bowler had been no-balled for throwing in English first-class cricket, but from 1959 to 1966 twelve were, most notably the South African Geoff Griffin, called eleven times by Frank Lee in the Lord's Test of 1960, and Derbyshire's Harold Rhodes, called controversially by Buller when close to an England recall in 1965.

"Syd Buller did what he thought was right," Derek says, "but he was a worrier. His wife reckoned it caused him an early death."

By 1961 Derek Pearson was on his way out, starting a career in the probation service in which he became a national expert in divorce court liaison work. His German wife had no interest in cricket, and for forty years he left the game behind. Now, however, he goes to the old players' reunions, and he wonders if somewhere there is film of his bowling.

"I can't think of any other sport where you can be fouled to such an extent that you can lose everything you had. But perhaps it did me a favour. Instead of scratching around as an OK cricketer, living an extended adolescence, I got down to a proper job."

*Derek Pearson and Syd Buller on the fateful day.*

## 64. After the batsmen ...

*Peter Smith of Essex* TWC, Feb 2005

When Peter Smith volunteered himself for an Essex trial in 1929, he was a 20-year-old batsman for Chelmsford, looking to while away the summer before a life of adventure in the Rhodesian Mounted Police.

In the nets his batting made no impression, and he was asked to keep wicket. Then he was shown how to bowl leg-breaks, and somehow by July he was bowling them in the county side. In five matches his only wicket, taken with a high full-toss, cost 233 runs, but the county persevered. 'A slow bowler of considerable individuality,' *The Cricketer* called him.

He played four times for England – though his first cap was a long time coming. In 1933 he was called out of a cinema and given a telegram telling him to report to The Oval to play the West Indies, only to find on arrival that it was a hoax. Six years later the call-up, for a tour of India, was genuine but war intervened and he ended up as an officer in the Middle East.

When he returned to Essex in 1946, only he and his cousin Ray were left of the pre-war bowlers. Now nearly 38, he finally won his England cap but, touring Australia that winter, he developed appendicitis and did not impress. So in 1947 he was giving his all to Essex once more.

Together that summer the cousins bowled 3,163 overs. Ray would swing the new ball, then put on his cap and send down off-breaks, while Peter would amble in hour after hour with his leg-spin.

"With his military moustache and bearing," team-mate Dickie Dodds says, "he looked like a major in the Indian army."

"He spun the ball considerably," Doug Insole remembers, "and his high arm action helped him to bowl a ball which dipped into the batsman late."

Ray and Peter Smith. There were no delays when they were in tandem, so much so that once at Leicester Essex got through 148 overs in six hours. Captain Tom Pearce's only idea for a bowling change, they say, was to get the Smiths to switch ends.

But if the bowling lacked depth, not so the batting which stretched all the way from one to eleven – never more famously than at Chesterfield in August 1947. Of the eleven that day, only Ray Smith at number ten had not scored a first-class century – and he would soon put that right, three times in the next eight years hitting the fastest century of the summer.

The Chesterfield pitch was typically green and Derbyshire, third in the table, grafted their way to 223. Then their trio of England seamers – Copson, Pope and Gladwin – reduced Essex to 65 for six.

Only Frank Vigar of the top order remained. A swarthy man of Cornish descent, he was a gangly batsman, but he had a formidable tail to keep him company: the youngsters Bailey and Insole, and the two Smiths. With Bailey, he took the score to 104; with Insole, to 160.

"After the batsmen," the Smiths would say, "come the run-getters."

"I remember how livid I was at getting out," Doug Insole says. "I'd scored 48, and I don't think I'd ever played better. They were bowling in-swingers, which for me were like oats to a donkey, and they were starting to get a bit tired. Ray Smith came in after me and banged a few. He was a magnificent hitter."

Next morning, when Ray Smith was caught, it was 199 for nine, and in came cousin Peter, fresh from a pair at Chelmsford.

"He was a good player of medium and slow bowling," Doug says, "but he wasn't the bravest if the ball was round his ear-hole. Chesterfield was quite a bouncy wicket, and Bill Copson was fairly quick. Peter was retreating and giving it the old wave, and the ball would go over the slips. And in between he'd hit some very good blows."

He took 12 off one Copson over, then – when the slow left-armer Eric Marsh replaced him – he thrashed him for 22.

'He may seem uncertain as a bat,' *The Cricketer* wrote, 'but he is a punishing one if permitted to remain at the wicket.' And he was still at the wicket after lunch, reaching his century in 105 minutes with a straight drive off the ageing seamer Stan Worthington. "I've never seen Derbyshire bowlers look so discomfited," Trevor Bailey says.

"It was enormous fun," Doug recalls, "but it wasn't dramatic. Just a tremendous turnaround. At 65 for six we thought we'd had it. Now we could see ourselves winning."

According to the local paper, Peter Smith was 'punishing all the demoralised Derbyshire bowlers relentlessly,' and he brought up his 150 with 'a mighty six' off Copson. Frank Vigar had been on 60 at the start of their stand, and he had reached 114 when Peter Smith was finally bowled for 163.

It remains the highest score made by a number eleven in first-class cricket.

In the second innings the Smiths bowled 71 overs, and Essex won by five wickets. The next day at Clacton Peter took eight for 98 in 50 more overs. The young batsman killing time before a career in the Rhodesian Mounted Police went on to become the greatest wicket-taker in Essex's history.

His 1,610 wickets for the county included four the following May at Southend when the Australians broke all records, hitting 721 runs in the day. In the words of Bill O'Reilly, 'it was a full-scale jollification at the expense of an attack, which was completely incapable of self-defence.' Amid the carnage Ray Smith took two wickets for 169, cousin Peter four for 193.

'Heigh-ho, it's a great game,' Peter wrote. 'On top of the world one day; the next you feel so low that you could sit on a cigarette card and swing your legs.'

## 65. The end of a long tour

*Sydney, Weds 17 Feb 1971, with Ray Illingworth* THE TIMES, 4 DEC 2006

"I liked playing at Sydney," Ray Illingworth says. "There was always something in the pitch for the bowlers, and you knew you were going to finish the game naturally. And that's the best type of cricket. It was a wonderful ground, the right size, with a lovely stand, and you could have a bit of fun with The Hill. But you couldn't let them get on top of you."

At Sydney in February 1971 Ray Illingworth played the most important match of his long career. The last Test of the series, with England 1-0 up. Win it, and he would follow his boyhood idol Len Hutton into the history books, only the second England captain since the war to win in Australia.

"It was a wonderful game of cricket," he says. "At several points it could have gone either way."

With the sun shining after days of heavy rain, the toss was crucial. Ray lost it and Ian Chappell, in his first Test in charge, invited him to bat. Boycott, the star of the series, was nursing a broken arm, and the batting conditions were so difficult that Illingworth was stepping out – 'to the rowdy clanking of beer cans' – at 69 for four. His top-scoring 42 helped the total to 184, but that suddenly seemed less inadequate when, in the last half hour, Snow and Lever sent back the Australian openers.

"It was a different pitch the next day and, if we hadn't taken those two wickets, I think they'd have got too far away from us."

The tension built on the second day, overspilling in the evening when John Snow, with a shortish ball, hit the ducking Terry Jenner on the head and The Hill responded by showering Snow with cans and bottles. Ray Illingworth gathered his men into the middle and, when the trouble flared a second time, he led them off into the pavilion.

A long tour had come to crisis point. For the first time the schedule had included six Tests and, when rain washed away the Melbourne match, the MCC manager David Clark – keen to spread goodwill – agreed to play the first one-day international and to add an extra Test, a seventh, in the break between the fourth and fifth.

"We were playing Test after Test in the hottest two months of the year. We were very tired, and we were having to go to Lord Mayor's parlours and the like, even once on the first morning of a Test. And you do get a siege mentality. It's difficult not to. We didn't get one lbw decision from the umpires in the whole series."

After a few minutes the crowd calmed down, and Ray Illingworth's men reappeared. The Australians established a lead of 80 and, with England battling their way to 302, the home team were left to score 223 for victory.

"We really wanted another 50 runs, but we batted well and it did give us a chance."

John Snow soon struck, removing the debutant Eastwood, but disaster followed when, attempting a swirling catch in the deep, he impaled his hand on a picket and retired with a bone jutting through the skin of his finger. No Boycott, no Snow. In the words of John Woodcock in *The Times*, 'If ever this Australian side were to win a game, this surely was the time.'

Peter Lever had Ian Chappell caught behind, but Stackpole – 'playing some rich strokes' – and Redpath took the score forward. Then Ray Illingworth came on, his eleven eight-ball overs his longest spell of the tour, and he removed them both. "Peter Lever said to me, 'You haven't bowled much, I wasn't sure you could do it.' But I'd bowled that much in my career that, to be honest, I could nearly bowl with my eyes shut. And I knew it."

Australia ended the day on 123 for five. They wanted 100 runs to win, with Greg Chappell and Rodney Marsh the not-out batsmen, and the journalists divided over who was the stronger placed.

Brian Luckhurst admitted in later life that, despite taking sleeping tablets, he had lain awake all night. "I was a good fielder, but such was the tension that morning that, when we went out, I found myself almost willing the ball not to come to me."

"We had a chap called Max who used to pick us up in the morning in his car," Ray recalls, "and I said to him, 'I hope the Old Boy up there is on our side today. We might just need a little bit of luck. Otherwise it's been four and a half months of hard work for nothing.'"

Only eight runs had been added when Underwood bowled Marsh. Then, after 50 minutes of rising tension, Ray Illingworth – in his best spell of the series – drifted his floater past Chappell and Alan Knott completed the vital stumping. "After that," Ray says, "I felt we would be all right."

The remaining wickets followed quickly so that by half past twelve the England players were chairing their captain off the field. England had not only won the Ashes in Australia but, for the only time since the days of three-match series in the 1880s, they had done so without losing a Test.

The next day they flew to New Zealand to play two more Tests, and Ray was brought down with a bump by his manager.

"David Clark was a nice fellow but he was besotted with the old MCC ways and, to save money, he decided we couldn't take our equipment with us. We had to go with a team bag, with five bats and five pairs of pads. 'Bloody hell,' I said, 'We're back playing Sunday School cricket here.'"

But Ray knew that his team, a team of strong characters, had won its place in history. "It was a wonderful tour. I like Australians; in many ways they're like Yorkshiremen. Frustrated Yorkshiremen perhaps. But on the field you've got to be as hard as them. Or they'll destroy you."

## 66. Where did it all go?

*Basil Bridge of Warwickshire* TWC, DEC 2005

"When you're bowling well," the Warwickshire off-spinner Basil Bridge says, "you don't think about it. You just come up and bowl."

All through the summer of 1961 the 23-year-old Bridge – with his distinctive quiff of hair – 'came up and bowled'. So successful was he that, on the first of August, at the Millfield School ground in Street, when he trapped Bill Alley lbw for one, he found himself being congratulated by team-mate Tom Cartwright.

"He was shaking my hand, and I was thinking, 'What's all this about?'"

Alley was the batsman of that summer, on his way to 3,000 runs, but the handshake was for more than that one victim. Basil Bridge had taken 100 wickets, the first slow bowler in the country to reach the figure – and that was despite missing two games with a stomach strain and despite having to bowl on the unhelpful Edgbaston pitch.

"He had a genuine talent," Tom Cartwright says. "He bowled out good players. We hadn't had a top-class off-spinner and I think we all thought, 'Here's somebody for a long time.' He was still young. It was going to be another eight or nine years before he was at his best."

Basil, a local boy from Balsall Heath, had been discovered by Patsy Hendren at Butlin's Holiday Camp in Filey, where *The People* newspaper were running a Find A Young Cricketer week. He was a 14-year-old batsman, dreaming of becoming the next Don Bradman, but – under the expert eye of Edgbaston's veteran 'Tiger' Smith – he was soon flighting off-breaks. "Keep it up there all the time," the old man would growl. "If you've got your field set right, you've got a chance of getting them out."

After National Service he was ready for first team cricket, and in his second championship match of 1959 he found himself bowling on "a ploughed field" at Stroud and taking eight for 66 in the Gloucestershire second innings. He finished that summer with 85 wickets, but in 1961 he topped that with 123 and set off to do a winter's coaching in South Africa.

Nobody could have guessed what would follow the next May. By the third match he was bowling head-high full-tosses and balls that rolled along the ground. He stayed on the staff for four more years, but he took just two championship wickets.

"It was a nightmare," he says. "I didn't know why it was happening."

His stomach pains had intensified, and later in that summer of 1962 the doctors discovered a haematoma, a blood clot in the muscle. "I'd had the pain on and off for at least three years. I remember coming off the field against the Indians in 1959 and being told that I should be out there bowling. All they ever did was give me heat treatment and massages. Now you'd get sent for a scan straightaway. The surgeon, who removed it, said it was the size of an orange. I'm sure that's what started my problems. It only became psychological later."

Others are not so certain, pointing to his father's death at the end of the 1961 season and his subsequent trip to South Africa. "He was a shy, introverted boy when he went out there," Tom Cartwright, a fellow passenger on the *Windsor Castle*, says. "And I think he felt he had to become an extrovert. A change like that is bound to have a bearing on how you do your job."

At Warwickshire's expense Basil Bridge found himself lying on a psychiatrist's couch, even at one stage being asked if he would mind being seen by a hypnotist attached to the New Zealand touring team.

"Next thing I know I'm in an office, and my arms are up in the air."

Then there were the technical suggestions: people trying to shorten his delivery stride or get him to run in just two yards. His team-mate Norman Horner had a bit of film of his bowling that day at Millfield, and they watched it together, trying to make out what his action had been.

"But you can't run up to bowl, thinking you've got to put one foot here, one foot there. Bowling is a natural thing, and I didn't know if I was coming or going. At the finish Tiger said, 'You can forget it. You've lost all your natural ability.'"

"It was a tragedy to watch it happen," Tom Cartwright says. "Wrenching. He was such a nice kid, and it was a romantic story: how he'd come through from Butlin's and had so much success. It was in people's minds that he'd go on and play for England."

Basil Bridge became a batsman, playing till 60 at Studley where he still looks after the square. He is a popular figure at the Warwickshire Old Players' reunions, and he treasures the cuttings of his brief spell of glory.

"But I couldn't tell you now," he says, "I couldn't even dream about how I used to bowl. The whole thing has gone."

## 67. Method in everything he did

*Herbert Sutcliffe of Yorkshire and England* TWC, July 2005

Woodlands. A grand mill-owner's house, built of stone and set in several acres of land. With a tennis court, an orchard and a stable block. High above Pudsey.

Here in the 1930s lived Herbert Sutcliffe, the orphan who had grown up with strict Congregationalist aunts above the bakery down in Robin Lane, who had started his working life at 13 as an apprentice boot-maker and who had risen through cricket and through his sports outfitting business to a social standing unknown to previous generations of paid cricketers.

'He gave to professional cricketers,' Jim Kilburn wrote, 'the same sort of status that Henry Cotton gave to professional golfers.'

"Everything had to be done to the highest standard," his daughter Barbara recalls. "He dressed immaculately, and he didn't like anything out of place. He bred pedigree boxer dogs, and he often sat with them in the evening in his office, doing his books for the shop, all in his beautiful handwriting."

He coached her younger brother Bill on a concrete pitch in the garden, together with some of the local boys. Roland Parker was one, and he remembers the magic of those sessions.

"Herbert was Pudsey's hero, the most popular man in Yorkshire, and he was very encouraging to us, showed us all how to play straight. Although he was a wonderful hooker, he was also a great straight player."

Bill, who was sent to Rydal School, captained Yorkshire as an amateur for two years in the 1950s, but he never quite coped with his father's overbearing presence. Barbara, by contrast, was a free-spirited girl, who suffered no such pressure. "I was a tomboy. I used to climb trees, and I was never tidy. But he accepted me for what I was, which was marvellous. We only ever argued once. There were two lovely trees on the lawn in front of the house, a weeping willow and an ash, and he had them cut down."

Herbert Sutcliffe was a self-made man, ambitious and thorough, and, according to his England partner Jack Hobbs, he turned himself from 'an ordinary speaker' into 'a wonderful orator'. Hobbs, the son of a college servant at Cambridge, was a different character, always deferential to his social superiors, while Sutcliffe broke barriers, acquiring the vowels of the amateurs and calling them by their Christian names. He exuded confidence, and he made it his mission to raise the standing of his profession. At Yorkshire he demanded as much from his younger team-mates. "Make sure your manners and bearing are better than those of the amateurs," he told them. "Remember that you are representing Yorkshire, not just yourself."

As a batsman he had three great shots: an off-drive, a back-foot push behind point and a fearless hook. 'There was method in everything he did,' his Yorkshire team-mate Bill Bowes wrote, describing how if there were two men back for the hook he would only take it on when he had 40 on the board. "By that time," he reckoned, "I've so much confidence I think I can miss them both." On such days he could be an electrifying sight. At Scarborough in 1932 he took on the Essex fast men, Farnes and Nichols, and he raced from 100 to 182 in 20 minutes.

He was also the master of the quick single. He opened with Derbyshire's Denis Smith against the Indians in a Festival match. 'If he was my regular partner,' Smith said, 'I'd average another 15 runs an innings.'

When he was out, he would return to the dressing room with not a hair out of place. 'The sort of man who would rather miss a train than run for it,' Robertson-Glasgow called him. After a wash and rub down, Bowes wrote, 'he would dress methodically, then produce a writing case and sit down to ten or fifteen letters.' Always a good team man, he would look up from time to time: 'How are we doing?'

If ever there was a cricketer for a big occasion, it was Herbert Sutcliffe. In a career that spanned the 21 years between the wars, he scored 50,138 runs at an average of 51.95. But in Tests he averaged 60.73, higher than any other Englishman, and in Ashes Tests his 66.85 is second only to Bradman among the major batsmen.

Len Hutton thought he had a higher level of concentration than any other player he knew, while to Bradman 'he had the best temperament of any cricketer I ever played with or against.'

His greatest innings was at Melbourne in January 1929. He and Hobbs set out in search of 332 for victory, on a 'sticky dog'. In his book, *'For England and Yorkshire'*, painstakingly written in long-hand by himself, he wrote of the wicket as a nightmare: 'It was so bad that before we went out for the tricky 25 minutes before lunch we were told by everyone (good judges, as well) that England would do well to score 90 runs on it.'

In the event, Sutcliffe was not dismissed till the following afternoon, scoring 135 out of 318 for four, and the Ashes were won a few minutes later. 'For many a day afterwards,' he wrote, 'I carried the marks of the ball which did such fearsome tricks on that rain-affected wicket.'

But, if that was his greatest innings, his most memorable remained the one at The Oval in 1926. Not since 1912 had England won the Ashes, and they reached the final Test all square. On Monday evening Hobbs and Sutcliffe had put on 49, to give England a second innings lead of 22 going into the third day. There was every hope of victory – till a tropical rainstorm broke over London in the small hours.

Tuesday 17 August 1926. 'What Hobbs and Sutcliffe achieved that day,' Sir Pelham Warner wrote, 'will be talked of as long as cricket is played.'

Len Hutton, then a boy of ten, was still writing about it sixty years later: 'If I could be granted one wish, I would be tempted to ask for a rerun of their famous stand. Wilfred Rhodes, who played in the match at the age of 48, used to talk about it with a faraway look in his eyes.'

Hobbs and Sutcliffe returned to the middle on Tuesday morning to find a pitch growing ever more treacherous as the sun broke through.

"Jolly bad luck, that rain," Hobbs said to his partner as they patted down the surface after the first over. "It's cooked our chances."

"Yes, it is hard luck," the umpire 'Sailor' Young agreed.

'The Australians were on tiptoe,' Hobbs wrote, 'and should have got many of us out before lunch.'

But somehow the pair survived into the afternoon. At one stage, surrounded by several short legs, Sutcliffe played out eight maidens from the off-spinner Arthur Richardson, with *The Times* reckoning that 'every ball cut out a little fid of turf as it pitched.'

'I was the happiest man on the ground to know I was still there,' he said.

The score was 172 when Hobbs was bowled for 100, but Sutcliffe did not follow till the day's last over, when he had reached 161. *The Times* marvelled at 'the graceful solidity of his defence, his subordination of self to side, and his almost uncanny wisdom.' But, according to Neville

Cardus, 'he smote his pads in open disgust, outraged that he, of all men, should be bowled a few minutes before the close.'

England took their total to 436 the next morning. Then, in front of Prime Minister Stanley Baldwin and the King of Iraq, they bowled out Australia for 125, with the veteran Rhodes – recalled after a five-year absence – taking four for 44.

Not since the War had England won an Ashes series, and the country was still suffering the after-shocks of the General Strike. So the vast crowd in front of the pavilion cheered themselves hoarse. "We want Hobbs," they chanted. "We want Sutcliffe."

Pelham Warner in *The Cricketer* was full of the significance of the moment: 'Had we been beaten, despondency would have crept over the land. As it is, our cricket will be fortified and refreshed.'

'Sutcliffe was cool beyond disturbance,' John Arlott wrote later of his match-winning innings. 'He was the master of survival and the ultimate pragmatist.'

Or, as Sutcliffe himself put it to the editor of *The Cricketer*, "Yes, Mr Warner, I love a dog fight."

At Woodlands, high above Pudsey, he enjoyed the fruits of his labour. He still attended the Congregationalist church, where the family sat in the cold through long sermons, and he did much to develop the young Len Hutton, also of Pudsey. "I'm only setting up these records for Hutton to break them," he once said.

'He was not born to greatness,' Neville Cardus wrote. 'He achieved greatness. His wasn't a triumph of skill only, it was a finer triumph, a triumph of character, application, will-power.'

'A personality as dependable as fallible human nature will allow,' AA Thomson called him.

But, beneath his well-cultivated exterior and his self-discipline, did there lurk a freer spirit?

Barbara still talks of him as "a very jolly person, with a great sense of humour, a wonderful father." Her childhood at Woodlands was a happy one, and he was proud of her success as a teacher.

He died in January 1978, at the age of 83.

"We'd only ever quarrelled once, about anything, and I can still remember his last words to me before he died. His very last words to me. 'I should never have felled those trees.'"

## 68. Always in the game

*Trevor Bailey of Essex and England* TWC, Nov 2003

Sabina Park, Jamaica. March 1954. England were 2-1 down going into the last Test, and the pitch looked a dream for batting. "Bat first, and you should make 700," the groundsman told Len Hutton and, with Brian Statham unfit, the England captain opted for a team with only two seamers, Fred Trueman and Trevor Bailey.

"Our only hope was to bat," Trevor recalls, "then bowl them out with spinners. And Len lost the toss. I've never seen him more depressed."

"Which end do you want?" the captain asked him as they took the field.

"Well, obviously, with Fred at the other end, I had to bowl into the wind – and that meant the cross-wind was going the wrong way for me. But it was just one of those dream days. Everything seemed to go right."

After 40 minutes West Indies were 13 for four, and Bailey had taken three of them: Holt, Stollmeyer and the prize scalp of Everton Weekes. Then in the afternoon he added another four as West Indies were dismissed for just 139.

The England team formed two lines, and Bailey – with seven for 34 – walked between their clapping. Ten minutes later, he was walking back the other way with Len Hutton, taking the score to 17 for no wicket at the close.

"That wasn't a bad day," he says with smiling under-statement.

'Unlike too many English players,' Len Hutton wrote, 'Trevor was able to play to the maximum of his ability on the big occasions.'

The next morning, enduring several blows, Bailey grafted a painstaking 23 before becoming the first Test victim of the 17-year-old Garry Sobers. In the judgment of EW Swanton, he was 'only a makeshift opener', but he had played a true all-rounder's part in setting England on the way to victory.

Fifteen years earlier his prep school headmaster, the Essex captain Denys Wilcox, had tried to persuade him to give up bowling – "He told me that I wasn't big or strong enough to be a fast bowler and that I should concentrate on my batting" – but he rejected the advice: "I loved bowling. And being an all-rounder suited me. I was always in the game. I wanted to bat like Bradman, bowl like Larwood. Straightforward. Simple."

It was his fast bowling that got him into the Dulwich school team at the age of 14: "Seeing my name on the team sheet for the first time, that was the greatest moment in my whole career. Undoubtedly. I was sitting in class, and I put my hand up to be excused. Just to see it again."

It was his bowling, too, that got him into the England team in 1949, where he took six wickets in the first innings. "I don't remember much about that. Only that I took my wife to Harrogate on the Sunday, to the seaside. When we got off the bus, I was looking for the people with buckets and spades, to follow them."

But it was his batting that made him a national hero, starting with the all-day partnership with Willie Watson that defied the Australians at Lord's in 1953. Originally a free-scoring player, he came to be the Barnacle, a man with an impeccable forward defensive. "It became part and parcel of me. Like the singer with his top hat. 'Give me the moonlight, give me the girl.' People expected it of me."

In South Africa in 1956/57 he topped the bowling averages, and he opened the batting all series. In 61 Tests he scored 2,290 runs at an average of 29.74, and he took 132 wickets. Until Ian Botham emerged, he was the only Test-class all-rounder that England produced in the post-war era.

Now he thinks that we might be seeing the emergence of a third. "I saw Flintoff get a hundred five years ago, and he looked very good indeed. He's very, very talented. I fancy he will make it. I may be wrong. I hope I'm not."

So why have there only been the three of them?

"It's a hard life for an all-rounder in county cricket. If you want a Test quality all-rounder, assuming he's a seam bowler, he's got to be opening the attack for his county. As a batsman he's got to be in the first four or five. And if he's a spinner, he's got to be the number one spinner.

"Ray Illingworth was pretty good, but he played for a county where he wasn't required to score quite as many runs as he would have been at a weaker county. And the boy Ben Hollioake, if he had played for Essex or Leicester, he might well have become an England all-rounder. He'd have come in at five or six, and his runs would have been needed. But Surrey will never produce all-rounders on their wicket."

With Essex he was always in the game. They were the only side in 1948 to bowl the Australians out in a day: "They got 721. Tom Pearce was captain. He had a pre-war approach. The idea was to get the opposition out, not to stop them scoring."

He took all ten wickets against Lancashire at Clacton: "And we lost by ten wickets." And now he has received a booklet from a statistician, setting out that he did the double of 1,000 runs and 100 wickets at both Southchurch and Chalkwell Parks. "I'm the only cricketer to do it on two grounds in the same town," he boasts.

Did the 14-year-old boy who wanted to be Bradman and Larwood expect all this? "Not quite like that. Not as it occurred."

And if he were 14 now, who would he want to bat and bowl like?

A smile comes across his face as he thinks. His 80th birthday approaches, but his enthusiasm for the game has not dimmed.

"Bowl like McGrath. Bat like Mark Waugh."

# 69. Wickets amid the bull's blood

*Brian Langford of Somerset* TWC, March 2005

Perhaps at another county Brian Langford would have waited longer for his chance. But in 1953 Somerset were at rock bottom, so short of players that they called on the services of 16 amateurs that summer. Sooner or later the fair-haired 17-year-old from Bridgwater was sure to have to make up numbers.

He had joined the ground staff the previous summer as an opening batsman who bowled medium-pace, and coach Harry Parks – after a brief experiment with leg breaks – had turned him into an off-spinner. Then he spent the winter with his fellow colt John Harris: "We had to weed the whole ground by hand. It took us about two weeks."

On Friday 5 June 1953 he was told to catch the train to Bath the next morning. "I thought I was going to be twelfth man. If I'd known I was going to be playing, I probably wouldn't have slept that night."

The rest of the Somerset team were much older men. As a lad on the ground staff he knocked on their dressing room door and ran errands. In fact, it was only three or four years since he had been queuing to collect their autographs: "Maurice Tremlett wasn't an easy one to get." Now he was playing alongside them, against a strong Lancashire side.

"Ben Brocklehurst was the Somerset captain. Not the greatest player but a nice man, a farmer. He turned up at The Oval one time in his scruffy, old Land Rover, and they wouldn't let him in. I think they thought he'd come to empty the bins."

It was the veteran Bertie Buse's benefit match, the first game to be played on the newly relaid square at the Bath Rec, and it was a disaster. The turfs had not knitted together, the top was unstable and, with Somerset losing by an innings at 5.30 on the first day, the newcomer's memories are a blur.

"It all happened so fast. I think I faced an over from Brian Statham. I wasn't used to that sort of pace, and I don't think I got a bat on one of them. …Running up to bowl for the first time was quite frightening, but I had Statham caught at short mid-off."

With bowling figures of three overs, one for 18, it was an unremarkable debut, but he remained in the team for Wednesday's match against Kent.

"We stayed up in Bath. At the Argyle Hotel, by the station. Air Vice-Marshal Taylor, the Secretary, gave me a few bob to go out and buy some better boots. I had a pretty old pair that were rather heavy, and some of the senior pros thought I might have a better chance if I had a decent pair."

Meanwhile the county took desperate measures to deal with the square.

"They went to a local abattoir and got some bull's blood, sprayed it on the wicket to bind it together and spent two days on the heavy roller."

On Wednesday, after Somerset had been dismissed for 123, the young off-spinner was handed the new ball: "In those days you could rub it in the dirt."

With the bull's blood?

"Well, I wouldn't have fancied licking my fingers."

Breaking in his new boots, he bowled 41 overs unchanged – "I'd never bowled so many overs, but I was used to bowling all day in the nets" – and he returned figures of eight wickets for 96. Then on Friday, in Kent's second innings, after Gimblett and Buse had put the pitch into perspective with fighting centuries, he took his match figures to 80 overs, 14 for 156.

'He has an easy action, plenty of confidence and keeps a steady length,' was the verdict in *The Times*. But Brian gives credit to his seniors: "Harold Gimblett set the field for each batsman, and Maurice Tremlett told me what pace to bowl."

In the final match at Bath, he took 11 Leicestershire wickets for 134 and, when the national averages next appeared, there was a new name at the top:

| | *O* | *M* | *R* | *W* | *Ave* |
|---|---|---|---|---|---|
| Langford | 134.2 | 45 | 308 | 26 | 11.84 |
| Bedser, A.V. | 458.3 | 125 | 917 | 70 | 13.10 |
| Lock | 262.5 | 111 | 515 | 36 | 14.30 |
| Tattersall | 209 | 53 | 548 | 36 | 15.22 |

He stayed in the side for the rest of 1953 but, away from Bath, took only 25 wickets in 15 games. He missed two seasons on National Service, then struggled to re-establish himself in 1956 – until Bath, that is, where three matches brought him another 27 wickets.

"The only way to enjoy county cricket is to be a regular in the side," he says. "I was too young to know it at the time, but those games at Bath did take the pressure off."

So much so that he was still floating down his off-breaks in the 1970s, the third greatest wicket-taker in Somerset's history.

And, in his hour of glory, did he dream of playing for England?

"Not really. There were some pretty good off-spinners in those days. Laker, for one. After those first games at Bath, we went down to Swansea and Allan Watkins said to me, 'You've just started, son. Remember, the bread and butter is county cricket. If you get picked for anything else, it's a bonus.' And he was right. Shortly afterwards I was playing in a Sunday benefit match, and this club batsman kept smashing me into the hedge. That brings you down to earth pretty quickly."

## 70. War stopped play

*August 1939* TWC, Apr 2006

"I went on the staff at The Oval in 1938 when I was 17 years old," Bernie Constable said. "I was a leg-spin-and-googly bowler, and the captain ERT Holmes loved to see people bowling leg-spinners. Whether you got hit all over the ground, it didn't seem to make any difference to him. He just liked to see leg-spin."

Holmes was a genuinely amateur captain, forever exhorting his batsmen to hit the ball over mid-off's head, so much so that they formed an OMO club complete with a tie, and his 1939 successor Monty Garland-Wells was another in the same mould.

"The only time we professionals saw the captain was on the field of play."

The amateurs changed and ate separately, and the Northamptonshire batsman Dennis Brookes recalls the special atmosphere at The Oval. "Before the war you could have as many drinks as you liked at lunch, and they used to have Pimm's No 1. I can remember some of our senior players, they used to be a bit high when they went out. In those pre-war days, it was very carefree. It was really enjoyable."

Bernie Constable's first-team debut came against the West Indian tourists in July 1939, standing in for the amateur Freddie Brown, "who couldn't play – or didn't want to play, put it that way." He was presented to King George VI at lunchtime on the first day, and he should have claimed George Headley as his first victim. "The Black Bradman, they called him. When he had about 20, he hit this little dolly up to mid-on, and Eddie Watts dropped it."

Constable bowled 19 overs, took two for 94 and returned to the second eleven. But four weeks later, with Freddie Brown again unavailable, he was called up for his championship debut against Lancashire at The Oval.

German troops were massed at the Polish border, and Prime Minister Chamberlain had been granted emergency powers in readiness for war. On Tuesday 29 August the War Ministry requisitioned The Oval, and the match the next morning was moved to Old Trafford.

The Lancashire team were playing at Dover, where Kent's captain Gerry Chalk – another dashing amateur – hit a thrilling 94 to secure an unlikely victory. That left Lancashire with a long journey north that came to a standstill at Crewe railway station where they waited three hours for a connection. According to Cyril Washbrook, 'the station on that chilly morning looked like a recruitment centre. As cricketers we felt out of place.'

They had already lost their captain Lionel Lister, a reservist who had been called back to his regiment while padded up to bat at Northampton the previous week. "We'd read what Chamberlain had said in the newspapers," Dennis Brookes recalls, "but we were playing cricket every day and we didn't really think there was going to be a war. But when Lionel Lister went off like that, that's when we realised how serious it had become."

The Lancashire players arrived at Old Trafford at 4 a.m., several of them sleeping the rest of the night in the pavilion. For two days the match was played in what Washbrook called 'an unreal atmosphere'. Then early on Friday morning, with Lancashire needing 352 for victory, the German Army entered Poland and the game was abandoned. "We caught the train back to London," Bernie Constable recalled. "When we reached Euston station, it was full of kids being evacuated."

Only one match was played that Friday, Yorkshire staying in Hove to bowl out Sussex for 33. 'It was difficult for the players to concentrate on the game,' *The Cricketer* reckoned, and Hedley Verity quickly wrapped up proceedings with seven wickets for nine runs. The feat, wrote his team-mate Bill Bowes, 'barely raised a handclap. The Scarborough Cricket Festival was cancelled, and in order to return to Yorkshire we had to hire a char-a-banc.'

They drove through blacked-out towns and villages, saw evacuee children and searchlights and, in the words of Len Hutton, 'The farther we got from Brighton, the deeper was our conviction that we would be lucky if we ever played cricket again.'

Some like Verity and Chalk did not return alive, while for others the long break halted their development.

"I went into the air force, working in despatch," Bernie Constable said. "I think I went about four years without bowling a ball. And if you're young and you bowl leg-spin, you need to be bowling it every day. When I came back, I found I'd lost it."

The Oval was a different place after the war, the spirit of carefree amateur captains and leg-break bowling never fully recaptured, and Bernie Constable turned himself into a grafting batsman: "I knew what I could do and what I couldn't do. Cricket is a game you've got to work out in your own mind, and I reckon I was good enough to do that. To me a batsman is a chap who can stay there on a dodgy wicket and get runs – collecting ones and twos, not belting the ball over mid-off's head and getting out."

In August 1949 he became a regular in the side, helping Surrey to win eight championships in the next nine summers. They were wet years, played on uncovered pitches, and the county had a great bowling attack. "Tony Lock, Jim Laker, Alec Bedser were bloody good bowlers, and we got enough runs for them to bowl at."

In fact, with Peter May often playing Test cricket, Surrey's leading run-scorer in those nine summers was the man who but for the war would have been a leg-spinner.

## 71. Your country needs you

*The Victory Test at Lord's in 1945* TWC, MAY 2006

It was Monday 9 July 1945. The war in Europe had ended two months earlier, but there was still fighting in the Far East. The previous summer Donald Carr had been captain of cricket at Repton. Now, aged 18, he was in the Army, training to be an officer at Wrotham in Kent.

"I was called to the Adjutant's office and told that I was wanted by my country. At Lord's. To play against Australia. I wasn't playing regular cricket at all. It was quite a shock."

The third 'Victory Test' was due to start that Saturday. The selectors – searching for young talent amid the makeshift cricket of wartime – had called up two 18-year-olds, the Cambridge freshmen John Dewes and Luke White. Now Donald Carr became a third, replacing the Derbyshire all-rounder George Pope who had calculated that he could earn more by turning out for Colne in the Lancashire League.

The series of five three-day matches, against an Australian Services XI, were not official Tests but, as England's Cyril Washbrook put it, 'the magic title, England v Australia, acted as a magnet to a sport-starved nation.'

On the first day, with the temperature in the 80s and railway stations overflowing with people heading for the seaside, more than 30,000 spectators filled Lord's. Admission was one shilling, with the advice from MCC to 'bring your own refreshments'.

The 42-year-old Wally Hammond was England captain. "When I arrived in the dressing room," Donald Carr says, "he looked straight through me. I think he thought that I was carrying somebody else's bag."

Dewes, White and Carr. Twelve months earlier they had been playing together for the Public Schools at Lord's. On that occasion a flying bomb had cut out overhead. "It landed just over the back of the practice grounds. We started running, and the umpires shouted, 'Get down.'" According to *Wisden*, 'pieces of soil fell on the pitch.'

"All I got was a little mud on my shirt," John Dewes recalls. "But it was very frightening."

Now they were to encounter a different fear: facing the young Australian airman Keith Miller.

Some were saying that the left-handed Dewes could fill the gap left by the great Maurice Leyland, and Dewes himself – making runs for Cambridge against sides such as the Metropolitan Police and the London Fire Force – was full of confidence. "I was in form. I thought I was going to make it. Little did I realise what a big jump I was making."

With Len Hutton at the other end, John Dewes scored 27 in a second wicket partnership of 65. *The Times* reckoned he had 'an old head on his

*Ground full but the crowd tries to push in.*

*John Dewes and Len Hutton.*

shoulders', but his sound defence and unruffled temperament was tested by Miller.

"The fastest bowler I'd seen was Trevor Bailey, and Keith was twice as fast. He came off about eight paces, but he was tall and he had this wrist action that gave him extraordinary lift. Bailey was fast, but he wasn't going to bowl a bumper to knock your head off like Miller would."

Several times John Dewes was hit on the body before his off stump was uprooted. "I had no idea that bowling could be that fast."

With White making only 11, Donald Carr's turn came when Miller bowled Hutton for 104. A thunderstorm was brewing, there was no sight screen in front of the pavilion and the light, according to *The Times*, 'varied in colour from green to black and then to yellow'.

"Keith was bowling from the pavilion end. He'd knocked Len Hutton's leg stick many a mile. And I thought, 'Len's just got a hundred. What chance have I got?' As I went past, Keith said, 'Good luck, kid.' First ball I started to prod forward, and the ball was already in the keeper's hands. So next ball I played forward as the ball was bowled, and it landed straight on my bat and went past mid-off for four. For a moment, I thought, 'This is easy.' Then he bowled me. Bowled Miller, 4."

That evening, Donald remembers, they went to the dog races at the White City and in turn the three youngsters had to place Wally Hammond's bets. "I was the only one who was successful. I had to collect his winnings. I think he got a couple of quid, and he gave me sixpence."

Hammond retired from the match with a bad back, Washbrook nursed a bruised thumb, and in the second innings the three newcomers made five runs between them, allowing Australia to win by four wickets. It was the end of England's experiment with youth.

Was it good to blood such inexperienced youngsters?

Luke White, heir to a baronetcy, was never going to be a cricketer, but Donald Carr has spent a lifetime in the game.

"I think I knew I was out of my depth before I got there," he reflects. "I didn't expect it to be anything else. And it did help me in the years that followed that I'd played in that match."

"It made me realise that there was a bit more to cricket than I had thought," says John Dewes, whose later Test encounters with Miller all ended in failure. "We had no really fast bowlers in England so there was nothing I could do to make me a better player of fast bowling. After that match at Lord's, all through my career, I always had Keith Miller at the back of my mind."

## 72. Lost to Test cricket

*Roy Marshall of Hampshire* TWC, June 2005

August 21, 1963. At The Oval England and the West Indies assembled the day before the final Test, and the talk in both teams was of frailty at the top of the order. West Indies were trying a third partner for Conrad Hunte while a desperate England toyed with the unlikely idea of sending Fred Titmus in first.

Meanwhile, on a wet wicket at Southampton, the Hampshire opener Roy Marshall was blazing his fifth century of the summer, with six sixes and 16 fours. A sugar planter's son from Barbados, he had settled in England ten years earlier, and he had become county cricket's most prolific run-scorer, the only batsman to hit more than 14,000 county runs over the last seven summers.

But, though he had been sounded out by both Walter Robins, England's Chairman of Selectors, and Frank Worrell, West Indies captain, he could not play for either side at The Oval. His four Tests for West Indies in 1951/52 made him ineligible for England, and a West Indies appearance would end his qualification for Hampshire.

"He could have played 60 Tests," Jimmy Gray, his Hampshire opening partner, reckons. "He wasn't up with Worrell and Weekes, they were very special, but he was as good as Walcott. He was certainly way above the England openers of that time."

He batted bare-headed, with thick glasses, a slim figure who stood upright and used his strong wrists to hit the ball hard. He drove through the covers, he lofted over the bowler's head, and so powerful was his flashing cut that he even hit sixes with it.

"We played Somerset," Jimmy Gray remembers, "and Bill Alley and he were drinking in the evening. 'I'll get you out, Marshall,' Bill said, and the next day he bowled with a gully, two more gullies half way back and one right on the boundary. Roy still whacked it through them. He was a beautiful striker of the ball. If he got it right, the ball just whistled."

Jimmy Gray was a good enough bat to top 2,000 runs three times but, when he and Roy Marshall put on 120 in 66 minutes against Kent in 1957, his share was 15.

"I had a problem in my first year with Roy. I used to bat according to the scoreboard. When we'd got to 50 or 60, I'd start to open up. But Roy would go off so fast that I'd be playing loose when I'd only got about 10, before I'd got myself in."

Marshall and Gray. John Arlott called them Galloper and Squire.

"Most teams would have batted Roy at number four," Jimmy says, "but he could never wait, he had to go in first. And it was a great success for

*Jimmy Gray (left) and Roy Marshall at Portsmouth.*

us. After the first year, you had experienced bowlers, taking the new ball, who really didn't want to bowl at him. It was lovely to watch the fast bowlers going back and the captains walking over. 'Keep going. Just keep it there.' I remember Fred Trueman once at Bradford. At first the ball pinged, it was going up the arm. And suddenly it didn't ping. 'I'm not going to waste my f---ing energy on you two buggers,' he said. 'I've got five wickets to take.'"

Roy Marshall was not an orthodox thinker. "County cricket was a routine and, when he first came, he queried everything. 'Why have we got that man there? ... Why isn't he bowling round the wicket?' He made us rethink our cricket. Then Colin Ingleby-Mackenzie came into the side, and he absorbed all his ideas. I think it's an excellent idea to have one overseas player."

In 1961 Ingleby-Mackenzie led them to the county's first championship, famously quipping that he liked his team in bed by breakfast.

"We were playing at The Oval," Jimmy Gray recalls, "and there was a party on the second night. I got in about half past three, and Roy, I don't think he ever did come in. But one of his great abilities was to have a lot to drink and never be drunk. My powers of recovery were terrible, but he'd sit down in the morning and eat egg and bacon."

Surrey set them 308 to win, and Gray was soon back in the pavilion. "But Roy, he smashed them all over the field, and we won with an hour to spare."

In an age of uncovered pitches Marshall scored 35,725 runs, with 68 centuries. "But you can't measure him in figures. He won so many matches. And I suspect that he got more runs against the better bowlers. He could be a bit sloppy against the ones he didn't rate. Then he'd sit in the dressing room. 'Fancy getting out to him,' he'd say."

He was a West Indian; he had grown up in a hot climate. "I played squash with him, and he wasn't keen on too much movement. He just stood there with those rapier wrists and made me do all the running. And if you batted with Roy, you were never sprinting ones. He went on a Cavaliers tour to Jamaica with Peter Richardson. Peter was all application and push and, with Roy at the other end, he couldn't get any runs. So they got into an argument. 'I'm not rushing up and down with you,' Roy said. 'You want to learn to hit the ball.'"

Jimmy Gray hit 22,650 runs, with 30 centuries. But how many more runs could he have scored with a more athletic partner?

"I don't look at it like that," he says. "Roy was a lovely batsman to watch, and I had the best seat in the ground. It was such a waste that he didn't play more Test cricket."

## 73. A wholehearted trier

*Tommy Greenhough of Lancashire* TWC, June 2006

"What do you bowl, lad?" the Lancashire coach Harry Makepeace asked.

It was 1948, the summer of Bradman's Invincibles, and the 16-year-old Tommy Greenhough from Rochdale, a shop assistant with the Co-op, was preparing to bowl in the Old Trafford nets.

"I'd been spotted playing for Fieldhouse," he recalls, "bowling off-spinners mainly. But I used to slip in an occasional leg-break. I'd also worked out how to bowl a googly from watching a mate of mine."

"I bowl off-breaks, leg-breaks and googlies," he replied.

"You can't set a field for all of them. Anyway, I don't want to see you bowl off-spinners. They're ten a penny."

So, for the first time in his life, he bowled a spell entirely of wrist spin, and he ended the day on the Lancashire staff. The next summer, with 55 wickets, he helped the second XI to their championship, and he appeared regularly for assistant coach George Duckworth's 'circus team', a side of international stars that played exhibition matches around the county. "I was only on four pound ten shillings a week, and he paid me a fiver a game. He used to cart me everywhere in his car; it didn't happen to anybody else. When he arrived, they used to say, 'Your Dad's here.'"

Then in January 1950 his progress was abruptly halted. Working for a wholesale newsagents, he fell forty feet and shattered the metatarsals in both his feet.

"Halfway through the summer I went across to Old Trafford and had a net. Ducky was there. He looked at me, said 'Oh my god!' and walked off. It was only Geoffrey Howard the Secretary who saved me. He persuaded them to pay me week-to-week and see how it went."

He was a whole-hearted trier but, after the accident, he could never get up high. "I spent hours skipping, skipping, skipping, but I could always hear two distinct sounds."

Encouraged by the captain Cyril Washbrook, he eventually got into the first team though, with uncovered pitches and wet summers, he was never an automatic choice. "I could have a good match but, if there was rain about, I'd be out for the next one."

He was capped in 1956 and in the winter went with the Duke of Norfolk to Jamaica, rooming with Kent's veteran leg-spinner Doug Wright. "He said to me, 'You're going to get people coming up, telling you what to do. Take no notice. You'll find out for yourself.' And by god I did. One of the things they used to say was, 'Bowl leg-break, leg-break, leg-break. They know you bowl a googly so keep them waiting for it.' And Doug said, 'The more I mixed it up, the better I did.' And I found out just the same thing. I could bowl three googlies an over."

Later in his career, he remembers, he bowled a leg-break first ball to Ted Dexter, a batsman he greatly admired. "He played and missed it. So I slipped in a googly next ball, and it went through the gate and bowled him."

At the end of 1958 Tommy had had enough, and he sought his release from Lancashire. "Washy called me into his captain's room. 'The wickets are being covered next year,' he said. 'You'll be in the side from the start.' And he was as good as his word."

He bowled 300 overs in the first four weeks, more than in the whole of 1958, and was in the England team for the first Test. His injury was not known outside Lancashire, and his England team-mates stared in amazement at his mis-shapen right foot.

In the second Test he had a golden half hour, taking five Indian wickets in the space of 31 balls, during which Godfrey Evans missed four stumpings off him. In his 91st game, Evans was hoping to be the first man in the history of cricket to reach 100 Tests, but he never played again for England.

"Whenever I saw him after that, he used to say, 'That's the fellow who cost me my Test place.'"

'If keenness and determination get their due reward,' *The Times* wrote, 'Greenhough's career will be full of blue skies.'

Alas, it was not. He had trouble running down the wicket, and he was not at his best that winter in the Caribbean.

Back in Lancashire he loved to bowl in tandem with his leg-spinning captain Bob Barber – "He could spin it like a racing top; I wish he would have bowled more" – and, towards the end of his career, with the legendary Sonny Ramadhin: "That was brilliant. The first time I bowled with him I got ten wickets, and he got eight. And I thought, what a difference it made having him at the other end. He made it so much easier for me."

Despite his determination, the old injury got worse. "At the end I just wasn't a bowler at all. Ray Illingworth said to me, 'I don't know if you realise, but you're bowling on your knees.'"

There have been few England leg-spinners since his day – Robin Hobbs, Ian Salisbury, Chris Schofield – but none has matched his five wickets in an innings. "It's such a pity about Chris Schofield. When I first saw him, I thought, 'He's the best thing that's happened to Lancashire since Brian Statham.' If I'd had his ability, they'd never have been able to leave me out."

## 74. A night in the abbey

*Peter Walker of Glamorgan* PREVIOUSLY UNPUBLISHED

The stained glass windows in the east end of Bath Abbey depict 56 scenes from the life of Christ, from virgin birth to resurrection, but in the dying light of the day the solitary cricketer who had wandered in through the side door was in no mood to find inspiration in them.

It was the evening of Thursday 14 July 1960.

Three days earlier Peter Walker had left the field at Trent Bridge, a happy member of an England side that had won all three Tests against South Africa that summer. He had hit useful runs in all three games, including a fifty at Lord's, and his brilliant close fielding had brought him five catches.

The previous summer he had scored 1,564 runs, taken 80 wickets and been the leading fielder in the country with 65 catches. 'Walker has all the gifts to make a Test all-rounder,' John Arlott wrote.

Yet, for all his success with England, the summer of 1960 was turning into a nightmare. His county Glamorgan were losing game after game, and his own contribution was in his stark contrast to his Test match form: 307 runs at an average of 12, 25 wickets at 37.

One moment he was in the middle of high drama at Lord's, his fifty punctuated by the repeated no-balling of South Africa's Griffin; the next, he was facing his angry Welsh team-mates, returning to the dressing room with another single-figure score. "I couldn't explain it then," he says, "and I can't explain it now. The harder I tried, the worse my county form became."

It did not help that he was something of an outsider in Wilf Wooller's Glamorgan side. Though he had family connections with Cardiff, he had grown up in South Africa and spoke in a different accent, even sometimes a different language, from his team-mates. He came from an artistic family, interested in political ideas; he played the clarinet. He was 24 years old, an adventurer who had run away to sea at the age of 16, and he was not reconciled to the life of a professional cricketer, the day-in, day-out treadmill of the circuit.

"There were times when we thought we'd lost him," his team-mate Don Shepherd recalls. "He'd wander off with his clarinet."

"I would often spend the evenings tootling away in the grounds of our hotel," Peter says. "It was a calming balm when I felt depressed."

That night at Bath, however, when he drifted into the abbey, he had gone beyond the solace of the clarinet. The previous day he had bowled 34 overs as Graham Atkinson and Peter Wight compiled a record-breaking 300 for the Somerset third wicket. And that day he had tried to hit his way out of his trough, as he had done with success of a kind two weeks earlier at Stourbridge.

"Something inside me snapped at Stourbridge. I had to open the batting in the second innings, Worcestershire had Flavell and Rumsey, and I just stood firm-footed at the crease and slashed, heaved and slogged at every ball."

"Call yourself a f---ing England player," the Worcester captain Don Kenyon said to him, but he made 68, his best score of the summer. The *Western Mail* called it 'one of the most startling displays ever of unorthodox hitting by a Glamorgan player.'

"Bernard Hedges, my opening partner, was so disgusted that he refused to talk to me for some weeks after."

Peter tried the same tactic at Bath, his first scoring shot a six that only just cleared the mid-wicket fielder, and he made 23. Then, when they followed on that evening, Wooller told him to open the batting and, according to the *Western Mail*, 'he essayed a strange stroke and was caught in the first over.'

"I was at rock bottom, and the hostile dressing room atmosphere was greater than ever. They told me my attitude was unprofessional and that I was having a bad effect on morale."

He sat alone in the abbey. "Peter," he thought to himself. "You've achieved everything you wanted to do when you ran away to sea. You've become a professional cricketer, and you've reached the highest level. OK, the clarinet has fallen away, but what's left?"

"Nothing," came back a voice inside him.

He stretched out on a pew, the fan vaulting high above him in the gloom, and he slept, waking only when the early morning cleaners arrived.

At the ground he sought out Wilf Wooller and tendered his resignation. Wooller, also an England selector, persuaded him not to act rashly. But the turmoil hit the headlines in the following days as he found himself not only dropped from the England side but left out at Glamorgan as well.

The Cardiff-based *Empire News* got him to unburden his troubled soul – 'WALKER TELLS ALL', the billboard read. Under the headline 'NEUROTIC! (That's what they call me)', he wrestled with his demons:

'My mind (and surely all things are basically played in the mind), with its early indoctrination of the arts, will not accept the stultifying effect of cricket. For the job, as opposed to the *game*, makes demands on us which leave little time for any action or thought outside cricket.'

Somehow he got back on track, and the next summer he became only the second man in cricket history to complete the treble of 1,000 runs, 100 wickets and 50 catches. And, though his England career was over, he was still playing for Glamorgan when they won the championship in 1969.

Looking back, he struggles to explain the events of that summer of 1960. "I just became too wound up in my inner nightmare," he reflects. "In fact, I've no doubt that, for six weeks or so, I could have been quoted as an even-money favourite to win the Introverted Cricketer Handicap Chase."

## 75. Two hundred not out

*Barwell versus North Coventry* TWC, Nov 2007

Saturday 22 September 2007. On an overcast morning the Coventry and North Warwickshire cricketers arrive by coach in the Leicestershire village of Barwell – to play a fixture that has taken place every year since 1807. It is thought to be the longest uninterrupted fixture in the history of cricket.

The teams assemble at 10.30 in St Mary's Church. '*Time, like an ever-rolling stream, bears all its sons away,*' they sing. The rector preaches from the pulpit where 200 years earlier his predecessor George Mettam had stood.

Mettam studied at Oxford University, where he played cricket with Robert Simson, vicar of St Michael's in Coventry, and they set up a contest between their parishes. The farmhands of Barwell against the textile workers of Coventry. They bowled under-arm, and they played with curved bats.

The 2007 teams make their way from the church by horse-drawn carriage, accompanied by the Wigston Brass Band. At the ground the Hinckley Town Crier issues a proclamation, a task he performed for the Queen in Moscow in 1994. "They'd never seen anything like it in their lives," he says. "Quite a crowd used to assemble for me." Then the captains toss with an 1807 George III halfpenny. Coventry's Tony Bristow calls "Tails", and it lands Britannia side up. "We'll have a bowl," he says, conscious that the pitch is still damp from overnight rain.

"In those days," comments the man who provided the coin, "they'd have called King or Queen."

Little is known of those early matches, not even the field they used, but Mettam and Simson stayed with their churches for many years and their annual cricket match became a tradition. Gradually the bowling became over-arm, the bats straight, and the St Michael's side acquired boaters and striped blazers. In 1895 the game moved to its current field, where across the road the following year houses were built called Cricketer's Villas.

In 1907 they celebrated the fixture's centenary, with the Barwell Brass Band playing a tune at the fall of each wicket. Alas, Barwell – who the previous year, thanks to an appearance by Leicestershire's Sammy Coe, had scored a massive 281 – managed only 34 all out. According to the *Hinckley Times*, the band was rarely silent.

A hundred years on, the match is taking a less dramatic course. The Barwell team are almost all born and bred in the village – though their score of 100 for two after 24 overs owes much to Richard Page, their "foreign import" from Bagworth five miles away.

After the first world war, Coventry St Michael became a cathedral. The cricketers became part of the Coventry and North Warwickshire Club, but the Barwell fixture survived, and there are several spectators today whose memories go back to the 1930s, when Barwell had some twenty boot-and-shoe factories and the September match against Coventry was held on the Tuesday of their Wakes Week. The village had a population of only 2,000, yet it ran four cricket teams, and the Coventry fixture was the most important one of the summer.

"It was always a needle game," says the 83-year-old Arthur Robinson. "You'd got to beat Coventry at all costs."

"Important?" says Coventry's 92-year-old Fred Dillam. "Oh gracious me, yes. Barwell never wanted us to win, and we never allowed them to if we could help it."

The first Eton-Harrow match was in 1805, but it was not played again till 1818. So Barwell and Coventry claim that theirs is cricket's longest continuously running fixture. Even in 1943, when Coventry could not raise a side, they managed to send across a handful of men. Stumps were set up, a few balls bowled and the tradition survived unbroken.

In the 1970s Coventry began playing league cricket, but the trip to Barwell retained its significance. "I started in 1980," their secretary David Robinson says, "and all the talk was, 'You've got to play at Barwell.' Even then they were calculating when the 200th game would be."

Out in the middle Barwell's innings is faltering against the leg spin of Zuhaib Akhlaque. Every time the batsmen try to accelerate, a wicket seems to fall and their 40-over total is a disappointing 145.

The Barwell sports complex is an impressive one for a village of fewer than 10,000 people. In 1919 they raised the money to acquire an army hut from Cannock Chase, making out of it a wooden pavilion that at the back served as a stand for the football pitch. Now they have not only a modern pavilion but also a large Indoor Bowling Club, where lunch is taken today.

"Club cricket is at the heart of cricket in this country," the ECB Chief Executive David Collier tells the diners. "More than that, it is at the heart of the whole community."

"Barwell has always been known as a cricketing village," 91-year-old Stan Lockley says, and the conversation turns to its county cricketers: Sammy Coe, whose 252 was for many years Leicestershire's highest score, Albert Lord whose bat and old leather bag are on display in a showcase, and George Ball.

"George could bat," Arthur Robinson says with a chuckle, "but he'd never play at Kirkby Mallory, would he? The wickets there were dodgy. Whenever we had to go there, there was always something wrong with George."

Above all, there was the great George Geary, a key all-rounder in the victorious England side in Australia in 1928/29 who – at the end of the following summer – was playing for Barwell against Coventry.

"He was a splendid figure of a man," Stan Lockley says. "He grew up in the Cricketer's Villas. There were 16 in the family, and it was only a two-up, two-down. Some of them used to sit on the stairs to have their meals."

For Coventry and North Warwickshire there was Bob Wyatt, the England captain who more than once did battle with Geary in this fixture. Briefly there was Tom Cartwright, between school and county cricket. Then in recent years Ian Bell, who first played this fixture in 1995 as a 13-year-old.

Coventry are batting, and the scoreboard after 18 of their 40 overs shows 41 for two.

In 1991 Barwell, by now the lesser club, were tired of losing, and they recruited Tim Boon and the young Darren Maddy to play for them. Roger Goadby, then Leicestershire Treasurer, offered Maddy a £25 match fee – "or would you rather be paid a pound a run?" Maddy opted for the latter and won the game with a much-remembered century. He was keen to play this year, but the Twenty20 World Cup took him to South Africa.

The Barwell change bowling is not so testing, and Coventry's runs flow freely from the bats of their captain Tony Bristow and leg-spinner "Zed" Akhlaque.

Barwell may still be a village, but the modern Coventry is a cosmopolitan city. Zed, a 20-year-old graphic design student, is from Newcastle, County

Durham, while the accent of Bristow, the club's groundsman, still carries traces of another Newcastle, in New South Wales.

All day the sun has struggled to break through, but it appears at six o'clock as Coventry complete a six-wicket victory and the Man of the Match award is presented to Akhlaque.

The umpire Ray Julian has watched him closely from the middle. "He's got a lovely action for a leg-spinner," he says. "I talked to him a lot, and he's a nice guy with it. He's definitely one to watch for the future."

Wyatt and Geary, Bell and Maddy. Perhaps the old men in 2057 will be talking about Akhlaque.

The teams no longer compete on the coconut shy of the Wakes Week fair nor do they play skittles in the Queen's Head. But the beer flows in the Sports Club, where a giant screen is showing the rugby world cup.

Little can those two churchmen in 1807 have imagined how their contest would survive so long: through industrialisation, through two world wars, through the destruction by bombing of Coventry's St Michael, into an age of satellite television and easy international travel.

"I went on holiday to Lahore last winter," Zed says. "Mushtaq Ahmed is a family friend, and he gave me some help with my bowling."

Fred Dillam leaves the ground with a smile on his face. "It's been a wonderful day," he says and, before he is driven away, he repeats his words in the morning service, words that echo back across the two centuries of this fixture.

"We're celebrating cricket. Friendship and kindness but also keenness. But not only that. We're celebrating the love of God."

## 76. Victory amid the sawdust

*The Oval, Tues 27 Aug 1968, with Derek Underwood* THE TIMES, 14 JULY 2005

It had been a frustrating summer for England. They had lost the first Test at Old Trafford. Then, when victory seemed certain at Lord's, rain washed away much of the last day. It was a similar story at Edgbaston and, after a draw at Headingley, the Ashes could not be regained.

At The Oval, with only honour at stake, England set Australia 352 for victory and, as lunch approached on the final day, the visitors were 86 for five. The pitch was responding to the spinners, Kent's slow left-armer Derek Underwood had taken three wickets, and only Inverarity remained of Australia's front-line batsmen.

Then the rain of the summer returned, a torrential storm that – with covers only allowed for the bowling ends of the pitch – soon flooded the ground.

"It was an amazing sight," Derek Underwood recalls. "You could see the gasometers reflected in the pools of water. And we were thinking, 'That's it. It's another Lord's. We're not destined to win this summer.' Most of the boys were looking to pack their bags."

But not their captain Colin Cowdrey.

"He knew that the forecast was good and that The Oval was a good drying ground. 'Don't give up, boys,' he said. 'We're going to win this match.' Then this extraordinary scene developed, with the spectators coming out to help the ground staff. A few youngsters first, then adults."

Hessian bags were rolled into the turf, then wrung out. Forks were spiked into the earth to improve the drainage. One group of barefoot volunteers swept away a large pool with wooden planks.

"It's amazing where the water went, how it all disappeared."

At 4.45, with 75 minutes remaining, the players took the field. There was sawdust everywhere, and the pitch was too damp to help the bowlers.

"We just thought we'd play for half an hour or so, then all shake hands and walk off."

At 5.25 Australia were still only five wickets down, but Colin Cowdrey would not give up, trying all his bowlers in turn. Basil D'Oliveira finally rewarded him, bringing a ball back to trim Jarman's off bail.

Derek Underwood replaced D'Oliveira at the pavilion end and, with all ten fielders hovering like vultures around the bat, his first over saw both Mallett and McKenzie caught at forward short leg by the tall David Brown.

"There was nothing in the pitch to suggest that it was treacherous. Nothing at all. Never did I bowl a ball that beat the outside edge. It was just the pressure of having everybody up around the bat. Especially David

Brown. He was so close he could have finished up in hospital. But he was really psyched up. After one of the catches, he hurled the ball back at me, and it almost knocked me over."

Gleeson bustled out, and after two aggressive sweeps he defended watchfully. Then at 5.48 Derek Underwood, who had probed him from over the wicket, went back round and the next ball saw Gleeson offering no shot and bowled off stump.

The clock ticked. Connnolly survived several balls, and at 5.55 Inverarity – playing in only his second Test and after four tense hours at the crease – faced another over from Underwood. The third ball drifted in with the arm, and he thrust his pad at it. Immediately the bowler spun round.

"Sometimes you appeal when you hope it might be out, but I just knew with that one. It was a straight ball. And Charlie Elliott was a brave umpire. If it was out, he would give it."

The finger went up.

"If you asked Inverarity to play that ball again, I'm sure he'd play it with ease. But he succumbed to the pressure."

With five minutes to spare, England had levelled the series and the spectators, who had played such a vital part, swarmed triumphantly in front of the pavilion. They cheered with gusto as the young Derek Underwood stepped forward and waved.

"Everywhere I go, that game gets mentioned. All the drama of the mopping up and the sawdust, we'll never see the like of it again."

Deep down, however, he is just as proud of his bowling eight years later on a parched Oval, when Viv Richards hit 291 in the August of a long, baking hot summer. "I put in 61 overs, and I finished with three for 165. In the circumstances it would have been very easy to have flagged. When the wickets aren't turning, when you have to keep going, those performances mean just as much – if not more."

He now sells artificial pitches to schools and clubs. "The game has moved onto another level in terms of entertainment and batting skills," he reflects, "but I do fear for the future of spinners in this country."

He lists the factors: covered pitches, modern top dressings, heavier bats, the emphasis on containment in limited over cricket. "Spinners need to bowl in tandem, and now most teams only play one."

In his 42 Tests in England, he took five wickets in an innings ten times. By contrast, English spinners have taken five only three times in the last 76 home Tests.

"I'd love to see Ashley Giles bowling this summer on a big turning wicket, with England having runs on the board and the fielders up close in catching positions. But it's a much tougher task for him than it was for me, especially against these present Australians."

## 77. From tree trunk to Indian palace

*Les Lenham of Sussex* TWC, March 2008

Groundstaff boy, first-team batsman, county coach, national coach for the Southern Region, then back part-time with Sussex. For 55 years Les Lenham has been based at Hove, and finally he has called it a day.

"I want to finish while I am still fit," he says. "I don't want people saying, 'Poor old Les. He's hobbling about.' We've got the best set-up I've ever seen at Sussex. Last year we won the championship and the second eleven championship. It's a nice time to ease out."

It was August 1952 when he started. A 16-year-old cabinet-maker's son fresh from taking 'O' levels at Worthing High School.

"I was a groundstaff lad, selling cushions and scorecards, manning the scoreboard. I even had to lay the floor in the groundsman's hut. If you look, you'll see it's not quite even."

His had been an outdoor childhood – "running, walking, climbing trees, over the downs, only going home at night when it was dark" – and he learnt his cricket playing with friends against a tree trunk in Lancing Park. "It's never played against now," he says sadly. "I give it a wave every time I drive past."

Through the next two summers, he played Club and Ground and 2nd XI matches. But there was almost no help on offer. Sussex had no coach in 1952; then they gave the job to Jim Langridge, whose 30-year playing career was ending.

"Jim was one of the loveliest men I've ever met. He made us all feel we could play. 'Well played, Les,' he'd say. 'Well bowled, Don.' But he wasn't a techniques man. None of the coaches were in those days. They'd played the game in their own natural way, and they'd learnt by watching other people."

Times were changing. In 1952 MCC published its *Cricket Coaching Book* and initiated a Coaching Award scheme. "Leslie," the Sussex Secretary Colonel Grimston told him one day. "You're going to attend an MCC coaching course. Arthur Holt, the Hampshire coach, is coming over."

For three days the young pros, together with some top club cricketers, were shown the basics of coaching, with Holt returning later to examine them. "I really took to it," Les recalls. "It inspired me. I found I had a gift that, when an action took place, I could replay it in my mind clearly. Colonel Grimston called me over afterwards. 'Well done, young man,' he said. 'You came out top of the course.'"

At Cardiff, in the last match of 1956, he got leave from National Service to make his first-team debut. "Rain got under the covers, and I went in at number five, facing Don Shepherd with fielders all round me. The ball exploded off the pitch, I got a bit of mud in my eye and the ball flew to short leg. Caught Devereux, bowled Shepherd, 0. I walked off, trying to get the mud out of my eye."

The following spring Alan Oakman returned unfit from the MCC tour of South Africa, and Les Lenham found himself opening the innings in the county's first match – against Gloucestershire at Hove.

The wet conditions forced the game to be played close to the edge of the square, and Les hit a patient 95 in the first innings. Then in the second he pushed singles and watched his partner Don Smith repeatedly sweep the off-spinners into the stand. In all Smith struck nine sixes, one of them breaking the jaw of a spectator. "He was really middling it. This chap with an umbrella came running out onto the square. 'This must stop,' he said. 'It's too dangerous.' We put on 163 together, and I made 34."

At Worthing he won his county cap with 89 against Notts, mastering the Australian leg-spinner Bruce Dooland, "the best bowler I ever faced", and he ended his summer in glory with a maiden century against Derbyshire's Jackson and Rhodes, then an unbeaten 66 against the mighty Surrey, the only opener ever to carry his bat against their full attack.

Also, as the result of a trip to Lilleshall, he became the owner of an Advanced Coaching Certificate, making a great impression on the scheme's director Harry Crabtree.

For the next twelve summers he was a regular in the county side, and out of season his coaching was in demand. He went out to South Africa for four winters. Then in 1964 he found himself invited by Prince Shatrusalyansinhji, nephew of Duleep, great-nephew of Ranji, to be his personal coach in India.

It was a winter in dreamland: sailing into Bombay and being escorted straight to the Royal Box at the Test where Sussex's own 'Tiger' Pataudi was making runs against Australia; staying in Ranji's Guest Palace and admiring the jewellery of Shatrusalyansinhji's wife, a Nepalese princess; playing in front of 20,000 people at Jamnagar where he, a workaday county cricketer, put on 100 with one of his heroes, Vinoo Mankad.

"It was a wonderful experience but, away from the palaces and the plush hotels, there was the most ghastly poverty. I couldn't come to terms with that.

"Tony Buss came as well. 'Sat' wanted somebody to bowl fast at him. He hired the Brabourne Stadium, had a pitch cut and employed three Test bowlers. 'I will practise in the heat of the day,' he said. Poor Bussy was my pace after about ten minutes; he was wet through with the humidity. We practised six afternoons a week for six weeks. 'Sat' was a good player; he scored a first-class century. But he wanted to be a Ranji and a Duleep, all rolled into one, and he played too exotically."

Sussex, with its tradition of Ranji, Duleep, Pataudi and 'Lord Ted' Dexter, had its own aristocratic grandeur, and they became the first champions of the new one-day game. But Les, though technically immaculate, was never a glamorous batsman. "I was a good player on bad pitches. But on a good pitch, if I came off at lunch with 38 or 40, I was never told 'Keep going.' I'd get out, and there'd be all this applause. And it wouldn't be for me, it would be for Ted Dexter walking out."

Les Lenham played 300 times for Sussex, scoring 1,000 runs in a season six times, 2,000 once. Then in 1970 he retired early to become county coach.

For 38 years, summer and winter, he has coached, as far afield as Sri Lanka, Zimbabwe and most notably the West Indies, where he ran their first Advanced course: "I hold a world record," he boasts with a smile. "I've been involved in the tutoring of more than 300 certified courses for coaches."

Through it all he has witnessed great changes in the English game.

"Today the pitches are much more uniform. The batsmen never play forward and get a lump of mud in their eye. But then today they have to adapt to so many different forms of cricket, and that's not easy. Jack Hobbs made 197 hundreds, but he only played one type of cricket.

"The bats have changed, too. The modern bat is fantastic. The old bats had a small sweet spot, and it showed up more the difference between the average player and the great one. Ted Dexter hit the sweet spot all the time, where with me the ball would hit the splice and the lower part of the bat. All the red marks on Ted's bat were around the one spot.

"It's hard for bowlers now. The batsmen can hit through the ball so much more easily. So many who bowl today would have been fantastic years ago. Jason Lewry is the best left-arm swing bowler in England since the second world war. But in my time he'd not only have swung it, he'd have seamed it and it would have stopped on wet ones. … Monty Panesar would have got 100 wickets every season. On good pitches he'd have had to bowl tight, but then he'd also have bowled on wet ones and he'd have got 5s, 6s, maybe 7s and 8s. It would have given him the inner belief. The great Jim Laker never really fancied bowling when it was flat, did he?"

More than all this, though, he has lived through a coaching revolution.

"Even now technology is moving on. The camera can go click, click, click, and you can see every frame. You can score a hundred or bowl 30 overs, and you can come in and look at every ball. That can help in the coaching, because sometimes with top-class players they only half-believe what you tell them.

"Each county club has an extremely efficient coaching set-up, and a boy who shows flair will be getting a lot of assistance from the age of 12 or 13. By the time he reaches 18, you should have a guy who can play. … But there is a danger that you finish up manufacturing cricketers and you lose the natural flair. People have got to work things out for themselves. You can't play for them in the middle."

His mind drifts back sixty years to that tree trunk.

"In a way it's better if the initial flair, the natural ball sense, the hand-eye co-ordination come from playing for hours with your mates in the park. Then the coaching just adds the tighter technique."

Has he really called it a day?

"I'm doing another summer at Christ's Hospital School, and I'm only a phone call away if anybody needs me."

He walks towards his car, bumping into the young Sussex keeper, Andrew Hodd. "The best coach in the world," Hodd says without prompting.

That telephone is going to be ringing.

## 78. What on earth did he say?

*Roly Jenkins of Worcestershire* TWC, May 2004

No English leg-spinner has ever returned all-round figures to rival those of Worcester's Roly Jenkins in the summer of 1949. With 183 victims, he was the country's leading wicket-taker, his 'dogged batting' yielded 1,183 runs, and his 'live-wire fielding' resulted in 27 catches, the majority of them off his own bowling. *Wisden* named him as one of their Cricketers of the Year, detailing also his outstanding success in South Africa the previous winter when in all matches he took 103 wickets. 'Worcester people are proud of him,' it wrote, 'the only man born in the city itself to be chosen by MCC for a tour.'

'The keenest man playing first-class cricket today,' the *Guardian's* Terence Prittie called him. 'He loves the game as much as any man living.'

Nine years on from his death, his widow Olive remembers his enthusiasm.

"He never stopped talking about cricket. Not long before he died, we were in the doctor's waiting room, and he met this chap. They were talking away for hours. In the end, the doctor came out. 'Is one of you two going to come in?'"

As a bowler, always in his cap, he had a short, fidgety roll to the wicket, a distinctive mix of muscle and anxiety as he threw the ball high and spun it prodigiously. 'Spin for Roly,' he would tell the ball, but his quest for perfection rarely left him satisfied.

"I've seen him take eight wickets and go straight into the nets," his team-mate Martin Horton says. "He particularly hated batsmen sweeping him. He used to say to Bill Alley, 'I hope your chickens all die.' Jim Parks used to sweep him first ball, whatever. 'Haven't they got any proper batsmen today?' he'd say."

"George Emmett hit him for three successive fours at Cheltenham once," Bomber Wells recalls. "When the clapping died down, Roly walked down the pitch, put his hands on his hips. I can see it now. 'Emmett,' he said, 'if you don't like me, that's fair enough. But for God's sake, don't keep taking it out on the ball.' You should have heard the laughter all round the ground."

"He and Eric Hollies would sit together in the evening," Warwickshire's Ray Hitchcock recalls. "Roly was so proud of the fact that he could pitch one on leg stump and second slip would catch it. How many feet it had turned."

The phlegmatic Hollies was not impressed. "My best ball, Roly," he would reply, "pitches on middle stump and hits middle stump."

One year in Glasgow Roly beat the Reverend Jim Aitchison repeatedly but without success, and he came down the wicket. "They say you're a vicar. Well, with your luck, you'll be the Archbishop of Canterbury.'" Later, as he nursed a sore finger, he turned to the umpire: "I'll borrow the one you're not using." Then he broke down in tears, returning to Worcester in a state of nervous distress. He did not bowl again for a month.

"He was always talking," Olive says. "And he never bothered what he said. He just said it."

In the war he was admonished by an officer batting with him. "Now listen, Jenkins, you don't say 'come one,' you say 'come one, sir.'" And Roly, with his insistent Worcester vowels, had to have the last word: "And if I'm wearing a cap, sir, should I salute when we cross?"

He wrote a piece on spin bowling, and Walter Robins commended him. "That was a very good article, Jenkins. Who wrote it for you?" Quick as a flash he came back: "I wrote it myself, sir. Who read it for you?"

But in May 1949 he made one remark too many and, for all his success in South Africa and during that golden summer, it cost him his Test place. The selectors picked six slow bowlers that summer – including three leg-spinners at The Oval – but there was no call-up for the man from Worcester.

Olive produces eight pages of typed script from an envelope marked Unpublished Article: 'There are those who assert that he was omitted because of a frivolous (and harmless) remark made while batting for MCC in a friendly match. He was certainly carpeted at Lord's for his levity and, it seems, lost his Test place because of it.'

"What on earth did he say?"

"Ah well, I don't suppose it matters to repeat it now. He was batting on the last morning, and he said to this fancy cap, 'I'm going to play as an amateur today. I want to catch the early train back to Worcester.'"

Fifty-five years on, with abuse traded routinely on the field of play, it is hard to comprehend. 'I'm going to play as an amateur today. I want to catch the early train back to Worcester.' The words had cost him his England place.

The irony is that no cricketer ever tried harder or took the game more seriously, ever looked after its spirit more lovingly. In his final radio interview, he read Lord Harris's famous words: 'Cricket. It is a moral lesson in itself, and the classroom is God's air and sunshine. Foster it, my brothers, protect it from anything that will sully it, so that it will be in favour with all men.'

"What would he do in his grave," Roly added, "if he could see what was going on today?"

But if there was no England place for Roly that summer, at least he had time for the wedding he had had to postpone during the winter. Worcester released him for a week in June, and he sent them a postcard from Llandudno: 'They say it's sunny outside.'

He reappeared the following Saturday, bowling 49 overs on a hot day at Dudley and glowing with the joys of married life: "I never realised you could have so much fun without laughing."

## 79. The accidental cricketer

*Peter Wight of Somerset* TWC, Oct 2005

"There was always a lovely ring to his bat," Graham Atkinson says of his Somerset team-mate Peter Wight. "He seemed to middle the ball so well. If he'd gone out with an old chair leg, there'd still have been a nice ring to it."

"Peter was such a good player of fast bowling," says Brian Langford. "He'd step back a little, give himself some room and let the arms go."

"He had a magnificent eye," Atkinson says. "He picked up the length so quickly, and he had such strong wrists. He was the first person I saw who hit the ball at the top of the bounce. And, when it was short, his square cut was like a rifle shot. Crack. His timing was so good."

Only Harold Gimblett has scored more first-class runs for Somerset. Yet Peter Wight would never have been a professional cricketer if his employer in Burnley had released him, as promised, for his motor mechanic exams.

He had grown up in British Guiana, his family a mix of Scottish and Portuguese. His cousin had been West Indian vice-captain in England in 1928, his brother Leslie played one Test in 1953, and other brothers represented Guiana at cricket, hockey, tennis and soccer.

He came to England on a cargo boat in 1951, shivering in his tropical clothes, shocked by the rationing and outdoor toilets. "I came to learn engineering, not to play cricket." But, after missing his exams, he emigrated to Toronto, then returned to work in a factory. He was scoring runs in the Lancashire League and in the summer of 1953, when he visited his sister near Bridgwater, her husband Bill offered a suggestion. "'Why don't you play for Somerset? They've got no players.' We went down on the bus the next day."

After two nets and a second eleven match, he was picked to play the tourists. "A trial game against the Australians?" Graham Atkinson laughs. "It's amazing how Somerset did things."

He followed a first innings duck with a century, and Somerset offered him £250 a year. He preferred his factory wages but the offer was improved and, for the next 12 years, he delighted the county faithful.

He was not a hard-living extrovert like the Australian Bill Alley. He never swore, never lost his temper and believed in an early night. A white man in the Caribbean, his darker skin earned him the nickname Rajah.

"He was a quiet guy," Atkinson says. "His bat did his talking."

A frail-looking figure, he often seemed to be under the weather, and fast bowlers grew excited when he did not get behind their short-pitched balls. "Even Statham used to bowl bouncers at him," Ken Palmer recalls.

"And Fred Trueman used to chirp away. 'Your room mate, Ken,' he'd say to me. 'He's turned white now.'"

Trueman, with his banter, always got the better of him, but he made runs against all of the other quicks – especially Surrey's Peter Loader. "He could be the most vicious of them all," Brian Langford says, "and Peter used to murder him."

"To tell you the truth," Peter says, still with a high-pitched West Indian lilt to his voice, "I'd heard so much about county cricket, but I thought it was just as ordinary as anything else."

The shining rolled clay of The Bourda was very different from the uncovered pitches of England, and he never really changed his technique. But on a wet wicket at The Oval in 1956, batting at number four, he played two of his finest innings.

Against Loader, Lock and the Bedsers, he hit an unbeaten 62 first time. "I came in and sat down. We had to follow on, and they said, 'Don't take your pads off.' So I had a drink and a stretch and blow me down, within minutes, 'You're in, Peter.'" Loader took seven wickets as Somerset were dismissed for 196, but the waif-like Guianan came off with 128 not out.

Two years later, at Taunton, he hit the Surrey attack for 175 while suffering from all manner of ailments. "I used to love it when he came in and said he wasn't fit," Brian Langford says. "He always seemed to bat better."

"I put on 300 with him at Bath," Graham Atkinson remembers. "I think he was dying that day. I remember saying, 'Keep going, Rajah'. He always played better under duress."

He was the first to 2,000 runs in the summer of 1960, he reached 2,000 again in 1962, but in 1965, after a poor season, Somerset released him and he went onto the umpires' list, where he stayed for 30 summers. In all, he officiated in 567 first-class matches, more than Dickie Bird or David Shepherd, yet he never stood in a Test.

"I've never been at an international match in my life," he says.

With his benefit money he built an indoor cricket school in Bath, where for 35 years his cheerful patience made him many friends.

"He's done so much for cricket," Brian Langford says. "He doesn't get the recognition he deserves."

"He was the best player at Somerset in the years I was there," Graham Atkinson says. "I used to stand at the other end and drool at the shots he played."

And Peter Wight, how does he think of himself?

"I don't think of myself as anything," he says with a cheerful simplicity. "I never even thought of myself as a cricketer."

## 80. Knowing the score

*Percy Holmes and Herbert Sutcliffe at Leyton* TWC, Aug 2007

Leyton Cricket Ground. Thursday 16 June 1932. One o'clock.

The crowd roared with delight as Herbert Sutcliffe struck the four that took the Yorkshire score to 555 for no wicket. After 7½ hours of batting, hours of intense concentration and growing fatigue, hours when his partner – the 45-year-old Percy Holmes – had struggled with lumbago, the two of them had broken one of cricket's greatest records.

"I don't think I ever hit a ball with such joy," Sutcliffe said.

The old record of 554, set back in 1898, stood so far ahead of all its rivals that it seemed – in the words of the *Yorkshire Post* – to have been 'like a roc's nest on some mythical and impossibly high and unscalable Everest.' Yet Holmes and Sutcliffe had climbed above it.

The cricket writer Alan Gibson was a seven-year-old Yorkshire exile watching from the top-floor balcony of his home across the road. 'The cheering was rapturous,' he recalled. 'I saw Holmes and Sutcliffe stride down the pitch towards each other, majestically, and shake hands. Life, I felt, had not anything to show more fair, and I am not sure that it has had.'

When the applause died down, Sutcliffe – his concentration broken – carelessly played the next ball onto his stumps. The innings was declared, and the two record-breakers returned in triumph to the pavilion.

*

Leyton Cricket Ground. Saturday 16 June 2007. One o'clock.

75 years on, to the minute. Leyton County are playing Tennyson in a second eleven league match. On a damp day the Tennyson openers Ken Smith and Paul Fredericks are making their way to the middle, walking on the same stretch of grass where Holmes and Sutcliffe walked. The old pavilion, the Essex headquarters in 1932, is still standing, but the great scoreboard has been replaced by a little hut.

"For goodness sake, make sure you're not out for nought," I tell them.

The pitch is lively after rain, and in the first over Paul Fredericks pulls a two through mid-wicket. Then he tries to repeat the shot and is caught at mid-on. Two for one. A few minutes later, with the score on eight, a downpour – with thunder and lightning – drives them from the field.

I sit in the office with Dorian Thorne, wicket-keeper and long-time stalwart of the Leyton County club. It was formed by the local Caribbean community.

"I grew up with a passion for the game," he says. "Even when I first came over to England in 1964, every evening in the summertime I was running over to Downs Park in Stoke Newington. And it was cricket,

1932

2007

cricket, cricket. Now the youngsters, cricket's too long for them. They want something with more impact, a shorter game. And they want instant money. So it's football and basketball. Even in the Caribbean now, everywhere you see the ring on the pole, not cricket anymore. We were a Caribbean team. Now we're becoming more Asian. They're the ones who still have the passion."

We are so engrossed that we never notice that the sun has come out, the sawdust is down and the game is only waiting for a wicket-keeper.

I watch for a while, then – as the rain thickens once more – I head off to the local studies library.

*

When Essex came to Leyton in 1886, half the population of the county lived in the four boroughs of West Ham, East Ham, Walthamstow and Leyton, and for many years the ground, supported by a new railway line, brought in good crowds. In time the pitch became known as a perfect batting track in good weather. The *Cricketer* magazine even wrote that the phrase 'as good as a Leyton wicket' was 'an idiom in cricket language'. In 1927 Leyton hosted the BBC's first radio broadcast of cricket. Then in 1932 it was the stage for the breaking of a great record – followed by an almighty rumpus.

Percy Holmes and Herbert Sutcliffe. No opening pair in the history of first-class cricket can match their 74 century partnerships. Holmes was the older of the two, a jaunty figure, dainty on his feet, full of perky optimism, while Sutcliffe was the great Test cricketer, a self-made man with immense resources of will power and concentration.

When they came through the gate, Robertson-Glasgow wrote, 'Sutcliffe walked out as if to lay with a golden trowel the foundation-stone of some Hostel for Deserving Cricketers; Holmes, as if he were off to Aintree in merely incidental white flannels.'

At one stage on that Thursday morning at Leyton, as the record drew near, Holmes played a loose shot and Sutcliffe called down the wicket to him with magisterial severity. "Percy, do you – or do you not – want to go for this record?"

Then at one o'clock they enjoyed their finest moment, and they were led to the scoreboard where they stood beneath the 555. They shook hands for the cameramen but, to the gasps of the assembled crowd, the 555 suddenly turned back to 554.

Perhaps Holmes could see the funny side of it – but not Sutcliffe!

'He was outraged,' Don Mosey wrote. 'Recalling that moment even more than forty years afterwards, I have known his voice rise in high-pitched crescendo of horror.' And many in the crowd around the box were horrified too. There was even a man who had travelled specially from Hull that morning; he had come to see the record broken, not equalled.

What did happen next? There are so many conflicting accounts. It was a full twenty minutes before the Essex innings got under way, and their opener Leonard Crawley was bowled third ball for 0. They then had lunch, and at some stage of the interval it was announced that a no ball had been discovered and that the Yorkshire score really was 555.

I have pored over the scorebooks and the newspaper reports. It is like trying to do a giant and deadly Su Doku with a note at the bottom, saying 'Some of these numbers may have been misprinted.' Nothing ever adds up.

But it is in *Wisden* as 555 and, though the record was broken in Karachi in 1977, it remains to this day the highest ever partnership for any wicket in England.

When they went back out, play was stopped each time a telegram arrived. But the interruptions grew too frequent so the messages were stacked up in the Yorkshire dressing room, alongside a crate of State Express '555' cigarettes. "The team smoked themselves silly," the fast bowler Bill Bowes remembered.

Essex were all out for 78 and 164, and the following week Percy Holmes found himself recalled at the age of 45 to play in the summer's only Test, the first-ever match against All-India, at Lord's. He had been out of favour with the selectors all his career, and now he was one good performance from being on the boat to Australia with Douglas Jardine's team.

But it was not to be. His knee gave out in July, and he never scored another century.

EW Swanton was not on the boat to Australia, either. He was at Leyton for the *Evening Standard*, and he was beaten to the only telephone box by a rival, causing his paper to be scooped. In fury his editor sent the lawn tennis correspondent to Australia instead of him.

*

After years of neglect the Leyton ground is on the way back up. The pavilion has been extensively renovated, and the square is receiving the attention of Peter Sherwood, Essex's pitch advisor. "The old pitch is a long, long way down," he says.

I arrive back to find they have played through the rain. The box shows Tennyson's score to be 144, and Leyton County look to be winning comfortably. Then wickets fall and suddenly they are 139 for nine.

A single, a wide, another single – but the box is still showing 139.

"Telegraph, please!" they shout, and it turns out to be Dorian on scorer's duty in the box. Up goes 142. It's three to win.

There is another wide, followed by several forward defensives. "Perhaps we're going to get a tie," I say hopefully to the Leyton club secretary Bilal Mahmood. The over is called, and the fielders move to their new positions.

Dorian then appears from the box, the book in one hand, and he is waving the players off with the other. The game is over. It seems the Tennyson score was only 142, not 144.

Bilal and I walk across to the box to see that the last digit only shows a 4 because the 1,2 and 3 are missing. "What a farce!" he says in embarrassment.

All day the ghosts of Holmes and Sutcliffe have hung in the air. Now I sense them afresh as I linger in front of the broken scoreboard. What *would* Herbert be thinking?

"It's perfect," I reply. "It's how it all ended 75 years ago."

## 81. Too good a start

*Roger Harman of Surrey* TWC, Oct 2006

"In some ways it might have worked out better for me if I hadn't done so well," Surrey's slow left-armer Roger Harman says, reflecting on the 136 wickets he took in 1964, his first full summer. "If I'd only got 60 or 70 wickets, there'd have been less pressure on me the next year."

The previous summer Tony Lock had still been on the staff, limiting Roger's opportunities. But the 21-year-old, who had given up an engineering apprenticeship to be a Surrey cricketer, took the chances he had. At Blackheath he dismissed four front-line Kent batsman in five balls, including a hat-trick, and he was not overawed when Lock pulled out of the May fixture against the West Indian tourists.

"I turned up on Saturday morning, not expecting to play, and the next thing I knew I was bowling to the great Frank Worrell. He played back. It bounced and turned, and he gloved it to slip. At the end of the summer he said I was the best young bowler in the country."

Tony Lock emigrated to Australia, and in 1964 Roger Harman stepped into his boots, taking eight wickets for 12 runs at Trent Bridge in mid-May and eight for 32 against Kent in early June. By July 27 he had taken 97 wickets and was leading the race to 100.

"Stuart Surridge, the old Surrey captain, turned up with two crates of champagne in the dressing room, and I think it did play on me a bit."

Although it took Roger Harman another 11 days to take the three wickets, his final tally was second only to Hampshire's veteran seamer Derek Shackleton. And in August a fine performance for the MCC President's XI at Lord's, when his first ball to Bill Lawry span past the obdurate Australian's forward defensive and bowled him, came just too late to win him a place on the boat to South Africa.

He was a classic left-arm finger-spinner, capable – according to John Arlott – of 'vicious spin', and by August he was bowling in tandem with the 17-year-old off-spinner Pat Pocock. The Surrey members, yearning for the triumphs of Laker and Lock, were starting to say what their former captain Michael Barton had said when he had been to a second eleven match the previous year: "I've just seen the next England spin combination."

In all, Roger Harman bowled 1,131 overs that summer, over 500 more than any of his team-mates, and he wonders now if it was too many.

"By the end of the summer I think my arm had dropped a bit, and they said, 'You're knackered, don't come back till January.' It was the first winter I hadn't trained right through. And, when I did come back, things weren't quite right."

There was a buzz of expectation when summer began.

"Whenever the pitch started to take turn, they'd lob the ball to me. 'Come on, Airy.' And they'd expect me to bowl the other side out. When you're bowling well, you never think about what your body's doing; you think about what you're going to do with the ball. 'I'll toss one wide of off stump' or 'I'll bowl one quicker on leg'. But I got to the point where I couldn't do it, and I was thinking about what I was doing wrong. And of course I became tight, and that made things worse."

He also had to contend with the disappointment of the spectators.

"The previous year, when I was taking wickets, the members would all see me. Now, when I walked through them to the dressing room, they looked the other way. Progressively I lost confidence in my own ability."

The decline was dramatic: 136 wickets in 1964, 63 in '65, 50 in '66, 18 in '67 and no longer a regular in the side.

"It's not very nice when you're in the nets and you see the first team go off," he recalls – though there was one last hurrah in July 1968 when he travelled to Ilkeston and bowled on a pitch where the top came off. In the first innings he took six for 97; in the second, eight for 16 including a hat-trick.

Alas, four more appearances yielded only two more wickets, and Surrey turned instead to the young Chris Waller and to the Pakistani leg-spinner Intikhab Alam. "I was hoping I'd done enough to be retained, but I half-expected it was going to come to an end."

Now he is back at The Oval, as Chairman of Cricket, and the game he watches is a very different one: "Everybody says, 'Don't give the batsman any room. Tuck them up, and you can control where they're going to hit it.' When I was playing, if you wanted to get somebody out, you tended to bowl it higher and wider; you made them reach for it. But I'm not sure I'd like to bowl now some of the deliveries I bowled. With today's bats, instead of looping to cover, they'd probably go one bounce for four."

But maybe the mental side of cricket has not changed.

"I was never particularly confident as a player and hopefully, if someone is having a bad time, I'll be able to say more of the right words. In a way I was a similar type of bowler to Monty Panesar, a traditional left-arm spinner, and everybody now is so desperate for an English spinner to be a winner. I just hope people give him the opportunity to develop and are tolerant if he hits difficulties along the way."

## 82. A trio of club stalwarts

*Claude Kellaway of Sampford Arundel* TWC, May 2008

The little postage-stamp ground of Sampford Arundel, in West Somerset, is far from the bustle of the world. It sits at the bottom of a rough track, an enchanted spot nestled between farm fields and the grounds of a rarely occupied millionaire's mansion.

There for ten or twelve hours each week in summer you will find the lone figure of Claude Kellaway, 86 years old and still preparing the wickets – as he has been for nearly 40 years. "It's getting harder," he says cheerfully, puffing on his pipe. "I have to wind the roller up, and it takes some turning to start it."

A Cornishman, his job with the Ministry of Agriculture brought him to the village in 1963, and he was soon keeping wicket for the club. "Cricket was *the* recreation in the village in those days. Cricket and the Women's Institute. Now there's so much else for youngsters to do."

Within a few years he was the captain, the fixtures secretary and the groundsman. One summer he found time to turn out in 61 games – including several against touring teams. "Billy Butlin used to bring a side with quite a few county players. I remember hitting David Allen of Gloucestershire for a six. He said, 'You won't do that again,' and I didn't."

The team became quite successful in the 1970s. "When I was skipper, I didn't pick a side. I'd just say, 'See you next Saturday, next Sunday.' And everybody knew where to field. I played to win, but that wasn't the main thing. It was the people I played with."

He was keeping wicket till the age of 75, though by then Sampford had joined the Somerset League. He still does the fixtures, and he is always there on match day, watching quizzically from the seat of the mower. "I used to stand up to almost all the bowlers but, even if I was young, I couldn't now. They all try to bowl too fast instead of getting a length and an action. So many balls go down the leg side."

When he started, there were only four strips; now he looks after eight. "I don't do it properly," he says, "but I do the best with what we've got. It's a beautiful spot. It's quiet. There are trees all round, and I'm quite happy on my own." Then comes the mischievous twinkle. "I don't get any lady friends down here, though."

In 1955, at Ealing Cricket Club in West London, Mervyn Mansell, brother of the South African Test cricketer Percy, founded a colts section. "Cricket in schools was declining," Mansell, now 90, recalls. "So we had to start producing our own youngsters."

What youngsters he produced that first year! Three of them played at Lord's in 1971 in the National Club Knock-Out final: wicket-keeper and captain Bob Fisher, off-spinner Alan Price and pace bowler John Lindley. In 2008 all three are still playing for Ealing, as they have done every summer since 1955. On Saturday 23 August, playing for the fifth eleven, the 67-year-old Lindley took his 4,000th wicket for the club.

His leg-cutters are increasingly gentle, but his arm is high and he still practises what Mansell taught him: line and length and bowling straight. "The game's changed," he reflects. "There aren't too many who bowl at the stumps now."

In 1962 he took ten for 14 against St Benedict's School, his last victim the future politician Chris Patten. Several times against Brondesbury he dismissed the young Mike Gatting: "usually caught at short leg." And at Ealing he bowled in tandem with the young Simon Hughes: "I told him to take a few yards off his run-up, but he never listened to anything anybody said."

Eleven times he took 100 wickets for the club, his best 158 in 750 overs in 1973. He was working full-time as a credit controller for Visnews, and not even family holidays got in the way of his wicket-taking. "We used to have a fortnight in West Sussex, and I'd drive up each weekend to play."

Now the car journeys are longer. In 2003 he retired to Dorset, to the Blackmore Vale where little villages with mellow stone cottages are scattered along winding lanes. From there, at eight o'clock every Saturday morning in summer, he starts the 113-mile drive to the bustle of cosmopolitan Ealing, returning on Sunday night. In 2005, in all fixtures, he was the club's leading wicket-taker, the secret of his continuing success to be found in aerobics classes in Wincanton Sports Centre and in his back garden where in February he erects a makeshift net. "I do far more getting fit than I did when I was playing first-team cricket," he says.

For 43 years he has also been the club's fixtures secretary. But there is no sign of his retiring from bowling: "The fire is still inside me; I want to carry on playing into my 70s." And no sign of his transferring his allegiance to a club in Dorset: "That devotion to Ealing is there. It always has been, and it always will be."

*Claude Kellaway*

*Ken Wilson*

Little can the 15-year-old Ken Wilson have realised what he was letting himself in for when he was volunteered as "fresh blood" for the Wirksworth Cricket Club committee in the autumn of 1954. Though everything has changed around him in the Derbyshire Dales club, he is still there 54 years later: president, fixtures secretary, treasurer, scorer, amateur weather forecaster and much more besides. His efficiency is legendary.

He played his first game in the week Roger Bannister broke the four-minute mile, and one Sunday he did his first stint in the scorebox. Here he had to learn the intricacies of the club's social structure. "There were three classes of player. A quarryman, you had to write Sanders V. The local shopkeeper who'd been to Repton, the initials went first. He was DJO Marsden. Then one day we had a company director playing, and he created a real fuss. To be distinguished from the shopkeeper, he had to be HE Bowmer Esq."

The committee met in the pavilion where there was no electricity. "By September it was dark. People had to strike matches so the secretary could read the minutes. I was the only one who thought it was funny. You could hear people speaking, but you couldn't see them."

The club ran two elevens, playing friendly matches against other teams along the old LMS railway line, and they travelled with a large communal kitbag. They bought six balls to last the summer, and they renewed them by applying a liquid potion supplied by a German chemist in Belper. "There's some of it somewhere in my garage."

He was still a young progressive in 1971 when they finally decided to join the Derbyshire League. "There were quite a few against, but we had a good team and some of the younger ones would have gone somewhere else if we hadn't."

Now Wirksworth runs three elevens, a ladies' team and several junior sides. It is a Focus Club, with a budget of nearly £30,000. It has Clubmark recognition, and it hires an overseas professional.

The quarries have closed, and the work now is all in Derby and Matlock. But the cricket still has a community feel. "It's not quite what it was, but things are picking up at the moment. We've got a lot of good young lads. Unfortunately so many of them go to university and they don't come back."

Ken Wilson was bright enough, but he did not attend university. He stayed among his own people – and Wirksworth Cricket Club has been the richer.

## 83. The little fellow with the big bat

*George Emmett of Gloucestershire* TWC, Sept 2004

Time passes. Cricketers leave behind statistics and memories; in time the memories fade.

George Emmett, Gloucestershire, 1936-1959. 25,602 runs, average 31.41.

'A very ordinary county cricketer,' according to the historian Derek Birley.

It is not a verdict shared by those who saw him.

"Never a day goes by at the Cheltenham Festival," says Bomber Wells, "when somebody isn't talking about one of his innings."

"He was magical," Arthur Milton says. "A little fellow who wanted to be big, and he did it with the bat."

"A much under-rated player," Tom Graveney calls him. "Although he was a little man, gosh, he used to hit it hard. He played some of the best innings I've ever seen."

Emmett's early years with Gloucestershire suffered from the dominance of Hammond. 'George had to stifle his wonderful array of strokes,' his team-mate Charlie Barnett wrote. 'Anyone batting with Hammond had to take one run and leave the scoring to him.'

After an eventful war, in which he was wounded in the invasion of Italy, Emmett found himself dropped by Hammond in 1946.

"Hammond called him a second class cricketer," his daughter Gill remembers. "Dad didn't show his feelings, but he was really upset."

The following summer Hammond was gone and, according to Barnett, 'Gloucestershire came to life again with exciting and attractive cricket.' In the most golden of summers they challenged for the championship, with Emmett scoring six polished centuries.

"He batted right-handed," Arthur Milton says, "but, like Denis Compton, he was naturally left-sided. So he controlled the bat with his top hand, and he had a wonderful eye."

In 1948 Emmett was picked instead of Hutton for the Old Trafford Test but, twice dismissed cheaply by Lindwall, he was condemned to Gloucestershire's unequalled list of one-cap wonders.

His revenge came five years later at Bristol. Now 40 years old, he hammered Lindwall and Miller in a brilliant 141.

"I'm not sure they were the force they'd been in '48," Gill says, "but I guess he felt his honour had been satisfied."

The son of a Scots Guard, he grew up in India and returned there with a Commonwealth side. His fellow tourist Frank Worrell called him 'one of the greatest English batsmen I have seen in the tropics.'

For four years he captained the county, a disciplinarian who was always looking to move the game forward.

"He was the best captain I played under," Arthur Milton reckons. "He loved the game; we always had good games of cricket. And he kept us in good order. Gave us our manners, not just for the game but for life."

"Everything had to be correct with George," the late Geoff Edrich of Lancashire said. "Spot on. Nothing slipshod."

"He had a glare that would melt icicles," Gill says. "But in a way the more insulting he was to you, the more he liked you."

"At the time," Tony Brown says, "we didn't realise what a good influence he was. I wish the youngsters now could be pushed and stretched like we were."

Well into his forties and with a bad knee, he still hit his runs with panache. At a time when batsmen were adopting a less adventurous approach, he scored the fastest century of 1954, blazed 91 in 67 minutes against the 1957 West Indians, then at Cheltenham in 1959, in his last match as county captain, he hit 85 in 75 minutes against the Indians. In the words of *Wisden*, 'he gave them a lesson in brilliant stroke play.'

Nine years later, at the age of 55, he was still taking the county's indoor nets, and David Green recalls the evening that they persuaded him to put on his pads for ten minutes.

"He was most reluctant, and at first he scratched about. Then suddenly, with Allen, Mortimore and Smith all bowling, he started playing these beautiful drives and sweeps. For five or six minutes he was bloody dazzling."

David Green had arrived from Lancashire where he had lost his touch, and Emmett transformed him. "He told me that anxiety was getting in my way; it was making me move before the ball was bowled. He got me back to playing my natural game." Such was the transformation that only Barry Richards scored more runs than David Green that summer.

But, underneath his controlled exterior, was Emmett also a nervous batsman? A heavy smoker with an anxious cough, he reached 90 on 58 occasions, going on to 100 on only 37 of them.

"He deserved so many more hundreds," Bomber Wells says. "Other batsmen played for them, but he played exactly the same from start to finish, and they're the people you remember, aren't they? People like Boycott are nothing in comparison. They've only given the game facts and figures."

'A very ordinary county cricketer'?

Geoff Edrich did not think so. "If I could turn back the clock," he said, "and see one batsman in full flow again, it would be George Emmett. I've seen Hammond and Bradman score hundreds but, if George was batting as he could, he was the neatest of the lot."

## 84. The unlikely philanthropist

*Sir Julien Cahn* TWC, Sept 2005

Sir Julien Cahn wanted to be an English country gentleman. And what better way was there to do that than to buy a country house, become a Master of Hounds and run his own cricket team?

What a team it became! He owned grounds at West Bridgford in Nottingham and at Stanford Hall near Loughborough. He signed up Test cricketers from the Southern hemisphere, and he entertained all the touring sides except the Australians. His team lost only 19 of the 621 matches that they played between 1923 and 1939, and their winter tours – to such places as Canada, Argentina, Jamaica, Ceylon and New Zealand – were spoken of for years afterwards.

His father, a Jewish immigrant from Germany, had built up a furniture business in Nottingham before the First War, and Julien – seeing a fresh market in hire purchase sales – expanded it to the point where his "Jays" and "Campbells" stores could be found in towns all across Britain.

By the 1920s he was a wealthy man, and he spent lavishly and generously. It is said that he fell in love with cricket when, as a boy, he sat under Parr's tree at Trent Bridge, listening to the great Arthur Shrewsbury. In 1925 he joined the committee at Nottinghamshire, where his donations covered much of the cost of a new scoreboard, indoor nets and two new stands.

In 1926 he completed his West Bridgford ground, building a luxurious pavilion that housed a collection of ancient bats and that could also be converted into a badminton court. Two years later he bought Stanford Hall, where he created a second cricket ground, a nine-hole golf course, a bowling green and a large lake stocked with trout. He built a pond for performing sea lions and an art deco theatre with a Wurlitzer organ and a secret tunnel for the magic tricks that he loved to perform.

He became a notable philanthropist and was made a baronet. He saved Byron's home, Newstead Abbey, buying it and donating it to Nottingham Corporation. He funded research into the grass used by impoverished Welsh hill farmers. With Stanley Baldwin's wife he founded the National Birthday Trust, funding a maternity home in Stourport and introducing the use of gas and oxygen in childbirth. He was a patron of musical concerts in Nottingham, and such was his generosity towards the Leicestershire hunts that he became Master of three of them, the first Jewish man ever to acquire such status.

But cricket was his first love, and such was the strength of the sides he assembled that several of their matches were accorded first-class status.

So it happened that, in Kingston, Jamaica in March 1929, aged 46, he made his first-class debut, captaining a team containing eight Test cricketers – including the former England captain Lord Tennyson and Surrey's Andrew Sandham, who would return to the island the next winter and make Test cricket's first triple century. Cahn batted at eleven, broke a finger and was bowled for nought – but he made his contribution in other ways, bringing with him plenty of Fortnum and Mason hampers. When his grandson visited the island many years later, he was introduced to an old Jamaican who, as a boy, had carried Cahn's bags and had been so taken with him that he had changed his name to Julien Cahn.

No English first-class cricketer of the 20th century can have had less ability than Cahn. He was a hypochondriac, often preferring his electric wheelchair to walking, employing a nurse and thinking nothing of hiring a private train to bring Lord Horder, the King's reserve physician, to Stanford Hall. Conscious of brittle bones, he batted in special inflatable pads that it was his chauffeur's duty to pump up. His umpire 'Tommy' Gunn, the old Notts cricketer, never gave him lbw, and – keen to retain this fixture – neither did opposition umpires. According to Jim Swanton, 'the pads were very large, and the ball bounced readily off them for leg-byes, which the umpires conveniently forgot to signal.'

Philip Snow, younger brother of the novelist CP Snow, recalls playing for the Leicestershire Gentlemen at West Bridgford on the occasion when the pads deflated: "He'd no sooner come out to bat than there was a loud hissing noise. I liked him, but he was a real autocrat, a martinet. He stalked off the pitch, sacked his chauffeur on the spot and declared the innings."

Nevertheless, Cahn hit a match-winning 64 against the London Press in 1930, and ten years later, at the age of 57, he scored 35 in an opening partnership of 178 with 'Lofty' Newman, the former Surrey batsman who was his personal secretary.

He also loved to bowl, throwing the ball high in the air and relying on athletic fielders to take boundary catches. As one observer remarked, 'his bowling was not so much up and down as to and fro.' Yet on a mantelpiece in Stanford Hall, his elder son Albert recalls, there were several mounted balls, "each with a little inscription of what he'd done." In Ceylon and Malaya in 1937, he finished with tour figures of 10 for 159 in 29 overs, and he nestled in the averages between the Australian Jack Walsh and the South African Test all-rounder Denys Morkel.

By the mid-1930s Cahn's philanthropy had extended to the near-bankrupt Leicestershire County Cricket Club, and he arranged for 'Stewie' Dempster, the great New Zealand batsman, to work as his store manager in Leicester so that he could captain the county.

"At that time," Philip Snow says, "Dempster was regarded as the best player of slow bowling in the world. He was incredibly quick on his feet."

He was outstandingly successful at Leicester, but his appearances were limited by Cahn, who often took him off to play for his own team. It was the same story with Jack Walsh, whose chinamen took 216 wickets for Cahn's XI in 1938 but who was only released for four county matches.

Such was his financial clout, and such was the fun of his cricket, that he retained the loyalty of many first-rate cricketers. Dempster and Walsh would have been assets in any county side, as would Morkel, the outstanding all-rounder of the 1929 South Africans, and the adventurous fast bowler Bob Crisp, who took 107 wickets for the South Africans in 1935. Wicket-keeper Cecil Maxwell represented the Gentlemen on the strength of his performances for Julien Cahn, and both Ian Peebles and Walter Robins, the England leg-spinners, could often be found at West Bridgford and Stanford Hall.

Not everybody was lured, however, with 'Topsy' Wass, Notts' greatest wicket-taker, expressing his disapproval of Cahn's hire purchase business: "I'm not working for a fellow who sells you a lot of furniture and takes it back six months later."

Sir Julien Cahn's XI were far too strong for most of their opponents, and that was how he wanted it. Minor County sides were often beaten by an innings, and beside the West Bridgford pavilion the fox's tail that was raised for victory was rarely down. "Lunch was terrific," Philip Snow remembers. "He always saw that the opposing side were well-victualled. But he kept an eye on his own team not to have too much wine."

The British establishment fascinated him. "His parents were strict Jews, but he was an atheist," son Albert says. "He got great fun out of finding out about Freemasonry and all the secret handshakes. He used to pull their legs."

He became a member of MCC, acting as its intermediary in approaching Harold Larwood after the Bodyline tour, but his Jewish roots and his trade background were not easily accepted at Lord's and he fell out with the club when he was not allowed to serve on any of its committees.

He sent Albert to Harrow – a smaller school than Eton, there would be more chance of his making the cricket eleven – but, alas, the boy had no more ability than his father. A message was sent to the coach Patsy Hendren that he would be amply rewarded if Albert were selected. Back came the reply: "You could pay me a thousand pounds; I still couldn't manage it."

Sir Julien was a driven man, requiring his office staff to start at 5.30 a.m. on cricket and hunting days and, when he was advised by his doctor to slow down, he refused, dying at his desk at Stanford Hall in September 1944 after a day on duty as a magistrate at Nottingham Guildhall. Upset by bad publicity about rationing irregularities at some of his stores, he had already sold his business to Sir Isaac Woolfson.

His widow sold Stanford Hall to the Co-operative Society the following year, retiring to Sussex where she never watched another cricket match.

But another Julien Cahn, Albert's son and born after his grandfather's death, has revived the family tradition, playing cricket with no great skill in fund-raising ventures for cancer research at the Royal Marsden Hospital and supporting "the real grass roots of cricket" with the London Community Cricket Association.

"My grandfather could be impossible at times," he says, "but he was a great man. He lived his life to the full, his staff adored him, and he took his civic duties very seriously. His work for the National Birthday Trust lives on today."

So, too, does the pavilion at West Bridgford. After a spirited local campaign against demolition, it is being renovated by Rushcliffe Council: a memorial to one of cricket's greatest eccentrics – and most generous patrons.

*Sir Julien Cahn's XI, 1935*
*back: GFH Heane, CR Maxwell, GF Summers, TB Reddick, RC Blunt, SD Rhodes*
*front: DPB Morkel, FCW Newman, Sir Julien Cahn, RWV Robins, IAR Peebles*

## 85. A break in the clouds

*Eric Hill of Somerset* TWC, JAN 2004

"As a kid," Somerset's Eric Hill recalls, "I had assumed my first appearance at Lord's would be opening the innings for England. With Len Hutton."

Instead, he stepped onto the hallowed turf for the first time in February 1942. "Signing on for the RAF. With a slight sleet falling and snow on the ground. The Swearing Office kept saying, 'King George the Sixth, his Hairs and Successors.' It was the most solemn moment of our lives, and none of us could stop giggling. Then we did the signing in the Long Room."

County cricket got going again in 1946, but it was a damp summer and there were few new faces. Then, while the England team were being thrashed in Australia, bitter winter weather brought the country to a standstill. With relief the crowds returned to the cricket in May. 'Pale-faced, dowdy, worn,' Cardus called them, 'existing on rations, the rocket bombs still in their ears.'

Travelling to Lord's for their first fixture, the Somerset team included two newcomers, both from Taunton: Eric Hill and Maurice Tremlett. Eric was bowled second ball by Bill Edrich for a duck – "He was about three times as fast as anybody I'd ever faced before" – but Tremlett, a young fast bowler, captured the headlines with a spell of five for eight in the Middlesex second innings. "The story went round," Eric remembers, "that Tremmy hit Leslie Compton on the thigh, and Leslie had to go to the doctor to get blood moving through the vein. We thought this was highly dramatic. Even the old 'uns did. It suggested that Maurice was a tremendously fast bowler. He was quick, but he wasn't that quick."

England was crying out for a young fast bowler, and the pressmen were full of enthusiasm. "A wonderful bit of bowling," Jim Swanton told Jack Meyer, the Somerset skipper. "He's certain to be England's first choice fast bowler for the West Indies tour."

In the Caribbean, Eric says, "Gubby Allen tried to get him swinging the ball. He was very different when he came back. Said he'd got a lot to learn about bowling." Within three years Tremlett was concentrating on his batting.

By Tuesday morning at Lord's Somerset were chasing 176 for victory, and in a hazy atmosphere they subsided to 113 for seven. Then the young Eric Hill stepped out to join Wally Luckes, to what Swanton called 'a nightmare of a situation: in his first county match, with 0 in the first innings and Middlesex round his bat like vultures.'

But the young batsman had known worse nightmares than this. Navigating a Mosquito aircraft on a reconnaissance mission to the Lofoten Islands, he and his pilot Frank Dodd had come under enemy fire.

At the furthest extent of their plane's fuel capacity, they descended for close-up photographs. Then the German fire began. "Frank did a quick turn, and the perspex bubble top of the cabin blew off, with all the maps, the navigation bags, the telegraph equipment."

Open to the wind and not far from the Arctic Circle, they returned for more pictures, then away they went. Cloud everywhere. They were desperate for navigational help – but their answering code was lost in the sea. "I sent them our names, ranks, service numbers, but they just used the code challenge."

They flew unaided for four hours, high above the clouds. The fuel gauge neared empty as the sky grew dark.

"We were both trying to disguise our fear. Frank wasn't a talker, and I suppose I wasn't, either. We were thinking what we would have to do if we ditched, but neither of us said a word. Then I saw this gap in the cloud and I said, 'Frank, there's land.' We went straight down onto an airfield near Wick."

Now he was back at Lord's, on a pair in his first match.

"Compared with what we'd been through, I couldn't feel that anything was tremendously serious. I think we all felt, 'Thank God we got away with the war, and we're able to play cricket.'"

He survived two overs without scoring. "I was hopeless. I kept playing and missing, and Wally at the other end kept making these 'keep your elbow up' motions. Well, eventually I did get a run. I can't remember how."

Slowly the score crept up and the pair added 38, mostly in 'painful singles', before they both fell. That left Maurice Tremlett and tubby Horace Hazell to score another 25 for the last wicket.

The sun had broken through the hazy cloud, the temperature soared into the 80s and, on either side of lunch, the last pair drew close to a famous Somerset victory. There was tension – "We were all smoking like chimneys, and I was twittering away like an old fool" – but not tension as he had known in the Mosquito: "It was just an ordinary cricket match, there to be won."

Tremlett, graduating from the Rowbarton Brewery side in Taunton, lofted Jack Young for a six over long-off that landed just wide of the pavilion.

Then, with one run wanted, he drove the ball past mid-on and, as he told John Arlott later, "I made Horace run three, just to make sure, as you do in village matches."

176 to win. *Wisden* records the score as 178 for nine.

The Middlesex fielders lined up and clapped the Somerset pair into the pavilion. 'Test matches may come and go,' *The Times* declared, 'but a county match with a finish so tense and yet so friendly can in enjoyment never be excelled.'

The sun was shining once more on English cricket, and a golden summer was in store.

## 86. First-class cricket on holiday

*Festival cricket* TWC, Oct 2007

In the years after World War Two, when the Test and county programme was all over by the end of August, Festival crowds would gather at Scarborough and Hastings, to catch their last glimpses of the summer's tourists and to enjoy such contests as Gentlemen versus Players, North versus South, an England XI versus a Commonwealth XI.

The Scarborough Festival dated back to the 1870s, and Yorkshire's Ted Lester, born in a nearby house in 1923, recalls how as a small boy he was captivated by the mix of cricket, crowd and music.

"During the lunch interval the spectators would parade across the ground. The band would start playing, and they'd go right through to the close, ending with the National Anthem. And the players would take tea on the field, being served by a chap wearing white tie and tails. He usually had a bottle of whisky with him, too."

In 1934, as an 11-year-old, Ted Lester was throwing back the ball when Bradman hit 132 in 90 minutes. In 1945 he saw the Australian Cec Pepper strike the ball high over the rooftops into Trafalgar Square. Then the following year he was in the Yorkshire team himself.

"The cricket was played competitively," he says. "You expected the quick bowlers to bowl quick, but they didn't bowl bouncers at you. And the batsmen would play their shots – except Bob Wyatt. They used to say he was picked to make sure the games lasted three days."

The amateurs stayed at the Grand Hotel, the professionals in nearby guest houses. According to Ted, they lunched together in the marquee – though Jim Laker, playing there in 1948, reckoned he and his fellow professionals were told to stay in the pavilion. 'I think I may have made a few comments,' he later wrote. 'I was never asked to play in the Festival again.'

The match fees were a welcome end-of-season bonus for the professionals, many of whom brought their wives for a seaside break. "A capped player at Yorkshire was paid £13 for a match," Ted says. "But Scarborough paid £20 plus travelling expenses."

The amateurs, with their parties at the Grand, were even keener to be there. "I remember them talking. 'Have you been invited to the Scarborough Festival yet?' They all wanted to come."

The cricket was to be entertaining, with the umpires entering into the spirit. The story goes that at Hastings in 1899, in front of a large Saturday crowd, the dashing Gilbert Jessop was clearly stumped on 30: "Not out," the umpire said, muttering, "Near thing, near thing – but not near enough for the occasion."

It was subtly done and not always easy for newcomers to fathom. Ted Lester, playing for North against South at Scarborough, went out to bat on a pair. "Alec Bedser gave me a ball to get off the mark. I'd never played cricket like that, and I hit it for six."

There were opportunities for players to reach personal milestones. At Hastings in 1947 Denis Compton passed Tom Hayward's 1906 record of 3,518 runs in a season, hitting the final four off a leg-side full toss from Northamptonshire's Vince Broderick who remembers his captain's instructions. "Don't give him anything. It would be unfair on Tom Hayward. Not till he wants four." The umpire Alec Skelding, however, took a different view: "It's no good shouting for lbw," he said. "You'll have to bowl him or have him caught."

At Scarborough in 1951, Yorkshire's Bob Appleyard – in his first full summer – entered the last day of his last match, against MCC, on 197 wickets, and he bowled almost 40 overs before he reached his 200. At one point he asked his captain Norman Yardley to take him off – "It's spoiling the game" – but Yardley just smiled. "Keep going," he said.

He had bowled more than 1,300 overs in four months. Had he set some time aside for a break before returning to his winter job? "No, that was the holiday. We'd been to the Scarborough Festival."

The Hastings Festival withered away in the 1960s. Meanwhile at Scarborough the Gentlemen-Players fixture passed with the death of the amateur in 1962, and in the all-professional age the personal targets grew in importance. Essex's Robin Hobbs wanted five wickets for his 100 in 1967.

"Eddie Phillipson was umpiring. 'How many do you need?' he said. 'No problem.' He gave Boycott lbw when he was near a century. I don't think he was very happy."

Robin was the last leg-spinner in England, a good mixer, and he was a regular at Scarborough. His 1,099 first-class wickets include 111 there, more than he took on any other ground. "Batsmen would play more shots than in county cricket; you had more of a chance. It was a smashing way to end the summer. It was £30 a game, paid in cash out of a large tin."

Scarborough has survived, but it has lost much of its traditional atmosphere. A certain batsman, complaining that his concentration was being disturbed, had the band stopped during play, the Grand Hotel was bought by Butlins, and in the late 1970s the tourists were leaving for home after the final Test. By the 1990s the Festival was staging normal county matches.

"There's no room on the fixture list now," Robin Hobbs says. "But, if there were Festival matches, they'd still be an attraction. Some bloomin' good sides played at Scarborough, and there were great crowds. We all used to look forward to the Festival. It was like an end-of-term party."

## 87. Still alive

*A centenary at Hambledon* WCM, Nov 2008

Broadhalfpenny Down. Nestled in the rolling hills about the Meon Valley, north of Portsmouth. A quiet spot among farm fields, two and a half miles away from the village of Hambledon. Set across the road from the ancient Bat and Ball Inn.

We do not arrive in thousands, as apparently they did in the 1760s and 1770s when little Hambledon regularly took on All England and beat them. 'Half the county would be present,' John Nyren wrote sixty years later, 'the multitude forming a complete and dense circle round that noble green.'

Nor do the organisers need to arrange for the accommodation of 650 bicycles, as they did in 1908 when cricket returned to the field after an absence of 116 years. Then a memorial stone was unveiled, and in a three-day match Hambledon once more triumphed over an England side – though this Hambledon team, with CB Fry, Phil Mead and Jack Newman playing, were hardly men of the village.

Our gathering, on Saturday 13 September 2008, is a more modest affair. A 40-over contest to celebrate the centenary of that 1908 match. This time Hambledon, fortified by several Hampshire players past and present, will take on a team raised by the Broadhalfpenny Down Association, led by the former Sussex captain John Barclay whose great-uncle FGJ Ford had been in the England team a hundred years earlier.

Back in the 1770s the winner of the toss could choose where to pitch the wickets. Now, with the tinkling 1908 coin landing tails, all John Barclay has to do is to ask Hambledon to bat first – and to find out what exactly his assembled team has to offer. "Well, last time I bowled," one youngster replies cheerfully, "I managed three straight ones."

Meanwhile the Hambledon team are still arriving. Nic Pothas is coming on from a wedding while Michael Brown is said to be at the opticians. But then the Hampshire players have had quite a night: celebrating a victory at The Oval that has not only rid them of the season-long spectre of relegation but taken them improbably to the top of the championship table. It is impressive that they are coming at all.

Groundsman Harry Bates has worked long hours against the odds to provide a playable pitch, but it is something of a pudding and Hambledon's early batsmen struggle. Will Kendall bats patiently, but others perish trying to force the pace. John Stephenson, the only Test cricketer on view, faces 15 balls without scoring, finally hitting a catch to mid-off, while James Fry, trying to live up to his great-grandfather's name, manages only one run.

"I'm always surprised," James says, "how many people ask me if

I'm related to CB Fry. You think these days they'd say Stephen Fry or something."

His father Charles and uncle Jonathan reflect on the Edwardian world of 1908 in which CB was a hero blessed with "the effortless superiority" that he derived from being an English gentleman. What a world away September 1908 now seems – with Orville Wright keeping a plane in the air for an hour, the government preparing for the start of old age pensions and *The Times* lamenting the change in the playing of cricket: 'from an occasional pastime, marked by geniality and rapture, into a more or less mechanical trade.'

At the scorers' table Broadhalfpenny's Peter Danks is writing in pencil just as he would have done in 1908, though Hambledon's Penny Taylor has moved on to coloured pens. Their predecessors of the 1770s would have been cutting notches in sticks. But would they have recorded the individual scores as well? And how would the total have been displayed? Nobody seems quite sure.

"I'm fascinated by the period," historian David Rayvern Allen says. "If only we could discover a little more about it."

"They had a wonderful system in the West Indies," Peter Danks explains, happy to go off at a tangent. "When the first team batted, they would put a leaf in a bucket for each run. Then, when the second team went in, they would take out the leaves. When they took out the last leaf, they needed one run to win."

History is on all our minds. From those glory days of the 18th century, immortalised by Nyren, when here on the Down cricket made vital steps towards the modern game: when a new law had to be written after Thomas White of Reigate appeared with a bat as wide as the wicket, when a third stump was introduced forcing James Aylward to adopt a more defensive technique, when David Harris started to pitch on a length and John Small pioneered forward play. Over-arm bowling was still years away, but the days of Broadhalfpenny Down were vital ones in the development of the game.

In 1907 its memory was revived by the publication of EV Lucas's book *The Hambledon Men*, and that led to the return of cricket on the Down. The first suggestion was to build on the farm field 'a national asylum for the decayed professional', but that soon gave way to the idea of a monument and the revival of cricket on the ground. The prime mover was Edward Whalley-Tooker, the captain down at the Hambledon club, whose grand-daughter Christine Pardoe watches today's game, sitting alongside Ida Barrett, who can remember as a girl in the 1920s watching cricket here.

"It hasn't changed," Ida says. "Wherever you look, there are lovely clouds. It's so clear and open. You would never know there are 2,000 people living down the road."

Lunch is served in a marquee. We queue up for a range of delicate dishes far from the cuisine of Nyren's day when 'there were fellows who would strike dismay into a round of beef.' Nor would they have enjoyed the beer from boxes, compared to the 'barley-corn, such as would put the souls of three butchers into one weaver.'

At a table former England cricketer Bob Barber recalls the great part played by the Winchester schoolmaster Harry Altham in the revival of the ground. Bob had been the outstanding schoolboy cricketer of his generation, and Altham had become "a friendly uncle" figure, writing to him weekly at school when an injury kept him out of action and bringing him here to Broadhalfpenny Down where he passed on a burning sense of the ground's importance.

The FA Cup appears on the ground, as it did in 1939 on the only other occasion when nearby Portsmouth won it. It remained in Portsmouth's possession for seven years, kept through the war in the upstairs room of a pub. But now, is this the cup itself or is it a replica? The sceptics have their say.

Back in 1908 the memorial stone was to be unveiled by WG Grace, but a telegram arrived to say that he had missed his train. When a burly, bearded figure was later driven from Droxford station to the ground, it turned out not to be the Doctor. The lifting of the tarpaulin sheet was performed in a howling gale by the Hampshire captain Edward Sprot.

There is no gale today – not even the chill wind that caused the *Times* correspondent in 1908 to write that 'looking on at cricket, on the Hampshire Downs in September, is uncommonly cold work after 4 o'clock.'

Hambledon's innings ends on 166 for eight, with a few late runs from Nic Pothas, whose previous innings at The Oval brought him a century. "This was much harder work," he says. "I've renewed respect for club cricketers who have to play on pitches like this."

John Barclay is pessimistic about his young team's chances but – with runs from their two MCC Young Cricketers, Stuart Ransley and Oliver Saffell, and from Gerry Northwood of the Broadhalfpenny Brigands – they reach John Stephenson's last over needing twelve to win.

In 1908, when Fry led Hambledon to victory with an unbeaten 84, *The Times* admired his 'vigorous and beautifully timed hitting. If the ghosts of the former men of Hambledon were present on Broadhalfpenny Down, they must have felt, as they watched his play, that there is still something rather admirable in English cricket.'

The batting on show is not of that order, but the excitement is sustained to the last ball. With six to tie, Harry Chichester of the Butterflies pulls the ball through mid-wicket, and it bounces away for a four. Hambledon – thanks to Kendall, Pothas, Raj Maru and all – are triumphant once more.

One hundred years have passed since the ground reopened, and it is looking as good as it has ever looked. And, thanks to the hard work of the Broadhalfpenny Down Association, chaired by Peter Tuke, it now extends its pleasures to a wide range of cricketers, including Hampshire juniors (boys and girls), Hackney Community College and special needs children.

The sun is at its brightest as the day draws to a close, and Christine Pardoe returns to her car. What would her grandfather Edward Whalley-Tooker have thought about the day?

"He'd be glad that cricket's still alive," she says simply. "And glad that so many people are interested in the history of the game."

"The more the game changes," Bob Barber says, "the more important I think places like this are. I can't see how cricket can expect to survive as part of our culture if it's confined to concrete stadiums. Village grounds are so much at the heart of our game."

*1925*

*2008*

## 88. One match, three lives

*Somerset versus Yorkshire, Taunton 1954* TWC, JAN 2008

Wednesday 12 May 1954. At the County Ground, Taunton. Somerset's first home match of the summer. Against the mighty Yorkshire, a county they had last beaten in 1903. For three cricketers, it was – in very different ways – a match that stood out in the memory.

For the 21-year-old fast-medium bowler, Ken Biddulph, though he was not in the Somerset side, it marked a beginning.

A fortnight earlier he had travelled down from Essex and been offered a six-month contract. "I was so excited, but I had a good job in the Borough Treasurer's Department in Chingford Town Hall. And I thought, 'Six months, what happens after that?'"

He knocked on the door of the professionals' room, where the highly strung 39-year-old Harold Gimblett was putting on his pads. "I wonder if I could have a word with you after close of play, Mr Gimblett."

"Never mind the close of play. Come in and sit down."

"But they'll be waiting for you."

"Let them wait. You're more important at the moment. What's on your mind?"

Gimblett heard him out and was quick to respond: "You can go back in and tell that stupid Secretary of ours to shove it up his arse."

"I can't do that, Mr Gimblett."

"No, I suppose you can't. I'll tell him."

Later in the day the Secretary called the youngster in: "What do you want? A two-year contract? Yes, certainly."

On the morning of the Yorkshire match, Ken arrived bright and early, to bowl in the nets. "Half past nine, maybe. And, walking through the main gates in St James Street, I bumped into Harold Gimblett. All these small boys came running up for his autograph. So he was signing away, and I was standing to one side, waiting. Then they turned to me. 'Can we have yours?' 'Oh no,' I said, 'you don't want mine.' And I started to walk through the gates. It was the first time anybody had asked for my autograph.

"Gimblett didn't half give me a bollocking. 'You sign those autographs. Don't you ever refuse a boy an autograph.' 'But they don't even know who I am. They've never seen me play.' 'Yes, and by this time next week they will have seen you play. And they probably won't want your autograph.'"

That evening Gimblett went out to bat in poor light against a particularly fast Fred Trueman. By this stage of his career he was wracked by inner demons, the strain of being both the entertainer and the mainstay of the

Somerset batting having taken its toll. He had spent the winter having electro-convulsive therapy on his brain, and he tried to get off the marking by hooking Trueman.

According to the *Yorkshire Post*, it was 'an indeterminate shot', and he was caught off his glove at short leg. As he returned to the pavilion, he told a spectator, "It's no good. He was too fast for me. I've had it."

Then there was Yorkshire's Bob Appleyard. He was making one of cricket's most remarkable comebacks. Three summers earlier he had taken 200 wickets in his first full season. Then, in the first match of 1952, also at Taunton, he had been taken ill and had driven home in mid-match to be told that he was suffering from an advanced case of tuberculosis. He had half his left lung removed, had to learn to walk again and for a long time was given no chance of playing any more cricket.

The match at Taunton in May 1954 was only the third of his comeback. With an action remodelled to cope with his reduced lung capacity, he took five wickets for 72 runs in the Somerset first innings and seven for 16 in the second. "It was one of my best performances ever," he reflects now, "and extra special because it was at Taunton, where I was taken ill."

That summer would yield him 154 wickets and an England Test cap at the age of 30. "People always talk about the year I took 200 wickets," he says, "but really that summer was the greater achievement. I felt I was carrying a torch for everybody who had had tuberculosis. That gave me a great determination to do well."

On that first evening Gimblett walked out before close of play, and only a great diplomatic effort persuaded him to bat a second time when he was lbw to Trueman for five. "I never saw him again," Ken Biddulph said. "He just packed his bags at the end of the match and went."

Ken Biddulph. A journeyman cricketer, who never lost his enthusiasm for the game. He died of a heart attack in January 2003. "If it hadn't have been for cricket," he used to say, "I'd have finished up a wizened old stick in Chingford Town Hall."

Harold Gimblett. Still Somerset's greatest run-scorer. In March 1978 he took an overdose of tablets and died. "Perhaps he was a lot better player than he thought," was Ken's view. "Tony Hancock never thought he was a very good comedian, did he?"

And Bob Appleyard? Fifty-five years have passed since his TB operation, and he is just completing a two-year term as Yorkshire's President. Still full of determination, he has barely missed a day's duty in two summers.

A beginning, an end and an extraordinary return. Three lives meeting in one match.

## 89. The oldest county cricketer

*Cyril Perkins of Northamptonshire* TWC, OCT 2008

There are few survivors from pre-war county cricket, and Cyril Perkins – born in June 1911 – is the oldest of them.

A genial slow left-arm bowler, he played for Northamptonshire from 1934 to 1937, when the county was at its lowest ebb: not one win in his 56 games for them. His one later first-class match, for Minor Counties, also ended in defeat, leaving him the holder of an all-time record in English cricket: most first-class matches without a single victory.

"We did get a bit despondent at times," he says. "We had first innings lead in quite a few matches, and we didn't win any of them. But in the end you get so used to not winning that you just accept it. The members got used to it, too. They saw some cricket."

In 1935, according to *The Cricketer*, his bowling was 'by far the most cheering feature' of the county's summer. 'He possesses a nice action and can spin the ball. With careful coaching, he might attain to representative cricket.'

Alas, the next summer, he had less success. By 1937 he was rarely in the team, and the county released him.

"Sorry," they said, "but there's no money in the kitty."

He had worked previously for a landscape gardener, but times were hard and he went on an MCC list of unemployed cricketers, from which he was approached by Suffolk. They found him a job in a sugar beet factory outside Ipswich, and by 1939 he had qualified to play in the Minor Counties Championship.

So began his second cricketing career, one that lasted till 1967 and saw him named in 2000 in the Minor Counties Team of the Century. No other Suffolk bowler comes within 300 of his 779 wickets, and on his mantelpiece is the ball with which in 1960, aged 49, he took all ten Hertfordshire wickets for 23 runs. When he finally retired, Bill Edrich, by then with Norfolk, said of him: 'Cyril was one of the most accurate and effective bowlers not only in Minor Counties cricket but in the whole country.'

"As a boy I played a lot of cricket on the brick path alongside the chapel," he recalls. "The path was only four foot wide, and you had to be accurate to pitch the ball on it."

He cannot explain how, naturally right-handed, he came to bowl with his left arm, but he knows that he was never in the same class as Yorkshire's Hedley Verity. "He was so accurate. Arthur Mitchell could stand there and almost pick the ball off the bat. At Northampton once he bowled me this ball, and it turned and bounced so much my eyes stood out like hat pins. 'Oh, they never get anybody out,' he said. He was a real gentleman."

For Suffolk in 1939 Cyril Perkins played alongside Phil Mead, formerly of Hampshire, the greatest run-scorer in the history of the county championship. "A funny chap. He'd take guard, stand right away from his bat and do this shuffle towards the bat when the bowler was running in. He was an awkward man to get out."

That first summer he took 55 wickets in eight matches. With one game to play, at Lowestoft, they were top of the Minor Counties table.

"That was the best Suffolk team I played in, but war was coming and the game ended in a tedious draw because nobody was interested. As we were packing our bags and leaving the pavilion, the Navy came in and took over the ground. It became a barrage balloon site."

He joined the Royal Artillery, finishing up in Cairo. His scrapbook contains cuttings from the *Egyptian Mail* that he sent home to his mother, reports of cricket matches that featured Jim Laker and the New Zealander Martin Donnelly. "He gave me a right pasting. No matter where I set the fieldsmen, the ball went somewhere else. He was the best batsman I ever bowled at."

Not Bradman? "I didn't play against him. I was in the Northants team for the previous game, but the local amateurs used to come in for the tourist match." Not Wally Hammond? "We didn't play Gloucestershire. When I read about him, I used to think, 'Thank God we don't play *them*.'"

In 1946 he returned to Suffolk, where his 46 wickets at 7.21 runs each helped them to their first championship. He became coach and groundsman at Ipswich School, and each summer he bowled for Suffolk, often in tandem with Herbert Hargreaves, the fast bowler from Yorkshire, who did not appreciate the speed with which Cyril got through his overs.

"Herbert was a fiery character," their team-mate Brian Gibbons recalls. "He used to swear at having to bowl again so soon. But Cyril just carried on. Cyril was a classical slow left-armer, very accurate and with a good arm ball."

Cyril was still in post at Ipswich, an ever cheerful presence, when in 1966 the school hosted Suffolk's first appearance in the Gillette Cup – against Kent. A month short of his 55th birthday he rolled the pitch through the week, and on Saturday, while Colin Cowdrey scored a century, he bowled his 12 overs for 31 runs. "I think the captain was kind to me. I bowled before the hammer started."

He is one of the last men alive to have faced Larwood and Voce, to have bowled to Sutcliffe and Leyland. He was bowling at Northampton when an 18-year-old Denis Compton scored his first hundred, and now at Ipswich he was up against a 20-year-old Derek Underwood. Only one cricketer – Lincolnshire's Johnny Lawrence – has played in a one-day competition at a greater age.

"I've been lucky," he says of his longevity. "I've lived in the fresh air all my life, and I do believe this East Anglian air is good for you. It's so bracing."

## 90. From stumping to stomping

*Frank Parr of Lancashire* TWC, June 2007

In clubs and halls up and down England in the 1950s the Mick Mulligan Band played revivalist jazz to enthusiastic audiences, their singer George Melly rasping out the songs of the American poor.

*I wanna pay a visit to the devil down below*
*Hung and killed my woman, wanna reap just what I sow*
*So judge, judge, good time judge*
*Won't you send me to the 'lectric chair*

From 1956, playing the trombone behind him was Frank Parr – far, far from the world of county cricket where once he had been a wicket-keeper on the brink of England honours.

At The Oval in July 1952, in only his second championship match for Lancashire, his acrobatic catching made him the talk of the cricket world. 'This boy is the most promising I've seen in years,' the old England keeper Herbert Strudwick said while *The Times* wrote that he had 'strongly suggested himself as a successor to Evans.' This on the strength of one match.

"In those days most of the keepers, except Godfrey Evans, just stood and collected the ball," Frank says. "I was one of the first diving keepers, and I did have a very good game."

At Maidstone in the next match he stumped the young Colin Cowdrey down the leg side: "Colin remembered it when I met him more than forty years later."

A fortnight later, before a 10,000-strong Roses crowd at Old Trafford, he batted out the last hour, shielding his number eleven Bob Berry from the strike while defying Freddie Trueman and the new ball, and he came off to a standing ovation. He was, the papers said, 'a cricketer of great promise ... with an excellent temperament' and the following May he was playing for MCC at Lord's. Then the selectors wrote to ask if he was available, if chosen, to tour the Caribbean that winter.

It was everything he had dreamed of since as a small boy he had collected cigarette cards, since he had taken up keeping in the Wallasey Grammar School Colts.

But it all came to an end abruptly. He did not find it easy to take the brisk off-spin of the tall Roy Tattersall, and more significantly Nigel Howard, Lancashire's amateur captain, retired. His successor was Cyril Washbrook, a no-nonsense professional who believed in smartness and deference. They were not qualities found in the world of jazz, and Frank's star fell rapidly.

"All jazzmen are kicking against something," he says. "It comes out when they blow."

'Frank was a fine wicket-keeper,' Brian Statham wrote, 'but he was an arty, untidy type who looked what he was, a spare-time musician. Even in flannels, walking onto the field, he still managed to look anything but a cricketer.'

"We were playing in London," Frank remembers, "and we were invited by a group of Lancashire MPs to the House of Commons for dinner."

"We were under strict instructions to dress smartly," his team-mate Bob Barber recalls, "and Frank – to be fair to him – did wear a jacket and tie. But he had a blue shirt on. Cyril Washbrook went berserk."

"My card was duly marked," Frank says.

Throughout his cricketing days, on Sunday nights Frank blew his trombone with the Merseysippi Jazz Band in Liverpool who played in the style of King Oliver and Louis Armstrong. On match days, too, he would sometimes slip away at close of play for a gig.

On one occasion – just once – he played his trombone in the dressing room. At Oxford. With Bob Berry beating time with a stump. "Much to Washy's disgust." Cyril Washbrook's vitriolic words, on the origins and nature of jazz music, are perhaps best left unprinted.

Yorkshire's Ken Taylor was a jazz enthusiast, going to hear Frank some years later at the 100 Club in London.

"Frank was a very good keeper," he says, "and a good lad. But in those days jazz was looked on as the poor man's music. Playing for a county cricket club, especially one like Lancashire, was all about being smart and respectable. If you were involved in anything like jazz, in their eyes you'd be a drop-out. They'd be thinking drugs and all sorts."

"Jungle music," Frank says. "That's how they'd think of it. Played by 'niggers' or 'coons'."

In 1953 he was close to touring with England; the following year, with Washbrook as captain, he played just five games in the Lancashire first team.

"Ken Grieves said to me, 'You've got to watch it, Frank. Cyril's after you. One bad game, and you'll be out.' And I did have a bad game. Against Gloucestershire."

The team prepared to move on from Bristol to Edgbaston, but "Frank, you're going home," Washbrook said. Though he did not know it then, his first-class cricket career was over.

"We had five wicket-keepers on the staff at one time," Jack Bond remembers, "and Frank was the best of them."

Back in the second eleven his keeping improved further – "I don't think I ever kept better in my life" – and Worcestershire's new captain Peter Richardson tried to recruit him. Terms were agreed, but their committee wrote to say they had opted instead for Yorkshire's Roy Booth.

"I soon found out why," Frank says. "A girl in the office at Old Trafford showed me this letter. 'I hear that you are thinking of taking on Frank Parr as a wicket-keeper. I should inform you that he can be a grave social risk.' Signed: Cyril Washbrook."

Instead, Frank moved to London and became a full-time musician, joining Mick Mulligan's Band, a time described in great detail by George Melly in his book *Owning Up*. Melly was a games-hater from prep school days, but he was able to sum up the trombonist's cricketing career:

'The professional cricketer has a social role. He is expected to behave within certain defined limits. He can be 'a rough diamond', even 'a bit of a character', but he must know his place. If he smells of sweat, it must be fresh sweat. He must dress neatly and acceptably. His drinking habits must be under control. He must know when to say 'sir'. Frank had none of these qualifications.'

"Cricket was feudal at that time," Frank says simply. "Particularly at Lancashire. A lot of forelock tugging."

'We never knew the reason for his quarrel with the captain of Lancashire,' George Melly continued, 'but after a month or two in his company we realised it must have been inevitable.'

For a while Mulligan's band was a popular act, then one night their trombonist saw the future. In a cinema on the outskirts of South London, in front of an audience of unusually young girls, they played the first half to little applause. After the interval Tommy Steele appeared, the girls shrieked, and Frank sank into an alcohol-fuelled depression.

"I remember declaiming, and one did declaim in those days, 'He'll put us all on the breadline.'"

By the early 1960s the more conservative trad jazz had taken over, and Frank laid down his trombone to become Acker Bilk's manager.

"The jazz we played has all but died," he says sadly – but he is less gloomy about cricket. "I've watched almost every ball of the World Cup. Sangakkara is the best keeper. And I was sorry when Geraint Jones lost his place in the England team. He took some great diving catches. The best keeper I've ever seen, though, is Ian Healy."

The trombone has not been blown for forty years, but the keeping gloves survived till 1993, appearing regularly in the cause of The Ravers Cricket Club. Old Trafford's loss was the Paddington Recreation Ground's gain.

"Looking back, I've no reason to grumble," he says, sitting at ease in a flat that makes no concessions to tidiness. "I've been very lucky in my life, and I don't regret a moment of it."

# 91. Win – Win – Win

*Micky Stewart of Surrey* TWC, May 2008

For most of the counties in the 1950s, the championship programme was a way of life more than a competition they expected to win. Yorkshire had a culture of demanding success – "Second place is no good to me," their chairman of cricket Brian Sellers would say. "You might as well come second last" – but in the south attitudes were different.

Micky Stewart recalls asking Middlesex's John Murray whether in the pre-season the North Londoners ever talked about winning the championship. "No, never," he replied.

"If we were playing Yorkshire at the Oval," Micky says, "a large number of members would be hoping Len Hutton would get a hundred. The same with Middlesex and Denis Compton. That was their entertainment. If we'd enforced the follow-on, we'd go down the steps and they'd say, 'Don't get them out too quickly. I've taken a day off work for this.' It wasn't about winning like it was in Yorkshire."

Within the Surrey dressing room, however, that changed in 1952 when Stuart Surridge was appointed captain. Born into a family of sports goods manufacturers, Surridge was able to play as an amateur but he was not an old-fashioned amateur. He mixed with his team, and he never let up in his pursuit of victory.

He revolutionised the fielding. Wilf Woooller's Glamorgan had won the championship in 1948 with their close catching, and Yorkshire were always a physical presence in the field. But Surridge's Surrey set a new standard.

"We played Middlesex at The Oval," Micky remembers. "On a wet wicket. We fielded second, and you could see the footmarks where their leg-side catchers had been. They were nothing like as close as Locky, Stuey and I were standing."

In 1955 the three of them took an imposing 150 catches for Surrey. Two years later Lock and Stewart, with Barrington at slip, held 200, the three leading catchers in England.

They were mostly wet summers in the 1950s, the Oval square was no longer the batsman's paradise it had once been and Surrey had the bowling attack to force results in all conditions: Laker, Lock, Loader and the Bedser twins. Here were great gifts of spin and swing, cut and pace, but above all they hardly bowled a bad ball.

"Accuracy and consistency were the order of the day," Micky says. "I remember Derek Pratt coming into the team at Hastings; he bowled leg-breaks. His first ball was only fractionally overpitched, and Jim Parks timed it between extra cover and mid-off for four. And Stuey Surridge went mad. 'This is not the f…ing second eleven now,' he said. Accuracy was absolutely key."

In three-day cricket on uncovered pitches, it was vital to move the game forward at a good pace – and Surridge, armed with world-class bowlers, was a master of that. Micky Stewart came into the team in the middle of 1954 when they languished in mid-table, and in the wettest of summers they managed to complete nine victories in their last ten games, not one of their opponents reaching a total of 200.

They clinched the title dramatically at The Oval against Worcestershire. Starting after lunch on a wet pitch they bowled out the visitors for 25. Late in the day, with their own score on 92 for three and May and Barrington building a good lead, Surridge appeared on the balcony and waved them in.

"He's declared, Peter," Barrington said incredulously.

May, knowing his captain's liking for a lunchtime tipple, replied, "He didn't have a gin and tonic at tea as well, did he?"

By twelve o'clock the next morning Worcestershire were all out for 40, and the championship was once more being celebrated.

The next season they started with 12 straight victories. In all, across those two seasons, they won 18 consecutive matches, still a world record in first-class cricket – and in only three of them did batsmen hit centuries. Their job was simply to make *enough* runs. "In years to come," Bernie Constable would moan, "when they recall this Surrey side, they'll talk about the bowlers and they'll talk about Peter May. But there won't be one mention of we poor batsmen who've had to score our runs on these bloody pitches."

Surrey's sequence of championships ended in 1959 when a young Yorkshire side pipped them. By then the Bedsers were 41, keeper McIntyre had retired, Lock had had to remodel his bowling action and in a hot summer the Oval square was no longer so bowler-friendly. In the last match of 1958 they gave a debut to a young John Edrich, and it would be 13 years before he tasted the championship glory that was so familiar to his team-mates.

"That Surrey side of the fifties was exceptional," Micky Stewart says. "The environment was win-win-win."

Surridge retired in 1956, after five championships, passing the captaincy to the quieter but equally determined May. But Micky experienced the older man's leadership once more in the 1970s when he turned out for Surridge's President's XI in the Esher club's cricket week.

Surridge was now in his late fifties, but the fire in him had not abated.

"These poor old boys in his team, he was clapping his hands and shouting at them. 'Come on, come on.' He was still all keyed up."

*Stuart Surridge and Peter May with the newly created championship pennant*
*April 1953*

## 92. Thirteen of Surrey

*The Surrey side of the 1950s, profiled with the help of Micky Stewart*

TWC, May 2008

### Stuart Surridge (captain, 1952-56)

*Inspirational captain, whole-hearted all-rounder, brilliant close fielder.*

A loud and demonstrative man in the field, he brought a new competitiveness to Surrey. "As a close fielder he set the standard for everybody. He certainly set the standard for me to follow."

Surridge had grown up with the Bedsers, McIntyre and Constable in Surrey club cricket. "Before Stuey there was still the amateur-pro divide, and he totally changed that."

He knew how to get the best out of his side, bawling orders at Lock and gently encouraging Laker: 'I swore at Jim only once,' he said years later, 'and he couldn't bowl for an hour.' "Everything was for the team. When we went out to field, it was like going over the top out of the trenches."

### Peter May (captain, 1957-58)

*The greatest batsman of his generation.*

"Peter was a hard man, very competitive – but not loud like Stuey. He was a very good team player. He never played for his statistics, and more often than not – when runs were needed – he delivered."

On pitches on which bowlers dominated, he averaged almost 50 with the bat. On a dusty wicket at The Oval in 1958 Yorkshire's spinners, Wardle and Illingworth, were bowling by mid-day. "The first ball Ray Ilingworth bowled at me, I played forward and it hit me on the neck. Peter came in, and he scored 155. He kept hitting Johnny Wardle over extra cover – at a time when very few people did that. Johnny said he'd never seen a finer innings in those conditions."

### Ken Barrington

*Middle-order batsman, safest of slip fielders.*

Barrington, like Micky Stewart, established himself in the Surrey side in 1954, and such was the impact of his stylish batting that he was playing for England in the first Test the next summer. "He had every stroke in the book, but he was one of the biggest worriers. Before he went in to bat, he'd have two cigarettes going and the paper upside down."

Alas the selectors did not keep faith, and he turned himself into a more cautious player. "He built his game on consistency, and he restricted himself to his four main scoring shots. It's so sad that the cricketing public hardly saw the best of him."

**Tom Clark**

*Opening bat and occasional off-break bowler.*

"A fine player of pace bowling. He was very encouraging to me. I was lucky to have started my career, opening the batting with Tom at the other end."

Clark, also a footballer, was Surrey's leading run-scorer in 1954 and 1956. The England selectors picked him at the start of 1957 for the MCC–West Indians match, but by then his career was dogged by hip problems. "We played at Swansea, with all those steps. He said he was fit, and we finished up carrying him all the way up. Stuey was livid. He had hip replacements and lost the last three or four years of his career."

**Bernie Constable**

*Neat middle-order batsman.*

"He was a well-organised batsman, dapper and good looking, an exceptionally fine player of spin."

As a cover fielder Constable was quick, and he was also talkative. "They called him the Cockney Sparrow, though he wasn't a cockney. Stuey would move the field, and a voice would come. 'What you got him there for? He wants to be a bit squarer. Look at how he's holding the bat.' If new players came in, he'd watch them like a hawk, all the way from the pavilion. They'd take guard, and he'd be about three or four yards away, looking at how they were holding the bat. Staring. I learned more from Bernie than from anybody."

**Micky Stewart**

*Attractive opening batsman, one of the great catchers close to the wicket.*

In 1957 he took 77 catches, one short of Wally Hammond's record, including a world-record seven in one innings at Northampton.

"By the time I joined the team in 1954, there was this win-win environment. The result mattered, and that fitted with the way I'd been brought up. My father always said to me, 'If you're not going to be the best or thereabouts, forget it. Concentrate on what you're good at.'"

**David Fletcher**

*Opening bat.*

He had burst onto the scene in 1947 when he had been tipped as an England player. He was Surrey's leading run-scorer in their first championship year and did well in 1953 but after that, when Ken Barrington and Micky Stewart established themselves, he was in and out of the side.

"He was a pugnacious player, a good cutter and hooker. He was a good amateur boxer, and he was built like that, a lightweight boxer. He was always a quiet person. A nice man, like Tom Clark."

### Arthur McIntyre

*Wicket-keeper and useful lower-order bat. He played three Tests.*

"Up and down the country it was looked on that day in, day out he was the best wicket-keeper on the circuit. Standing up to Alec, then on wet or worn wickets keeping to Jim Laker and Locky. He had similar smooth hands to Keith Andrew or Bob Taylor, but Mac was also very strong. He was a quiet person, but he was very competitive – and, if somebody nicked it and didn't walk, he was non-stop in his ear; it used to go on and on. As a batsman he played some key innings. He was an outstanding contributor to the success of that period."

### Jim Laker

*The supreme off-spinner.*

"To me he was an absolute artist. I fielded in front of the bat, and I'd hear the snap of his fingers, then the zzzzz of the ball coming down the pitch. He was a real big spinner, with a shrewd brain. He'd work batsmen out."

Unlike Lock he maintained a calmness at all times, keeping his nerves in check with a leisurely way of doing everything. 'When things were going well, people would say, 'Look at the majesty of him, the control.' But when they weren't, it would be 'He couldn't care.' And that was wrong. He was a very emotional man."

### Tony Lock

*Aggressive slow left-arm bowler, predatory close fielder, belligerent batsman.*

"Locky was the country boy from Oxted, a real one hundred percenter. If he was true to himself, he was a great chap – but, when he tried to be suave and sophisticated like Jim, it didn't really work."

In all matches, in both 1955 and 1957, he took 200 wickets, the last bowler to do so, and his catching behind square on the leg side could be sensational.

"If I had to name one person, who did most match for match, bowling, fielding and even batting, it would be Locky. He had a real physical presence in everything he did, even down to kissing me if I caught a good 'un. 'Mi-kell,' he'd say. 'You're the best in the world … in front of square.'"

**Alec Bedser**

*The legendary fast-medium swing bowler with the devastating leg-cutter.*

"He hit the wicket hard, and his control of length and line, particularly when it was swinging, was magnificent. I came into the side in 1954, fielding bat-pad, and the first time I recall a horizontal bat shot played past me was Reg Simpson at The Oval, August Bank Holiday 1956."

As a bowler Alec Bedser benefited from huge hands and a huge heart. "Their mother was a great influence on Alec and Eric. She instilled a discipline in them – in their dress, manners, respect – and hard work was part of it. You had to put in the work – and that's what they both did, physically and technically."

**Eric Bedser**

*Off-spinner, opening or middle-order bat and slip fielder.*

With his huge hands he spun the ball from a great height. He might only be second to Jim Laker at Surrey but "if he had been about in recent years, he'd be the best off-spinner in the country by some way."

As a batsman he was good enough to score 1,000 runs in a season six times. "He should have been more aggressive. In the nets he was a magnificent timer and striker of a cricket ball but, having said that, with the pitches at that time, if it was your day, you had to stay in and make the most of it."

**Peter Loader**

*Wiry pace bowler with deadly bouncer, effective slower ball and mean streak.*

"If we declared half an hour before the close, he always seemed to knock two or three over that night. He was quick and he was accurate, quite like Brian Statham, and he would bowl them out or have them lbw."

A trainee dental mechanic, he came straight from club cricket at Beddington, and he developed his stamina felling trees in winter for Stuart Surridge. For England he took a hat-trick against the West Indies, but Trueman, Statham and Tyson were his rivals. "In any other era he'd have played a lot more Tests."

## 93. Coming to an end

*Retirement* TWC, Oct 2004

The cricket season draws to a close. For most counties in the 1950s, the last balls were bowled by the start of September. All that remained was to find winter work and to wait for news of next year's contract.

Some years the Somerset committee met as early as mid-August in the pavilion at Weston-super-Mare. "They came out of a pretty bibulous lunch," opening batsman Eric Hill recalls. "A lot of them didn't know a cricketer from a wombat. We had to keep our eyes open when we went in the bar. Make sure they didn't see *us* overdoing it."

At Southampton the meeting was held upstairs, and in 1962 fast bowler Malcolm Heath, struggling with injury, spent the day trying to prove his fitness. "I can see him now," says team-mate Alan Castell. "He was pounding round and round in his dark track suit, knowing that the committee was looking down on him."

"Next thing I was in the Secretary's office," Malcolm says. "To me it felt like the end of the world."

Mostly the bad news was delivered in person by the Secretary. Lancashire's Geoffrey Howard recalled how in 1955 he had to tell the seasoned professional Winston Place that his time was up. At the end of his first summer with the club, when asked where he would be going for his holiday, Place had replied, 'This is the last day of my holiday.' Now, after 13 summers of county cricket, he was in tears.

Some like Glamorgan's Louis Devereux read the bad news in the local paper, while Essex's Stan Cray heard by letter while coaching in South Africa. So shocked was he that he wrote to his MP, club chairman Hubert Ashton, comparing his figures with those of the team-mates who had been retained. "He sympathised," Stan remembers, "but he didn't go any further."

'Dear Sir,' the Yorkshire Secretary wrote to Bob Appleyard when he was first invited to play, 'Dear Bob' when he was laid up with tuberculosis. But at the end it was, 'Dear Appleyard, I am asked by the Committee to inform you that your services will not be required after the present season.' "You'd think they could have written 'Dear Bob'," he reflects. "I was a bit upset. The fact that it had come like that."

With hindsight most of them know that the decisions were right:

"I was really struggling," Bob Appleyard admits.

"I knew I'd had it," says Malcolm Heath.

"I'd been doing a bit of writing in the press box," Eric Hill says. "I was ready to make the switch."

Sussex's Alan Oakman retired voluntarily, becoming a first-class umpire, and he knows how hard it was for those who went out of the game.

"When you play cricket, it's the best years of your life. You won't find a job to compare with it. You're travelling round as a group; you have a few laughs. Then you find yourself working in an office, and you miss the camaraderie. You look out of the window, and the sun is shining. And you know that Sussex are at Bournemouth. And you remember what happened at Bournemouth last year. It's difficult readjusting."

Sometimes even the longest-serving could not choose their moment of parting, as Glamorgan's Don Shepherd discovered in 1972. Two years on from topping the national bowling averages, he was taken aside and told his time was up.

"It's difficult to know when you should pack up," he says. "You feel in your heart that you've passed your best, but there's always a lurking feeling that you'd like to have another season, and you could spend the winter getting back to the sort of fitness that you had when you were younger. But it's probably a pipe dream."

Their moment on the stage had passed, as Somerset's Ken Biddulph quickly realised when his contract was not renewed in 1961. "The sports shop in Taunton had a cut-out of me in the window, bowling. And the next time I walked past, it had gone."

Kent's Alan Dixon was only 23 when he called it a day at the end of 1957. A talented all-rounder, he was not in the first team, and he took up an offer to be a travelling salesman.

"But it came round to the spring, and I stopped the car by a cricket field where they were mowing the grass. And the smell of that new-mown grass meant so much. I got out of my car, and I rang Leslie Ames the Secretary. 'Leslie,' I said, 'it looks as if I've made a mistake.'"

When Kent won the championship in 1970, he was still playing.

"You miss it all so much after you retire," John Clay says, more than forty years on from his last game for Nottinghamshire. "In fact, I still miss it."

## 94. The end of an era

*Yorkshire's last championship for 33 years* WCM, Nov 2001

All afternoon blood had been seeping down Brian Close's trouser leg.

"You'll have to go off, skipper," his team mates had said to him several times. But he wouldn't hear of it.

Another blow struck him on his balding dome, and that too had no effect.

"Get on with the game," he snapped, and he took up his position once more at short leg. Helmetless and intrepid.

In most teams the junior player would field at short leg – but not at Yorkshire. "We called the position Boot Hill," Phil Sharpe says. "After the cemetery in the westerns. Peter Walker at Glamorgan might have stood as close as Brian – but nobody else."

"Closey was absolutely mental," Don Wilson reckons. "'Pain?' he used to say. 'It's all in the mind.'"

Friday August the 30th, 1968. At The Circle in Anlaby Road, Hull, where a weak sun took the edge off the east coast chill. It was ten minutes to five, Yorkshire needed victory to win the championship, and the Surrey eighth wicket pair had held them up since 3.15.

Fred Trueman had been brought back for a second spell. 'Come on, Fred,' a spectator called out. 'Yorkshire expects.' But he was 37 years old, his powers had waned, and he bowled just one ineffective over. "The saddest thing I've ever seen," Don Wilson says, and now it was up to Wilson himself to make the breakthrough.

There were just four overs left. A draw here in their last match, and the door would be open for Glamorgan to pip them to the championship.

Don Wilson's first ball was short, and Younis Ahmed pulled it hard, straight at Brian Close. "I braced myself," he says, "as you do when you know a blow is coming, with my arms tight to my sides, trying to make a smaller target, I suppose. The ball hit me somewhere between the side of my arm and the inside of my body, and it rebounded in the air."

The blow left an egg-sized lump, but Jimmy Binks the keeper was alert enough to hold on to the ricochet. Younis stood in his crease dumbfounded, and they turned to the umpire.

Albert Gaskell. A large, round man from Northallerton. "He drank an enormous amount," Don Wilson says, "and he had this great purple nose. Everybody seemed to like him so they gave him a couple of years on the first-class list."

"That's out," he said, and the crowd buzzed with fresh excitement.

"Albert," the Surrey captain Micky Stewart recalls, barely able to control hysterical laughter. "He was a lovely, happy character, always with a smile.

A real Yorkshireman. I got a pair in that match. Both lbw to Albert. The second one, from Illy, it would have gone two feet over the top and missed another two sets."

Two balls after Younis's departure, Don Wilson struck Robin Jackman on the pads and again the cheery umpire's finger was up. "It would have knocked out middle," Don reckons, but Micky Stewart saw it differently. "I think it was Albert who appealed."

Mike Selvey, in his first month as a county cricketer, came in at number eleven, and he survived the rest of the over. "I remember looking at Brian Close's boot," he says, "and seeing the blood spilling out of the eyelets."

Then Tony Nicholson bowled to Arnold Long, and off the final ball Long gave a catch to the keeper. According to *The Times*, 'the spectators swarmed around the Yorkshire team as they strolled triumphantly off the field.'

It was a great Yorkshire occasion. Michael Parkinson was doing interviews for *Yorkshire Television*, and Sir Leonard Hutton was teasing the young Surrey batsman Michael Hooper: "You're a batsman, are you? ... How many did you make? ... Four? Well, how were you out? ... Bowled. I see. ... Was it a straight one?"

And there was Albert Gaskell, celebrating his last match as a first-class umpire. "It was Albert's finest hour," Micky Stewart laughs.

"Is there a doctor on the ground?" the tannoy asked, and soon Brian Close was clambering into a spectator's Beetle, being driven away for stitches in his leg. "You know what hospitals are like," he says. "I missed all of the champagne and most of the party."

"He reappeared during the celebrations," Mike Selvey says. "With his gap-toothed grin, a fag in his palm and a cross of white sticking plaster on his head."

Seven titles in ten years – and this last one in a season when the other counties had overseas players: Sobers at Notts, Majid at Glamorgan, Asif and John Shepherd at Kent. Yorkshire's home-grown team had won without such help.

But Fred was retiring, Ray Illingworth off to Leicester, Ken Taylor emigrating. Next year Jimmy Binks would go. The year after, Brian Close.

"It was never the same again," Phil Sharpe says. "An era was ending."

But did they realise as they drank champagne that they would have to wait another 33 years for a title? "Oh no. We wouldn't have thought that."

"The tradition went," says Don Wilson, who soldiered on under Geoff Boycott's captaincy till 1974. "We lost the art of winning."

"I don't think at the time that the Yorkshire public appreciated how good the team was," Phil Sharpe says. "They expected us to win."

## 95. Against all the odds

*Geoff Edrich of Lancashire* WCM, Jan 2003

Nobody in English cricket after the war had a greater reputation for courage than Bill Edrich – with his fearless hooking of fast bouncers, his devil-may-care spirit and his DFC for low-level, day-time bombing raids. But what of his younger brother Geoffrey?

According to Geoff's Lancashire team-mate Ken Grieves, "Geoff was the ideal club man, the batsman who would fight hardest of all against the odds."

In 1951 he was struck a fearsome blow on the head by the South African Cuan McCarthy, retired for twenty minutes and returned to score a century. Then, after a nine-hour coach journey, he turned up the following morning at Portsmouth, his head still throbbing, and scored another century.

In August 1953 he played his greatest innings. An under-prepared Old Trafford pitch had been made spiteful by heavy rain on the second afternoon, and the Northants bowling attack was led by a young Frank Tyson, aided by a strong wind and determined to show his home county their mistake in rejecting him.

In 1939 Geoff Edrich, playing for Norfolk, had hit a fifty against the West Indians. "Martindale was playing, and he was a bit quick. But Tyson was the quickest I played against."

It was clear that none of his Lancashire team-mates relished the challenge. Ikin 0, Howard 6, Grieves 2, Wharton 4, Marner 5, Hilton 4. They were 94 for seven at close of play, with Edrich unbeaten on 59.

"When you watch from the pavilion at Old Trafford," he says, "it's side on, and it looks far worse than it is. The players coming in didn't fancy it."

Edrich was playing with a hand badly bruised in the previous game, and early in the innings he took a sharp rap on the left wrist from a Tyson lifter. But he kept in line and, when he resumed on the final morning, his grip on the bat was so light that Bob Clarke knocked it out of his hands.

'Edrich loves his cricket,' the *Manchester Guardian* reported, 'and a man will suffer and risk much for what he loves.'

Ten years earlier, under a tropical sun, he had been building the railway in Thailand. Dawn to dusk, seven days a week, with fever, cholera and dysentery taking their toll. "You had to have a bit of luck – and will power. A lot of the boys died of a broken heart. They couldn't see the end. There was one march, when we moved camp, maybe 20 miles, when some of us were ready to pack in. And if you dropped out, that was it – you got a bayonet through you from the guards. But 'Keep going,' my friend Dick Steward said. You had to have one or two decent chaps with you to get through. That's what's always made me feel a cricket team, to have success, has to have team spirit."

It was much tougher than the first months of captivity, when they worked in the docks of Singapore Old Town when there would be the occasional *yasume*, rest days when improbably they staged cricket matches. The battalion's sports officer Dick Curtis had carried their kit into the camp, and at Serangoon Road Geoff Edrich scored centuries in three makeshift matches. Then at Changi he played in the famous Tests, beating Ben Barnett's Australians two-one. They say that Jim Swanton arrived during one, saw Geoff run up to bowl with his rushing, slingy action and assumed that brother Bill had been captured.

It was serious cricket. Dick Curtis even found a typewriter and produced a team sheet. "He carried it with him right through to the end of the war."

But these were blurred memories by the time Geoff Edrich had spent 18 months building the railway. Down to six stone, with only five of his thirty-odd platoon comrades still alive.

"Work. Sleep. A bit of rice. Work. Time went on. It's amazing what you can put up with, isn't it? But then a lot of them didn't. I suppose there was somebody looking after me. When you were cutting the jungle down for the railway, if you got a bamboo scratch, it seemed there must be some poison in the bamboo or something. They used to form ulcers, and they would grow up quickly, from a shilling to half a crown. There was no antiseptic or anything to kill them. They used to remove their limbs. Oh dear, it was terrible."

He was put on a boat to Japan, was torpedoed and shipwrecked off Formosa, but somehow he got taken aboard another boat. "I think we started with a convoy of nine or ten ships, and only three survived."

When he eventually got back to England, he found his wife and son living on a widow's pension. Their lives had moved on, and he spent his first year in England apart from them.

"It's a bad dream now," he says, in his 63rd year of marriage.

He has survived cancer of the throat, though it is eight years since he has eaten any solid food. Life has greater challenges than a cricket ball propelled by McCarthy or Tyson.

He finished that innings at Old Trafford on 81 not out, Lancashire losing the game by one wicket. At close of play he drove to Cheltenham in his Austin 8, but the next morning in the dressing room he could not grip the bat at all. An x-ray confirmed that Tyson had broken his wrist.

"No matter how high the odds were stacked against him," Ken Grieves said, "he was the one man who would never quit."

"You have to have a bit of luck," Geoff says more modestly. "And you have to love the game. In the end, a lot of it comes down to how much you want to play."

## 96. All over in half an hour

*Edgbaston, Mon 19 Aug 1985, with Richard Ellison* The Times, 16 July 2005

"It's funny how some things happen," Richard Ellison reflects, "and so quickly. They're unplanned, or they're unintentional. They just materialise, and then they're gone. That's how that evening session at Edgbaston seems to me now."

It was 5.25 on the fourth day when England took the field. They had a first innings lead of 240, but time was running out – as it had at Old Trafford, where rain and an Allan Border century had allowed Australia to escape with a draw. The series stood at one-all and, with only the Oval Test to follow, England's chances to regain the Ashes were dwindling.

Here at Edgbaston there had also been intermittent rain, but England's batsmen had piled on the runs: Gower 215, Robinson 148, Gatting 100. Then at 572 for four Botham had come out to face Australia's premier quick bowler McDermott. He lofted his first and third balls for gigantic, straight sixes and sent the fourth to leg for a one-bounce four.

"It was a real psychological blow. Whether Gower planned it, I don't know, but it charged Both up for bowling, and it got the crowd going. The Australians had taken a pasting all day, and they had their noses rubbed in it by this amazing guy. They must have thought, 'Oh God, we've got to bat now.' Then it all just happened."

In his second over Botham, with his new blond rinse, bowled a bouncer and Hilditch top-edged it high towards Richard Ellison at long leg.

"The sun had come out. I'd just had a hat brought out to me, and I took the catch. So I was involved straightaway."

All summer the selectors had struggled to find fast bowlers to partner Botham. Cowans, Allott, Foster, Sidebottom, Agnew, Taylor. Now they were looking to the medium-pace swing of Ellison. He was heavily bunged up with a cold, but he insisted on playing and took six wickets in the first innings.

"Everything seemed to click that summer. I felt like I did when I was 19, when I thought that I could run in and bowl any ball at any time. I was fit, I was attacking the crease, and I seemed to have half a yard more of pace and to be swinging it later. You don't think about these things when they click, but it was a wonderful purple patch."

At 6.13, when the scoreboard read 31 for one, he came on to bowl at the City End. In his third over he sent down a widish delivery to the left-handed Wessels, who chased it, and it swung away to take the edge. Next ball he trapped night-watchman Holland lbw; and suddenly he was running in to bowl to Border on a hat-trick.

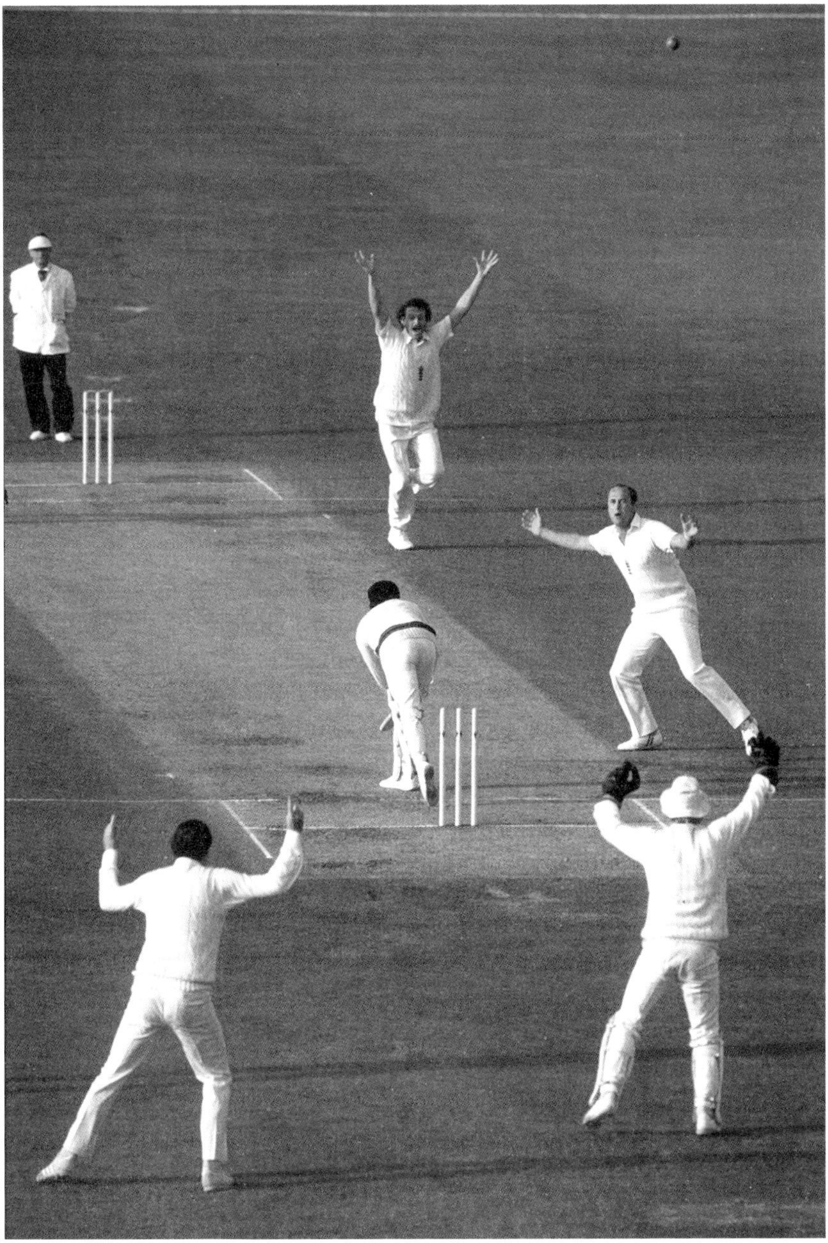

*Border, bowled Ellison*

"There was a hell of a roar behind me. I've played at Melbourne and Calcutta in front of 90,000, and the noise there was just the cacophony of the crowd. But at Edgbaston it was a crescendo of support. It wasn't around me, it was behind me."

As John Woodcock wrote in *The Times*, 'The crowd so warmed to this big, shambling, hirsute fellow that they roared their heads off in support.'

Border survived, but in his next over Richard Ellison had Wood caught off a leading edge. Then, as the clock neared five to seven, he bowled the ball of his life. It swung across the left-handed Border, pitched and came back to clip the off-stump.

Australia were 36 for five, and he had taken four wickets for one run.

"I don't think I could bowl that ball again. If I'm honest, it wasn't quite what I meant to bowl. But it was the crucial moment, and we all knew it. Everybody was jumping all over the place. There was so much euphoria. Then we were off the pitch, and the day was over. A meal, a beer, then bed. A job to do next day."

"That Monday evening," David Gower says, "was the moment we realised that England could regain the Ashes."

On the final day rain held up play till 2.30, and it was not till 4.40 – when a ball rebounded off Lamb's boot for a freak catch – that the breakthrough came. Then the last wickets fell, and Richard Ellison was declared Man of the Match.

"Afterwards I drove down to South London with Paul Downton. We went for a meal, and people kept coming up, congratulating me. I remember thinking, 'This is great, but don't get carried away with it.' At the end of the day it's just a game."

At The Oval he took seven wickets in another victory. He finished the summer top of the national averages, ahead of Richard Hadlee and Malcolm Marshall, and he was one of *Wisden*'s five cricketers of the year. Then the back problems and the self-doubt started, and his time at the top seemed to pass almost as fast as his Edgbaston triumph.

"It happened so quickly that evening. They chased wide ones and nicked them. The odd good ball came out. And it was all over in half an hour."

Now he is master in charge of cricket at Millfield School.

"I say to the guys here, 'Every ball you bowl can have a huge impact on the shape of a game. Every time you run in to bowl, you've got to believe that.' That evening at Edgbaston seems even more important now, because we haven't won an Ashes series in this country since. You're almost hanging on to it: 'The last time we won, I played a part.' I hope we beat them this year. I really do."

## 97. Ken Biddulph (1932-2003)

WCM, Mar 2003

Ken Biddulph was a fast-medium bowler for Somerset from 1955 to 1961, then for Durham till 1972. A tall, thin man who played his early cricket in Chingford in Essex, he was discovered by Alf Gover as part of an *Evening News* free coaching scheme that launched a dozen promising youngsters into county cricket.

He was signed by Somerset at a time when the county's fortunes were being revived by a wide-ranging recruitment campaign, and in 1958 their 'League of Nations' side reached an unprecedented third place. Moving north, he was the leading wicket-taker in the Minor Counties Championship in 1963.

As a professional cricketer he was a cheerful, whole-hearted performer, his immaculate appearance assisted by the coat hangers he introduced into the Somerset dressing room.

But it was in his later life that he achieved his real greatness, as a superb coach working in the Cotswolds. His sessions mixed skill development, humour and love of the game in a potent brew that attracted cricketers from all parts, young and old, myself included. Emulating Gover and his sidekick Arthur Wellard, his infectious enthusiasm could transform the dowdiest environment, and he always stayed afterwards to regale us with tales of his own modest career.

"I remember at Alf's once I was bowling at this chap and he didn't look very good. There was a club cricketer in the next net, and I said to Alf, 'Excuse me, Mr Gover, do you think I could go and bowl at that feller next door?' 'All right, old boy.' Everybody was 'old boy' to Alfred. 'But what's the matter with this one?' 'Well, he isn't very good.' Isn't very good. Afterwards, he said to me, 'That's Peter May.'

"I bought a new bat at the start of 1961. Took it out for a net, and Bill Alley bowled this ball at me. I played it back. 'Here, what's that bat you've got down there?' He banged a ball up and down on it. 'That's much too good for you. I'll give you one of mine.' And he went out that summer and scored 3,000 runs with my bat. You can see it in the museum at Taunton."

The stories enchanted me, and my attempt to weave them together in a short piece about his most memorable match led directly to the writing of my first book.

He may not have been a great cricketer himself, but it is only through the generosity and devotion of such people – not the cynics and the technocrats – that the fun and the magic of the game will pass to future generations.

With Ken there was always magic, and there was certainly always fun.

## 98. Geoffrey Howard (1909-2002)

WCM, JAN 2003

Geoffrey Howard was one of the finest administrators in the history of English cricket – some would say the finest.

Born in 1909 into a family imbued with Fabian ideals, he was a good enough batsman to play for Middlesex in 1930, declining an invitation to join the Lord's ground staff. But it was only after the war, when he found it hard to settle back into banking, that he turned to cricket to earn his living.

In 1947 he became Surrey's Assistant Secretary, making such an impression that within two years he overcame regional prejudice to become Secretary at Old Trafford. Sixteen years later he returned to The Oval where he stayed till retirement in 1974. They were not easy years, between the brief post-war surge in attendances and the advent of television's fat cheques. It took imagination and hard work to keep the game solvent.

At Old Trafford he insisted on ground improvements, realising that with affluence would come an intolerance of primitive conditions. At The Oval, he forced the Surrey aristocrats to accept advertising boards and pop concerts. He even turned up at a committee meeting in a coloured shirt. "Why don't we wear this in the Sunday League?" He was a man before his time.

He had only been Lancashire Secretary for three summers when MCC appointed him to manage a six-month tour of India. With just two journalists and 16 players, he set off with the words of the MCC secretary ringing in his ears: "Rather you than me, old boy. I can't stand educated Indians." Fortunately the new manager loved them, Indians and Pakistanis. He admired greatly their post-independence spirit, and he became their liaison man when they toured England.

Four years later he took an 'A' team to Pakistan. It was a happy tour, but he needed all his diplomatic charm to quell angry feelings when a local umpire got drenched in an out-of-hand rag.

His greatest triumph came in 1954/55 with Len Hutton's team in Australia. With no assistant and no funds in the bank when he arrived, he was a manager who played all the parts: ambassador, press relations officer, selector, travel co-ordinator, banker (albeit operating from a personal overdraft), gentle disciplinarian, convenor of the boisterous Saturday night club, even psychologist as he coaxed a dispirited captain out of bed on the morning of the third Test. After a disastrous defeat at Brisbane, when Hutton put Australia in, Frank Tyson became the Typhoon, Colin Cowdrey came of age, and they returned 3-1 victors.

"Nothing was more certain," Frank Tyson says, "than an enjoyable tour if Geoffrey Howard was the manager. Had he been able to spare the time away from his young family, he could have extended England's dominance of world cricket till the end of the decade." Trevor Bailey calls it "the happiest of all my tours" while, for Tom Graveney, "Geoffrey was in a class of his own."

It was typical of the Lancashire secretary that, on his first day back at Old Trafford, he left his mail unopened and cycled round the ground to talk to his staff. His early education had been a progressive one, with an emphasis on practical skills, and he never lost his respect for craftsmen.

After ten productive years at The Oval he retired, but he did not rest. He created a home out of a cow barn, he shook up the Minor Counties Association in eight years as its treasurer, and at the age of 92 he embarked with me on his memoirs. It was an exhausting undertaking, but he never let the pace slacken. "The clock is ticking," he would gently remind me.

He was the most valuable of witnesses: warm, humorous and wise. But I soon realised that I was not just writing a collection of memories. I was portraying a great man, a man who represented all that was best about England and about English cricket.

The late recognition startled him. "Do people really think these things about me?" he asked as the tributes poured in. Then he would ring me with delight: "You'll never guess who has just telephoned." And it would be Mike Brearley, Bob Appleyard, David Sheppard. Or a member of one of his hospitality tours. Or his secretary at Old Trafford. He remembered them all.

Like his grandfather, the pioneer of garden cities, he cared for people. He was the perfect English gentleman, always courteous, never succumbing to prejudice. But he also had a lovely sense of humour.

We had lunch one day at a garden centre where the only seats were at a table where two young women were talking rather earnestly.

"Excuse me," he said, "would you mind if we joined you at your table?"

"Not at all," one of them said, though she clearly did not mean it. "As long as you're not shocked by our conversation."

We sat and ate in silence. They dropped their voices, and Geoffrey looked across at them. "I'm sorry," he said finally, "but, if we are to be shocked by your conversation, you are going to have to speak up a bit."

He still loved cricket, admiring the Sri Lankan batting this summer at Lord's. "I always thought that they were the most naturally gifted of all the cricketers on the sub-continent."

As summer turned to autumn, he anticipated his death, facing it with the same clear eye as Shakespeare, whom he quoted with a smile:

*Golden lads and girls all must,*
*As chimney-sweepers, come to dust.*

His wife Nora had predeceased him, but he is survived by four daughters, who will miss him greatly – as will all of us who knew him in his second family, the world of cricket.

## 99. Charles Palmer (1919-2005)

TWC, June 2005

Charles Palmer was an easy man to underestimate: a much better batsman than his frail, bespectacled appearance suggested, a more testing bowler than he seemed from his innocuous-looking medium pace, and a far more determined and capable administrator than his self-deprecating, gentlemanly exterior led people to believe.

The son of a salesman in Old Hill in the Black Country, he attended Halesowen Grammar School and Birmingham University, making his cricketing debut for Worcestershire in July 1938 at the age of 19. He set out from home in style, chauffeured in his club president's Rolls Royce, but a prang en route left him making a less impressive entrance, perched with his bag on a milk float.

In June of the following year he hit three centuries, but war intervened and his great breakthrough did not come till April 1948. By this time he was teaching at Bromsgrove School, and he arranged three days' leave to play the visiting Australians.

Whipping Lindwall's first ball for four and hooking Miller with abandon, he hit a thrilling 85, an innings which Bradman rated the best played against them that summer by a batsman outside the England team. Such was his impact that, in early July, with only one more match under his belt, he received a letter from Lord's, asking if he would be available to tour South Africa that winter.

He missed out on the Test side in South Africa, but the following winter his life took another dramatic turn when he applied to become Somerset's captain-cum-secretary. Appalled by a disorganised interview panel of 43, he decided to remain in teaching. But Leicestershire, hearing of his application, courted him vigorously, and he ended up as captain and secretary there. They had finished bottom of the table the previous summer and were nearly bankrupt but, working with a forceful chairman Frank Smith, he transformed them to such an extent that the ground soon saw improvements and the team rose to an unprecedented third place in 1953.

His success led to his appointment as player-manager of the MCC tour of West Indies in 1953/54, where in Barbados he made his one Test appearance. It was a most difficult tour, set against the backdrop of a Caribbean on the verge of great political change, and he had no briefing before departure and no assistant to help carry the burden when the problems mounted up. Jim Swanton thought his appointment as player-manager a disaster, but the *Daily Mail*'s Alex Bannister reckoned that, without his great charm and intelligence, the tour would never have been completed.

He was primarily a batsman, a wristy stroke-player who hit 2,071 runs in 1952 and whose 33 centuries included two in the prestigious Gentlemen-

Players fixture at Lord's. But it was as a bowler that he had his greatest triumph. At Grace Road in May 1955, against the mighty Surrey side, he put himself on for one over to allow the spinners to change ends. He had a bad back and was under orders not to bowl, but he hit Peter May's stumps second ball, left himself on and after 12 overs had figures of eight wickets for no runs, seven of them bowled. It could have been nine for nought, but an aerial hit through the covers by Jim Laker narrowly missed a fielder and he finished with eight for seven. "I do beg your pardon, gentlemen," he is reported to have said in the Surrey dressing room afterwards.

His other speciality was the donkey drop, occasional deliveries that went 20 feet in the air and came down with unerring accuracy onto the wicket. Batsmen were bowled or caught, some trod on or smashed down their stumps, and his victims – thought to be at least 15 – included three of the 1957 West Indian tourists: Worrell, Kanhai and Asgarali. Somehow the ball summed up Charles: a seeming joke, delivered with an affectation of innocence but concealing a lethal skill.

After his playing days he worked for a steel company, but he stayed at the heart of Leicestershire cricket, as Chairman for 25 years, then as President. He had arrived in 1950 to find a county in dire straits, and it is a tribute to his leadership, in tandem for many years with Secretary Mike Turner, that the club has prospered, out-performing many of its grander rivals.

The greatest honour of his life was to become President of MCC in 1978, a rare achievement for one who had attended neither public school nor Oxbridge. In the accompanying role of Chairman of ICC, he dealt with the aftermath of the Packer affair and led a delegation to South Africa to inspect progress towards multi-racial cricket. He was an outstanding Chairman of the Cricket Council and of the TCCB, and he also chaired the committee which produced the Palmer Report of 1986, advocating the introduction of four-day cricket. He was made a CBE for services to the game.

At the time of his death, he was co-operating on a book about his life in cricket, and it is hoped that enough has been completed for it to be published this summer. On the surface he was an old-fashioned amateur, playing his cricket for fun and friendship, but – in the words of the book's title – he was 'more than just a gentleman'.

He is survived by Barbara, his wife of 63 years, and their two sons.

## 100. Vic Wilson (1921-2008)

TWC, Aug 2008

Born into farming stock in the East Riding, Yorkshire's Vic Wilson was a hard-hitting, left-handed batsman and an outstanding fielder, especially close to the wicket. He did not win an England cap, but he toured Australia under Len Hutton in 1954/55 and was on the field as twelfth man in all five Tests.

Educated at Malton Grammar School, he made rapid progress as a young cricketer: a century at 14 in the East Yorkshire Cup, two summers of success at Scarborough, then a wartime spell at Undercliffe where he equalled a Bradford League record of three successive hundreds. When he was out for 75 the next week, the local headline read 'Vic Wilson Fails'.

He played several times in Yorkshire's championship-winning side of 1946, scoring 74 against the touring Indians – though he remembered more keenly his pair at Sheffield, outwitted by Glamorgan's off-spinner Johnnie Clay. All through his career he was a better player of quick bowling.

His best summers were 1951, when he passed 2,000 runs, and 1954 when in the cauldron of a Roses match he played what he considered his finest innings, an unbeaten 130 on a difficult Old Trafford pitch.

Through the 1950s Yorkshire played in the shadow of the great Surrey side. But in 1959, captained by the amateur Ronnie Burnet, they became champions again. Ironically the 38-year-old Wilson had his worst summer, spending the final month in the second team. His career was over, it seemed, and he was granted one last appearance: for the Champion County against the Rest at The Oval.

He hit a century; then some weeks later, attending an open day at his children's school, he was called to the phone and offered the Yorkshire captaincy. Not since 1882 had a professional led the county, and many questioned the wisdom of the appointment.

He was a quiet, phlegmatic character in a team with several outsize personalities, and in his first game in charge his declaration backfired, leading the great Herbert Sutcliffe to express his displeasure. But, with a team with talents such as Trueman, Close and Illingworth, the victories soon came, the championship was won and his opponents were silenced.

"If I'd made a lash-up of it," he said, "it could have made trouble for years ahead."

He was named one of *Wisden*'s five cricketers of the year. 'Authority fitted him well,' Bill Bowes wrote. 'Almost overnight a quiet firmness crept into his voice, and there was purpose about his actions.'

He blamed himself for their finishing second in 1961, but at Harrogate in September 1962, in his final game for Yorkshire, he led them to a dramatic last-afternoon victory that regained the title.

That summer he had sent Fred Trueman home when he arrived late at the ground at Taunton. "You can't have one law for the rich and another for the poor," he said simply, though Trueman never forgave him. He also introduced the young Geoffrey Boycott into the team: "He was very polite. He even called me sir, which was quite remarkable, especially after what Fred called me."

On retirement he offered his services to the committee but was told he was not eligible. He went back to the farm, stayed out of the turmoil of later years and contented himself with visits to Scarborough, his favourite ground. He had played a major part in the county's history, but he was happy to sit without fuss on the terraces.

"I always used to look up at the clock when I was batting there," he said. "That was my aim, to hit that clock. But I never did."

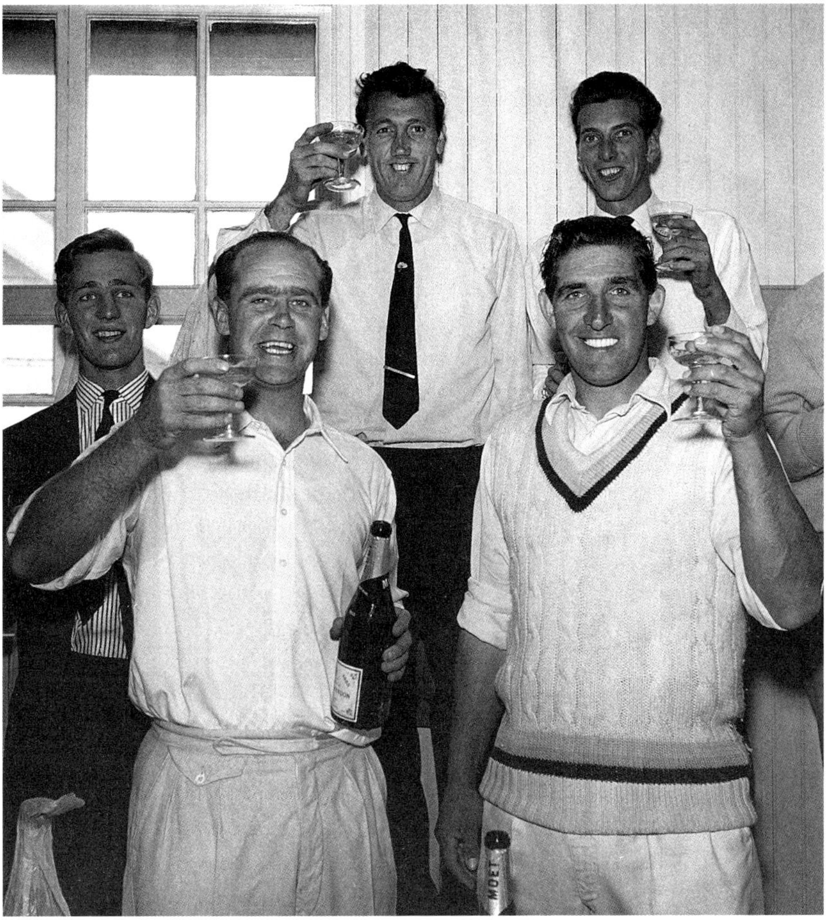


*The championship won at Harrogate, 1962*
*back: Richard Hutton, Mel Ryan and Don Wilson*
*front: Brian Close and Vic Wilson*

## 101. Tom Cartwright (1935-2007)

TWC, JUNE 2007

Tom Cartwright was a formidable medium-pace bowler, an outstanding coach and a man of the greatest integrity. He developed a passion for cricket as a schoolboy in Coventry in the late 1940s, and sixty years later, working with youngsters in Wales, that passion remained as strong.

His family worked in the car factories, Labour folk with a strong sense of right and wrong, and Tom retained their values throughout his life. He was a craftsman striving for excellence, an honest worker demanding an honest day's pay, a kind man, one who believed in sharing knowledge and passing it on.

He made his debut for Warwickshire in August 1952 at Trent Bridge. A shy lad, just past his 17th birthday, he hit a patient 82. He never quite fulfilled the county's hopes for his classical batting, but three times he passed 1,000 runs in a season, his best 1,668 in 1961. At Nuneaton in 1962 he hit a double century.

His bowling did not come to the fore till the late 1950s, but he quickly developed a reputation for unflagging accuracy, for an ability to move the ball even in unhelpful conditions and for a capacity for hard work. In 1967, when an experimental regulation prevented any polishing of the ball, he was the country's leading wicket-taker with 147 at 15.52 runs each.

He only played five Tests. In his first in 1964, when the Australian Bobby Simpson hit 311 on the flattest of old Trafford pitches, he bowled 77 overs on the first two days, never losing control and taking two wickets for 118. In his last in 1965, at Trent Bridge, when the South African Graeme Pollock hit a magnificent 125, he was at his most testing, taking six for 94. His thumb was fractured as he attempted a return catch, and he never regained his England place.

In August 1968, out of the game with a shoulder injury, he was surprisingly included in that winter's party to tour South Africa, a party that controversially did not include Basil D'Oliveira. He had wintered twice previously in South Africa – once as a coach in Johannesburg, then with Mike Smith's side in 1964/65 – and he had been appalled by the inhumanity of the apartheid system. Yet, like most English cricketers, he believed in maintaining sporting contact – until he read how the South African MPs, told of D'Oliveira's omission, had all stood up and cheered. "When I read that," he said, "I went cold. I started to wonder if I wanted to be part of it."

His injury did not clear up, he never liked leaving his family for long and, despite being put under pressure, he withdrew. D'Oliveira took his place, and the tour was cancelled. When the South Africans were due to visit England in 1970, Tom had just moved to Somerset and he made it clear that he did not wish to play against the tourists.

At Taunton he continued his supremacy with the ball – the country's leading wicket-taker in 1972, top of the first-class averages in 1973 – and, in the limited-over game, his economy rate of 2.78 runs an over remains the lowest of anyone who has bowled 1,000 overs.

Somerset appointed him as coach, and he successfully negotiated for £1,000 each for six young cricketers to join the staff for the summer of 1974. They were 'Tom's boys', and they included Ian Botham, Viv Richards, Vic Marks and Peter Roebuck. Botham had been on the ground staff at Lord's, where his bowling was considered a joke, but that changed quickly. "Ian was one of the most receptive people I ever worked with," Tom said.

In 1977 he moved to Glamorgan, where he played one last summer of county cricket and served as team manager. Then he became the full-time Director of Coaching in Wales. For 23 years he drove the length and breadth of the nation, selflessly passing on his great technical expertise and inculcating into every young cricketer the best values of the game.

In 1999 he was the first cricketer to be inducted into the National Coaching Federation's Hall of Fame, and he was still running the Wales Under-16s when he was struck down by a heart attack in March.

He had wonderful recall of the people and events of his life, and he had just finished collaborating on a book *The Flame Still Burns* that mixed his memories with his incisive views on the current state of English cricket. "I'm staggered by my thoughts now," he said, struggling to reconcile his socialism with the world he now encountered. "I'd rather see cricket go back to being controlled by the MCC of yesteryear, that type of person, than the hard-bitten professional who's come out of the City."

He lived for several weeks after his heart attack. He was in a bad way, quite confused, but he was still Tom, still a fighter, still talking cricket.

His last match took place in September 2005, on the magical occasion of his Warwickshire team-mate Bob Barber's 70th birthday party at Broadhalfpenny Down. His arm was high, and there was a leap in his delivery stride. "He wouldn't know how to bowl a bad ball," observed the former England captain Donald Carr.

In the marquee that evening the speaker was the former MCC President Dennis Silk, and in front of so many of the great names of post-war cricket, to great applause, he singled out Tom for special mention. "I've always had this thing about Tom," he said later. "He's tremendously respected by his fellow cricketers. He's kept up such high personal standards without making a meal of it. And he's put so much back into the game, patiently and generously. He's one of the great unsung heroes of English cricket."

## 102. Fred Trueman (1931-2006)

TWC, Aug 2006

He was Fiery Fred. He was Ferocious Freddie. It was enough just to say Fred.

The appeal of Frederick Sewards Trueman reached far beyond cricketing folk, beyond even the world of sport. Among English cricketers since his day, only Ian Botham has achieved such status.

He was the very embodiment of the fast bowler, bristling with menace as he walked back to his mark, black hair flopping, unbuttoned sleeve rolled up afresh. Then began that angled run, building to the beautiful side-on delivery, the expectation of a wicket with every ball. He understood the theatre that cricket provided, and he loved every minute of it.

He burst into the nation's imagination in June 1952. A miner's son from South Yorkshire, he was doing his National Service in the RAF when England called him up for the first Test against India at Headingley. Such was his pace and such the fear of the visiting batsmen that in the second innings he took three wickets in his first eight balls and the Indian number six found himself walking to the middle on a hat-trick and without a run on the board.

For six years since the war English cricket had suffered at the hands of the Australian pacemen Lindwall and Miller, even the South African Cuan McCarthy. Now at last, as the nation shook off the hardships of rationing, it had once more found a bowler of real pace. He took eight for 31 in the first innings of the third Test at Old Trafford, 29 wickets in the four matches and the next spring *Wisden* was writing of him as 'a second Harold Larwood'.

He had made his debut for Yorkshire at Fenner's in May 1949, on the same occasion as a shy 18-year-old called Brian Close. *Wisden*, in the error of the century, referred to 'Trueman, a spin bowler' when in fact he was a raw lad whose search for great pace was at the expense of the accuracy that the Yorkshire tradition demanded. For three summers, he found himself in and out of the first eleven.

"When he got it in the right place, he took wickets," Bob Appleyard, an early team-mate, recalls, "but he was erratic. I think Yorkshire persevered with him because he had this marvellous, late out-swing. He obviously had the potential to become a great bowler, but he hadn't developed the control."

The Yorkshire dressing room could be a harsh environment for a youngster, and one team-mate, rooming with him, recalls an evening in London in June 1951. "We were playing Middlesex at Lord's, and Freddie didn't do all that well against them. We were in the hotel bedroom, and we were all going out. And Freddie said, 'I don't think I'll go.' And he nearly started crying. 'I don't think I'll ever make it,' he said. He was really upset."

A week later he took eight for 68 against Notts but, with the team for the following match already announced, he found himself at Grimsby the next day, acting as twelfth man to the second eleven. The hurt of such moments was never forgotten.

He was back in the side soon enough, in the England team the next year, and at The Oval in 1953 he took four first-innings wickets when England regained the Ashes. He was a rising star, but his England career was blighted by the controversial tour of the Caribbean that followed.

He had grown up in a working-class community where people valued plain speaking. He enjoyed the persona of the fast bowler, hurling down bumpers and scowling at the batsmen. And he knew nothing of the politics of the West Indies in those troubled years before Independence. In the words of the manager Charles Palmer, 'He'd been pulled out of Yorkshire and put in a context which was entirely alien to his upbringing. There was no malice in him, but he spoke as a Yorkshireman would speak in Yorkshire and it didn't go down very well in a highly sensitive situation.'

Rightly or wrongly, whenever there was an incident, Trueman seemed to get the blame. His good conduct money was withheld, he acquired a reputation as something of a handful, and after that tour he played only three of England's next 26 Tests. He missed Len Hutton's Ashes-winning tour of Australia, where Tyson and Statham provided the match-winning pace, and he missed Peter May's tour of South Africa in 1956/57. His only foreign trip was a short tour to India in the New Year of 1957 when on one occasion the party shared a flight with the Indian Premier Pandit Nehru. The manager Geoffrey Howard sat next to Nehru, getting up only once during the journey: "When I came back," he recalled, "there was Fred Trueman in my seat, giving Nehru a real ear-bashing about the state of his country."

But Fred Trueman was far too good a bowler for the selectors to ignore for ever. 'He was a genuine and sometimes frighteningly fast bowler in the early 1950s,' Trevor Bailey reckons, 'but his vintage years were from 1958 to 1964. On all wickets and in all conditions, he was a complete fast bowler. He had fire, aggressiveness, pace, control, a glorious action, as well as limitless confidence in his own ability.'

He was also an outstanding fielder, both in the leg trap and in the deep, and he could wield his bat to mighty effect, scoring three first-class centuries, all of them in rapid time. Once at Middlesbrough, when the metronomic Derek Shackleton of Hampshire had reduced Yorkshire to 47 for seven, he arrived in the middle full of banter – "What the bloody 'ell's going on, Shack? Are there snakes in the wicket?" – and hit the bemused seamer for 26 in an over. In everything he did, he entertained.

In each of the four summers from 1959 to 1962 he bowled well over 1,000 overs, taking 623 wickets in all. His best year was 1960 when, in 32 matches, he took 175 wickets, the most by a fast bowler since the war. He had strong legs, a strong backside and was rarely troubled by injury.

In the words of his team-mate Ken Taylor, "Fred was the greatest fast bowler I've ever seen. He had everything: a beautiful action, speed, control, stamina. And he had the will-power to bowl as quick at half past five as he did at half past eleven. I only ever faced him in the nets, and he didn't like anybody to hit him, even there. He'd always be trying."

Trueman became a regular in the England side in 1957, but there were still those at Lord's who eyed him with suspicion. When he was finally taken to Australia in 1958/59, he was greeted on the gangplank by the manager Freddie Brown with the words, "Any trouble from you, Trueman, and you'll be on the next boat home."

Fred was a deeply traditional man, a lover of the Yorkshire countryside and a great patriot and monarchist, but he never forgave the amateurs who ran English cricket in the 1950s. His 2004 autobiography *As It Was* bristles with rage against them. He was the first bowler to take 300 Test wickets, and all his life he harboured the grievance that, but for those Southern amateurs in the MCC, he would have reached 400. He called them 'jazz-hats', and his bowling always seemed to grow fiercer when one arrived at the crease. "A good ball, Mister Trueman," they would say when their stumps went cartwheeling. "Ay," he would reply, his Yorkshire vowels at their thickest, "and it were bloody wasted on thee."

In his 67 Tests, 15 bowlers shared the new ball with him, from Alec Bedser to Fred Rumsey, but the one with whom he will always be bracketed, the one who opened with him in over half his Tests, was Brian Statham. 'Fiery Fred' and 'Gentleman George': in the public imagination they were the perfect pair, the rough-hewn, hard-drinking extrovert and his quiet, relentlessly accurate partner – though, away from the cameras, it was not Fred who did the drinking.

By the summer of 1963 Fred was starting to lose a little pace, but he had a formidable constitution and a great bowling brain, and at the age of 32 – not wanting to be upstaged by the West Indian Wes Hall – he had a golden summer, taking 34 Test wickets and topping the national averages. The following year, when the Australians came over, he suffered the ignominy of being dropped for the Old Trafford Test – when the visitors made 656 for eight – only to return at The Oval, where he took his 300th Test wicket. It was a triumphant moment for English cricket.

He played for Yorkshire till 1968, a key member of the side that won seven championships in ten years, and in his last summer – in his proudest moment with the county – he captained them to an innings victory over the Australians. Then that autumn he announced in his *Sunday People* column that he had retired, and he turned to a rich after-life: as a stand-up comedian, an after-dinner speaker, a charity worker and – above all – an instantly recognisable voice on *Test Match Special*, where his emphatic Yorkshire growl, his wonderful recall of the past and his increasingly trenchant criticisms of the modern game made sure that he stayed in our national consciousness. Whatever he did, once he achieved greatness as a fast bowler, he never again doubted that he could make it.

As a bowler he would usually start each match in the opposition dressing room, counting out the wickets he expected to take. "Ah, Ron, hit you on the head last year, didn't I? That's two wickets." And there's no doubt that he created fear. But, beneath it all, there was a warm-hearted, generous man, a great lover of the game, a proud Englishman and an even prouder Yorkshireman.

As his friend John Arlott once wrote, 'The God of cricket achieved one of his greatest triumphs of creation in Fred Trueman. Stories will be told about him as long as men talk about cricket. No one who ever saw him bowl will be able to forget.'

## 103. David Sheppard (1929-2005)

TWC, May 2005

So young did David Sheppard quit full-time cricket and so great was his later contribution to the Church that it is easy to under-estimate his achievements as a cricketer.

In his first summer in the Cambridge side, 1950, it was he more than his fellow freshman Peter May who caught the headlines. He scored a century in the first match, a double century against the touring West Indians and by August he was in the England team.

He liked to tell the story of his first Test innings at The Oval. When he had reached 11, the tannoy announced that Princess Elizabeth had given birth to a girl, and the West Indians in the crowd chanted "Let's have a wicket for the Princess." He was promptly bowled by Ramadhin.

Then, just 21 years old, he was fitting his study of history around a winter tour of Australia.

His game was still evolving. At Sherborne, a late developer, he had not broken into the first eleven till he was 17. But, thanks perhaps to a daily bottle of Guinness from his housemaster, he shot up a foot in two years and became a powerful young batsman, scoring so many runs that he was making his debut for Sussex at 18. After two years of National Service, he returned to the Sussex team in August 1949 and in successive matches reeled off scores of 204, 147 and 130.

In Australia runs came less easily, but he had determination and he managed to get the introverted Len Hutton to take him under his wing. At this stage, like many from the public schools, he had a predominantly off-side game, but Hutton got him playing over the line of the ball. Back in England the following summer, though he topped 2,000 runs, he became for a while rather an on-sided player.

The next two summers were the apex of his cricket career. In 1952, preferred to Peter May as Cambridge captain, he hit ten centuries – including a maiden Test hundred against India – and finished top of the national averages. 'Sheppard, tall and well built, looks a batsman from the moment he takes guard,' *Wisden* wrote.

Then in 1953 he played his only full season of county cricket, captaining Sussex so successfully that the county rose from 13th to 2nd in the table. In the seven years of the great Surrey's reign, no county ran them closer than David Sheppard's Sussex.

It was a time when young amateurs were expected to lead out seasoned professionals, and it is arguable whether any won their respect as completely as David Sheppard did. He was an outstanding batsman and a courageous close catcher, and he practised a leadership that combined a will to succeed with a gift for pastoral care. According to fellow amateur Hubert Doggart, he had "an extraordinary personal magnetism which his team found hard to resist" while Jim Parks, later to play under May, Dexter, Cowdrey and Close, has no doubts that "he was the finest captain I ever played under."

"He was only 24," wicket-keeper Rupert Webb says, "but he seemed older. He led from the front, he always had time for everybody, and the whole team admired him. If he'd said to me 'Try not to get out', they could have hit me on the head and I'd have stayed there." At the end of the summer, Alan Oakman recalls, they all received personal letters of thanks.

His batting was inspirational. On the final day at Leicester it seemed that the home team would never declare so he signalled the taking of the new ball and laboriously reset the field. Then Charles Palmer, captain and secretary of the impoverished club, waved his batsmen in. "I knew they couldn't afford a new ball," Sheppard joked as they left the field, and he put on his pads and scored an unbeaten 186 in 3½ hours. "It was the most exciting innings I ever played," he said. At Bournemouth he came down the track to the unhittable Shackleton and lofted him over his head for 22 in an over, and on an awkwardly green pitch at Guildford he battled for a 4½-hour century that brought victory over the mighty Surrey. "He was wonderfully single-minded," Colin Cowdrey wrote of him, "always hungry for runs."

Then he began his theological training – though, in the final words of his 1964 book *Parson's Pitch*, it was 'not so much a case of giving up cricket as of taking up something else which is infinitely worthwhile.'

He found time to play much of the 1954 season, even captaining England in Hutton's absence in two Tests, but thereafter his appearances grew less frequent. In 1956, he had played only four first-class innings when he was selected for the Old Trafford Test against Australia but, cheered on by a group of boys from his Islington parish, he went out to bat, was shaken up by a first-ball bouncer from Lindwall and went on to score a century that set up the game for Jim Laker to take 19 wickets. The following year, in the fourth Test at Headingley, he was walking out against the West Indies with only 32 first-class runs to his name, but he was equal to the task and made 68.

His ministry took him to London's East End, and his cricket became even more sporadic: ten games, with three centuries, in the next four years. Then in 1962, at the age of 33, he was persuaded to play more regularly and to make himself available for a winter in Australia, perhaps even as captain. On the eve of the decision he scored a fine century for the Gentlemen against the Players, but the vote went to Ted Dexter. Some say that he lost out because the MCC were nervous that he might criticise Australia's whites-only immigration policy, others that he did himself no favours when Walter Robins, Chairman of Selectors, left a message at the Docklands Settlement for him to ring back and, confusing him with another Mr. Robins, a persistent caller from the parish, he did not do so immediately. In the end, perhaps, he was happier to tour as a player and to spend his off-field time fulfilling invitations to spread the gospel.

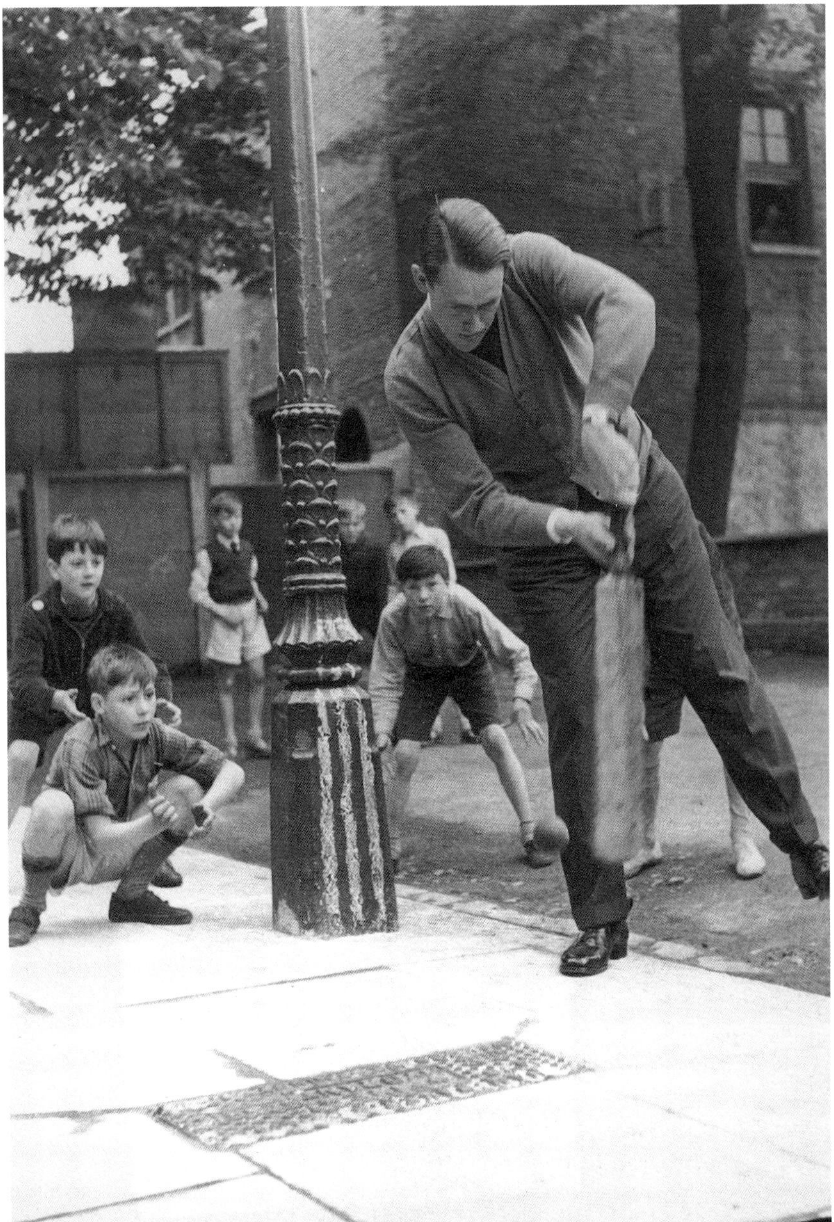

*In the streets of Islington.*
*Soon afterwards, he was hitting a century against Lindwall and Miller.*

In the second Test at Melbourne, when he went out to bat in the second innings, he was on a pair, had dropped two catches and was close to losing his place in the side. But he made a patient 113 – 'A triumph of character as well as technique,' Swanton called it – and England won a victory that allowed them to draw the series 1-1. In all, he made 330 runs in the five Tests, and the subsequent matches in New Zealand were his last first-class appearances.

As early as 1960 he had made it public that he would not play an all-white South African touring side, and in 1968 he returned to cricketing prominence in the wake of the D'Oliveira affair. He was asked by a group of MCC members – angered by the club's handling of events – to propose a motion of no confidence at a special meeting in December. It was an acrimonious time, and he suffered personal abuse, as he did again in 1970 when he campaigned for the cancellation of the next South African tour to England. But he drew strength from the words of Isaiah – 'Cry aloud, spare not, lift up thy voice like a trumpet' – and, as events unfolded across his life, though he regretted deeply the loss of his friendship with Peter May, he never regretted the position he had taken up.

In 1975 he was sent to Liverpool. He was at 46 the youngest diocesan bishop ever appointed, and the same qualities he brought to his cricket – the courage, the application, the pastoral care, the ability to transcend class and status and to treat all people the same, without condescension – were at the heart of his ministry.

They were hard years. The city was rapidly losing its economic position as a major port, and he championed the people in the face of a Conservative government determined to let market forces run their course and a Militant-led council eager to create conflict. He was a leading member of the Church Commission which produced the report *Faith in the City* that sought to bring 'the squalor and dilapidation of the inner city' into the consciousness of the people living in 'the green and wooded suburbs of middle Britain'. This brought him directly into conflict with Mrs Thatcher and, in his 2002 book *Steps Along Hope Street*, he wrote of a particularly bristly meeting at Chequers where she repeatedly interrupted him: 'It was like being heckled. Indeed my mouth went dry as I remembered it doing once when facing Lindwall and Miller!'

He retired in 1997, but in the following year he was returned to the House of Lords, to whose debates he contributed with perspicacity. His life's journey had taken him a long way from cricket, but he never lost his passion for the game and in 2002 he served as Sussex President. By this time, however, just as he was looking forward to some much-deserved years of quiet, he found himself locked in a long and ultimately unsuccessful battle with cancer. He died peacefully on the fifth of March, one day before his 76th birthday, and is survived by Grace, his wife of 47 years, and their daughter Jenny.

## 104. Bryan 'Bomber' Wells (1930-2008)

VARIOUS, 2008

Bryan 'Bomber' Wells was one of English cricket's greatest characters.

Born in Gloucester in July 1930, the son of a blacklisted trade unionist, he never really changed from the happy-go-lucky club cricketer he had been when he was first summoned to play for the county.

He learned the game during the wartime years of Double British Summer Time, when they played cricket in the street till the sun went down: rough-and-ready games with a tennis ball, a lump of wood for a bat and stumps made out of bean sticks. From that he progressed through various local sides: the Harlequins, the Nondescripts, Gloucester City.

He was an off-spinner but hardly a conventional one. He had a wide girth and a rolling gait, he ambled in off one or two paces, and he bowled whether the batsman was ready or not. This last aspect of his bowling was the subject of some wonderful stories, which he never tired of telling in that broad 'Glorster' accent of his.

One, from his early days, involved a Gloucester Nondescripts match at Witney where he bowled an opposing batsman, the Oxfordshire player Len Hemming, and the Nondies skipper, not sure Hemming had been ready, called him back. "We played all away matches, you see, and we didn't like to offend anyone." The batsman returned rather sheepishly and was immediately bowled a second time. Again it was not clear that he had been ready – "but, before our captain could say a word, Len Hemming swung round. 'Bill, if you think I'm staying here for him to get his bloody hat-trick, you've got another think coming.'"

By 1951 Bomber's bowling was attracting attention. He was summoned to play for the county second eleven against Glamorgan, and he took six wickets in each innings. Then the following week, in a story he told many times over the years, he was sitting with his girl friend on a park bench on Friday evening when Tom Goddard, Gloucester's legendary off-spinner, appeared.

"Are you Bomber Wells? … Well, get down to Bristol tomorrow. You're playing against Sussex."

"He was just a boy from the sticks," Arthur Milton recalled. "He strolled in, changed, came out. Nothing worried him."

"Why should it?" Bomber would reply. "It was just another game, wasn't it? All I ever wanted to do was to bowl."

The captain, Sir Derrick Bailey, did not ask him to bowl till after lunch. Then Bomber came in off his two paces. Some say that Sir Derrick, fielding at mid-off, walked in for the first ball, turned, went back to his mark and walked in again for the third ball.

Imagine what it was like to be a fast bowler at the other end. "One time I was walking down to third man at the end of my over," Frank McHugh tells, "and I heard this shout. And the ball whistled past me for four. Then I found out it was the second ball of the over. I'd hardly have my sweater on, and in no time I'd be taking it off for the next over."

But for all this Bomber was a fine bowler. He had powerful shoulders, a fast arm and a perfect action at point of delivery, and the ball came down much more quickly than the batsman expected. Not only that. His standard fare was off-breaks, but he had control of a wide variety of other deliveries: seamers, floaters and leg-breaks. And he could change his pace with no discernible sign. "It used to bore me silly to bowl two balls the same," he would say.

"He just stood at the wicket and turned his arm over," a later opponent recalled. "John Edrich had this ritual. He always looked down three or four times when the bowler was in his run-up. Well, Bomber would be standing there, ready to let the ball go. 'Are you ready, our John?' he'd ask in his broad Gloucester accent, and John couldn't get in synch. He couldn't get his four nods in."

Bomber took six Sussex wickets that first day, and he became a regular in the Gloucestershire side, alongside John Mortimore and Sam Cook, ahead of David Allen. In 1956, that golden summer for slow bowlers, only Don Shepherd and Jim Laker among off-spinners took more wickets than his 123.

Allen, Mortimore and Cook all played for England, but there were some on the county circuit who thought Bomber the best of the lot – though perhaps he offered less in the batting and fielding departments.

As a batsman his only aim was to entertain, the cry of 'Bomber's in' enough to clear the bars. He had only one real shot, a great agricultural mow over mid-wicket, but it was spectacular when it connected. His scrapbook contained a newspaper report of a Sunday benefit match at Stinchcombe, against several first-class bowlers, when he came in at 91 for nine and hit a hundred in 35 minutes. "They must have lost the ball four times," he said. "They were building houses next to the ground, and they kept scrambling over this wall into the building site."

His running between the wickets occasioned many stories – like the mix-up with Sam Cook that ended with Sam run out. "For God's sake, call," Sam cried out, and back came the reply: "Tails." Or the time Derbyshire's Derek Morgan picked up the ball and out-sprinted him to the bowler's end: "That's not fair, Derek," Bomber protested. "I've got pads on."

He even had a story of a day at Bristol when both batsmen had runners and such was the confusion he caused that all four men finished at the same end.

As a fielder he was even less like a modern cricketer. A leisurely figure on the boundary, he liked to chat to the nearby spectators, on one occasion – he reckoned – contriving to hold a catch while juggling a cup of tea in his other hand. His approach was not to everybody's taste, particularly when the game was nearing a tense conclusion, but even his disciplinarian captain George Emmett found it hard not to see the funny side of Bomber. As Michael Parkinson wrote, 'There was a summer's day in his face and laughter in his soul.'

In 1959, with Tom Graveney as captain, David Allen replaced him in the side, being picked for England before the year was out. Bomber played in the second eleven, where his captain was once more George Emmett. Then Tom Graveney was injured, George Emmett resumed the first-team captaincy, and Bomber took charge of the seconds, leading the team to first place in the newly established Second Eleven Championship. It became one of his jokes: "I'm the only man who's captained Gloucestershire to a championship title."

The following year he went to Nottinghamshire to bowl on the batsman's paradise at Trent Bridge. He was attracted, he said, by the beautiful ground and by the larger helpings served at meal times. "Not like the little salads we used to have every day at Bristol, one slice of cold meat so thin you could see through it."

"What do you want to go up there for, Bomber?" Sam Cook said. "You'll end up being cannon fodder." But Bomber enjoyed the challenge, and in his first summer there he bowled more overs than anybody else in England, taking 120 wickets. "The great thing about Bomber," Tony Brown says, "is that he was such a good bowler on good wickets."

He lost his place in 1965, and he had a story about that, too.

"Some statistician worked out that I'd taken 999 wickets so they offered me the game against Gloucester at Bristol. They said, 'Somebody down there will give you their wicket.' But I said, 'No. Plenty of people have got a thousand wickets. I bet no one's got 999.'"

Alas, the story had a sad ending.

"Three months later they found I'd only got 998."

For Bomber statisticians were in the same category as coaches, people who suffocated the natural fun of the game. He loved the stories, both from his own playing days and from further back in history, and he loved to watch people playing naturally, expressing their character and not moulded into a standard way of doing things.

"I could bowl standing still," he would say. "If you're a natural, everything comes easy. You can do what you like and get away with murder. If you're coached, unless you stay in that groove, you're struggling, aren't you?"

Bomber had started out as an apprentice printer, and after cricket he stayed for many years in Nottingham, working once more as a printer. Then, when his wife Pat died, he returned to his beloved Gloucester where he was lucky to meet Mary and to enjoy 18 happy years with her. He suffered a major stroke in 1998, but such was his spirit that, with

Mary's steadfast support, he fought his way back to enjoy another ten years, years in which he continued to tell his stories on the boundary edge throughout the county: at the Cheltenham Festival, at the Spa ground, at cricket matches of all sorts.

For Bomber, cricket was a people's game. Whether you played for England or for Gloucester City third eleven, it made no difference. It was a game of sunshine and laughter, of human beings revealing themselves – and, at its best, of wonderful artistry. He was not a religious man but, on a sunny day at Cheltenham, when he was settled in his favourite corner beyond the scoreboard, his conversation captured that sense of timelessness that makes cricket such a special game.

He expressed it superbly in a foreword I helped him to write to a book about Gloucestershire cricket:

> Robinswood Hill still looks down on the Wagon Works ground, but now the county plays in the shadow of Gloucester Cathedral – at the Archdeacon Meadow. When I was a boy, I used to pick bulrushes there, when it was just scrubland, and now it maintains the tradition of county cricket here in the city of Gloucester. How many runs Hammond would have scored on its placid surface, I can't imagine.
>
> The County Ground in Bristol is no longer the open field it was in my day. It is a modern cricket stadium with all the facilities. But for the true cricket lover there can be nowhere like Cheltenham College on a Festival day – with the sun shining, Matt Windows cutting his way to a hundred and the folk around the boundary reminiscing about days gone by. Reminiscing about Emmett and Zaheer, some even about Hammond and Parker, where once they sat and reminisced about Jessop and Grace. One day they will reminiscence about Russell and Windows.
>
> Generation upon generation of great Gloucestershire cricketers. Long may they keep coming – as long as the sun shines over the River Severn.

For certain, the crowds at Cheltenham will be reminiscing about Bomber for years to come. He brought so much joy into so many lives.

## 105. Step outside cricket and think

*Tom Cartwright*

Sledging is infantile playground behaviour, isn't it? I can't believe it goes on. The wicket-keepers are expected to orchestrate all this noise, and the players are telling you all the time who they're going to target. It's pathetic. It's a huge tragedy that it's been allowed to happen like this. Not enough people speak out against it.

Step outside cricket and think. Is that the sort of ethic we want to encourage in the world, the way we want adults to deal with each other? They say it's a test of mental strength, but it's got nothing to do with that. It's a complete abuse of what sport is about, and we just accept it. I can't watch the television with the sound on.

I say to my kids, 'The umpires are responsible for the laws of the game; the players are responsible for its spirit.' Unless people understand that, the real feel for the goodness of the game will go.

I had a boy keeping wicket in my final trials a couple of years ago, and he went up for a catch down the leg-side when he knew the batter hadn't hit it. I said, 'That's cheating.' 'No, it isn't, Tom.' I said, 'It is. You knew he hadn't hit it. I don't ever want to see that again on the field.' He came to me afterwards and apologised.

I remember one year my under-16s were playing against the West of Scotland, and they were making all these comments aimed at the batsmen. I just walked onto the field. 'Do you mind if I talk to my players?' And I said, 'I don't want to hear anymore. The next one that says anything doesn't ever play again.' I wish umpires would do it, but they won't.

Religion brought a semblance of order to the community, and it's gone. And sport did a similar thing. There was a discipline and an order. These things fashioned people's lives.

What was precious in our game is being destroyed, thrown away.

*Geoffrey Howard*

It isn't dignified to throw yourself on the floor when you've just beaten your opponent in a final at Wimbledon, is it? The manners have changed, and bad manners are accepted.

I said to Jack Simmons at Old Trafford, 'If I were in your position, I would say to the players that, when a wicket falls, they should stay in their positions in the field, not rush up and hug each other.' 'Oh,' he said, 'I couldn't possibly do that.' Well, why couldn't he? He's their employer, isn't he?

*Ken Taylor*

Cricket was a gentleman's game. You didn't put the umpires under pressure. If you were caught and you knew you'd hit the ball, you walked. And that's gone. Now, if you can get one over on the umpire or you can intimidate the batsman psychologically, then you're doing a good job. All these things have come into the game, and as a teacher I've seen how even the children are copying some of them. They're all in the field, hyping each other up, and that's not the spirit in which cricket should be played.

When I played, you didn't want to be known as a cheat. Now it seems cheating is part of the game. Football is exactly the same. You didn't hold players down at corners. You didn't have your elbows out; you kept your arms down at your sides. And if a forward went past you, you didn't pull them down. It seems in both games now that it's about winning at all costs.

*Bomber Wells*

I was watching Chelsea on the television last night. This chap came on, and he pretended he'd been tripped up, got a penalty. 'That's what I like about him,' the commentator said. 'He makes things happen.' Well, he'd cheated, that's all. And we're bringing the children up to think that that's how sport should be played.

*Keith Andrew*

What a fantastic thing it would be if somebody got a nick in a Test match and walked! What a message it would send out!

Peter Parfitt once walked at Lord's, and I hadn't appealed. What a game we could sell if cricket was like that! We'd be saying to people, 'That's how we play cricket.' And I think a lot of people would look up to us. Being successful is one thing, but we want to enjoy our lives as well – and part of that enjoyment is friendship between sportsmen.

If people are cheating, they don't respect one another, and the feeling for the game disappears. You don't go home at night feeling half so well.

The press quote the television all the time. 'Well, we haven't really lost, because he wasn't really out.' And once you've got that conflict, nobody's ever satisfied. It's not helping cricket. It becomes the talking point, rather than the quality of the play. Is it the cricket the television wants to film, or is it the argument? I wonder why they're going down that road. It's all detracting from the game.

Cricket is a game. You play to win. You play to be top of the pile. But that's not *why* you play cricket.

## Acknowledgements

I would like to thank all those who spoke to me while I researched these pieces, in particular:
Zed Akhlaque, David Allen, Keith Andrew, Bob Appleyard, Graham Atkinson, Trevor Bailey, Bob Barber, John Barclay, Gordon Barker, Ida Barrett, Michael Barton, Alec Bedser, Richie Benaud, Don Bennett, Ken Biddulph, Jimmy Binks, Jack Birkenshaw, Jack Bond, Roy Booth, Mike Bore, Ian Botham, Mike Brearley, Basil Bridge, Vince Broderick, Dennis Brookes, Alan Brown, David Brown, Tony Brown, Albert Cahn, Julien Cahn, Donald Carr, Bob Carter, Jeremy Cartwright, Tom Cartwright, Alan Castell, John Clay, Brian Close, David Collier, Bernie Constable, Stan Cray, Brian Crump, Peter Danks, Colin Davies, John Dewes, Fred Dillam, Alan Dixon, Dickie Dodds, Paul Donovan, Mike Eagar, Geoff Edrich, Richard Ellison, Aizaz Fakir, Duncan Fearnley, Gill Ford, Peter Forman, James Fry, Brian Gibbons, Lance Gibbs, Norman Gifford, Roger Goadby, Robert Godfrey, Tom Graveney, Jimmy Gray, David Green, Tommy Greenhough, Colin Griffiths, Michael Hall, Maurice Hallam, Roger Harman, Malcolm Heath, Ron Headley, John Hewie, Eric Hill, Ray Hitchcock, Robin Hobbs, Andrew Hodd, Ken Hopkins, Norman Horner, Martin Horton, Geoffrey Howard, Ray Illingworth, Doug Insole, Olive Jenkins, Alan Jones, Ray Julian, Claude Kellaway, Lilly Laker, Brian Langford, Les Lenham, Ted Lester, John Lindley, Clive Lloyd, Stan Lockley, Bilal Mahmood, Mervyn Mansell, Eric Martin, Geoff Miller, Arthur Milton, John Mortimore, Derek Oakley, Alan Oakman, Charles Palmer, Ken Palmer, Christine Pardoe, Jim Parks, Frank Parr, Derek Pearson, Richard Peck, Cyril Perkins, Bob Platt, Nic Pothas, Derek Randall, Alan Rayment, Harold Rhodes, Peter Richardson, John Rigby, Peter Roebuck, Arthur Robinson, David Robinson, Peter Robinson, Fred Rumsey, Jim Ruston, Peter Sainsbury, Phil Sharpe, Don Shepherd, David Sheppard, Peter Sherwood, Frank Shipston, Dennis Silk, Reg Simpson, Gladstone Small, Philip Snow, Terry Spencer, Michael Spurway, Micky Stewart, Vic Stocks, Bryan Stott, Michael Sturt, Chris Tavare, Bob Taylor, Ken Taylor, Penny Taylor, Ian Thomson, Dorian Thorne, Alan Townsend, Peter Tuke, Glenn Turner, Derek Underwood, Doug Verity, Peter Walker, Allan Watkins, Rupert Webb, Bomber Wells, Peter Wight, Barbara Wilcox, Don Wilson, Ken Wilson, Ray Wilson, Vic Wilson, Merv Winfield, Geoffrey Wooler and Carleton Wright.

I would also like to thank the many people who have been involved in the original publication of these articles, in particular:
Stephen Fay of *Wisden Cricket Monthly* and John Stern of *The Wisden Cricketer*, my two editors; Marcus Williams of *The Times*; Nigel Davies, the art director at *The Wisden Cricketer*, who has come up with some superb

photographs and who has been so helpful during the completion of this book; Jeremy Alexander, who originally suggested the title *The Way It Was* for my column; and everybody else at *Wisden Cricket Monthly* and *The Wisden Cricketer*, especially Paul Coupar whose chuckle on the other end of the telephone always lifted my spirits.

I am also most grateful to Rob Taylor of Midway Colour Print, who has done so much to make the photographs in this book as good as they can be – though my brother Andrew's effort on page 44 was beyond his powers, which I suppose is the point of its inclusion.

I have made use of a number of reference books, in particular:
*Wisden Cricketers' Almanack*
Bailey, Thorn & Wynne-Thomas, *Who's Who of Cricketers* (Newnes, 1984)

I have quoted from various newspapers and magazines, in particular:
*The Times, The Cricketer, Playfair Cricket Monthly, Wisden Cricket Monthly.*

I have made occasional use of other books, too many to list, but I would like to draw attention to two books that relate to these articles:
Douglas Miller, *Allan Watkins* (ACS Publications, 2007)
Miranda Rijks, *The Eccentric Entrepreneur* (The History Press, 2008)
Douglas's book came out at the same time as my article (number 13) and is an excellent short biography, with a good input from Allan himself. Miranda's book is a biography of her grandfather, Sir Julien Cahn, most capably researched, and was inspired by my article (number 84).

I have made regular use of the superb CricketArchive website and received from its mastermind, Peter Griffiths, several replies to queries that have astonished me with their level of detail and speed of response.

I have picked the brains of many others, most notably David Smith, Douglas Miller, Ron Deaton and Peter Wynne-Thomas, four cricket lovers who are always happy to share their great knowledge of the game's history.

Most of all, I am grateful to Sue Kendall, who puts up with me through all the ups and downs of this writing and who is so quick to spot when my prose has lost its way. And to Bomber Wells, who died this summer and who played such a special part in my life these last few years. In his own irreverent style he really did have an understanding of 'the way it was'.

Stephen Chalke
Bath, September 2008

## Further reading

Some of the subjects in this collection are explored further in other titles published by Fairfield Books.

The following are by Stephen Chalke:

*Runs in the Memory – County Cricket in the 1950s*

*Caught in the Memory – County Cricket in the 1960s* *

*One More Run – with Bryan 'Bomber' Wells* *

*At the Heart of English Cricket – The Life and Memories of Geoffrey Howard* *

*Guess My Story – The Life and Opinions of Keith Andrew, Cricketer*

*No Coward Soul – The Remarkable Story of Bob Appleyard*

*A Sporting Scrapbook – The Wimbledon Club 1854-2004*

*Ken Taylor – Drawn to Sport*

*A Summer of Plenty – George Herbert Hirst in 1906* *

*Tom Cartwright – The Flame Still Burns*

*Five Five Five – Holmes and Sutcliffe in 1932*

The following are by other authors:

John Barclay, *Life beyond the Airing Cupboard*

John Barclay, *The Appeal of the Championship – Sussex in the Summer of 1981* *

David Foot, *Fragments of Idolatry – From 'Crusoe' to Kid Berg*

David Foot, *Harold Gimblett, Tormented Genius of Cricket* *

David Foot & Ivan Ponting, *Sixty Summers – Somerset Cricket since the War* *

Simon Lister, *Supercat – The Authorised Biography of Clive Lloyd*

Douglas Miller, *Born to Bowl – The Life and Times of Don Shepherd* *

Douglas Miller, *Charles Palmer – More than just a Gentleman*

Peter Walker, *It's Not Just Cricket*

* currently out of print

If you would like more details of any of these, or would like to be placed on the mailing list for future publications, please contact:
**Fairfield Books**, 17 George's Road, Bath BA1 6EY
telephone 01225-335813

# INDEX – by chapter number

# INDEX – by chapter number

# INDEX – by chapter number

# INDEX – by chapter number

# INDEX – by chapter number

# INDEX – by chapter number